TAYLOR
in LOVE

Also by Anna Pointer

Beyoncé: Running the World – The Biography

TAYLOR
in LOVE

Inside Taylor Swift and
Travis Kelce's Love Story

ANNA POINTER

EBURY
SPOTLIGHT

EBURY SPOTLIGHT

UK | USA | Canada | Ireland | Australia
India | New Zealand | South Africa

Ebury Spotlight is part of the Penguin Random House group of companies
whose addresses can be found at global.penguinrandomhouse.com

Penguin Random House UK
One Embassy Gardens, 8 Viaduct Gardens, London SW11 7BW

penguin.co.uk

Penguin
Random House
UK

First published by Ebury Spotlight in 2026

I

Typeset by seagulls.net

Printed and bound in Great Britain by Clays Ltd, Elcograf S.p.A.

The authorised representative in the EEA is Penguin Random House Ireland, Morrison
Chambers, 32 Nassau Street, Dublin D02 YH68.

A CIP catalogue record for this book is available from the British Library

Hardback ISBN 9781529986709
Trade Paperback ISBN 9781529986716

About the Author

Anna Pointer is an author and journalist with more than 25 years' experience writing for the national press and media. She has ghostwritten celebrity memoirs and is the author of *Beyoncé: Running the World – The Biography*, translated into multiple languages globally, as well as *The Essential Beyoncé*. As the former Editor of one of Britain's most popular women's showbiz weeklies, Anna produces celebrity interviews and lifestyle features for a wide range of newspapers and magazines, including the *Telegraph*, the *Mirror*, *Daily Express*, *OK!* and *Fabulous*. She has also authored collectors' magazines focusing on celebrities such as Dua Lipa, Robbie Williams, Billie Eilish, Timothée Chalamet, BLACKPINK and Olivia Rodrigo.

PROLOGUE

On a perfect midsummer's evening at Wembley Stadium, 90,000 Taylor Swift fans are about to witness one of the defining moments of the singer's record-breaking Eras tour. It's Sunday, 23 June 2024 – the third night of her eight-date London takeover – and even after 15 gruelling months on the road, she is still capable of rewriting the script and finding new ways to surprise her audience.

Though Taylor has shared the stage with plenty of surprise guests before, there has been none quite like this. But there's no need for her to make any announcement; united in sequins and friendship bracelets beneath Wembley's iconic arch, the Swifties never miss a beat. As she comes to the end of a segment of songs from her album *The Tortured Poets Department*, an extended intro begins for 'I Can Do It with a Broken Heart'. Then, from out of the wings, a tall figure appears on stage, wearing a black tuxedo and patent Louboutin dress shoes. In a heartbeat, a chorus of screams and whistles erupts around the stadium, as loud as any heard that night. The broad-shouldered, 6ft 5in interloper heel-clicks his way towards Taylor, who is lying gracefully on the stage in a white Vivienne Westwood gown. As the handsome stranger cheekily doffs his glittery top hat, the giant LCD screens zoom in on his face. Then the sound reaches an ear-splitting crescendo. The Wembley faithful can hardly believe what they're seeing, because the man in front of them is none other than Travis Kelce, NFL superstar and Taylor's boyfriend of almost a year.

Instinctively, the fandom knows this is an unprecedented move: not only is it the first time Taylor has put Travis front and centre of her Eras tour, but in nearly two decades of performing live, she has never presented a romantic partner to the world in this way. Looking as if he belongs on stage, the Kansas City Chiefs ace effortlessly gathers Taylor in his arms and carries her to a red sofa, where she theatrically feigns a fainting fit. In a style mimicking a 1920s silent movie, Travis fans her with comedic devotion and uses a brush to apply powder to her face. Once she's back on her feet, two of her dancers whip away her dress to reveal a crystal-studded crop top and hot pants. Travis then hams it up with a few comedy dance steps, and as Taylor blows him a kiss, he waves goodbye and disappears through a hidden trapdoor.

The moment lasts barely two minutes, but it blows up the internet in just seconds. 'Travis Kelce just joined Taylor

Swift on stage at the Eras tour and the world as we know it has ended,' gasps one fan on X. 'Travis Kelce is on stage and he's wearing Louboutins!' screams another. As wobbly video footage circulates and thousands of amusing memes follow, the news media jump on the story, too. *Vanity Fair* calls it 'a jaw-dropping first' and the *LA Times* declares, 'Taylor Swift puts Travis Kelce where no boyfriend has gone before: on stage'. Later, Taylor gives her own verdict on social media. 'I'm still cracking up/swooning over @killatrav's Eras Tour debut,' she posts on Instagram. 'Never going to forget these shows.'

As the dust settles, Travis reveals that the Wembley skit was his idea. 'She started laughing, she was like, "Would you seriously be up for doing something like that?"' he says on his *New Heights* podcast with brother, Jason Kelce. 'I was like, "What? I would love to do that, are you kidding me?" I've seen the show enough, might as well put me to work.' But proving he's only human, he admits to a few nerves before his big debut. 'The one thing I told myself is, "Do not drop the baby. Do not drop Taylor on your way over [to] this damn couch",' he says, before hinting that his cameo could become a regular occurrence in future. 'Shout-out to Tay for letting me jump on stage with her. Who knows, might not be the last time.' Fourteen months later, the pair reminisce about the same night on another edition of the podcast. 'It was so good.

It was so special,' says Taylor, adding that Travis attracted 'the loudest screams I have ever heard on the tour'.

T hat was high praise indeed from the world's most prolific performer, but Travis's star turn under the Wembley floodlights revealed more about the Swift– Kelce dynamic than it did about his budding stage credentials. For Taylor, who spent nearly 20 years protecting the boundaries between her private life and her career, the decision to break the pattern seemed deliberate. It was a statement: she was ready to move to the next level with Travis, and wanted the world to know it – and be part of it. Commentators were quick to draw comparisons with her previous six-and-a-half-year union with the actor Joe Alwyn. Though the longest and most serious of all her relationships, it unfolded almost completely out of public view and was never acknowledged on stage in such a way. In stark contrast, Travis was written directly into Taylor's narrative, and his introduction at the end of *The Tortured Poets Department* sequence felt intentional, too. 'There is something extremely poetic about Travis Kelce carrying Taylor Swift away after her heart was shattered,' one fan wrote online. '"I Can Do It with a Broken Heart" tells a story of performing through heartbreak and masking misery,' *TIME* magazine noted. 'But it might be safe to say that Swift is no longer doing her shows with a broken heart.' From a star who has built an empire on scattering clues and hidden meanings through her art – commonly known as Easter eggs – the image of Travis lifting her into his arms resonated deeply. On the most primeval level, it felt like he was metaphorically carrying her away from years of hurt and trauma; an unshackling by her very own knight in shining armour.

Decoding the pain at the heart of Taylor's music has always been key to understanding the artist herself. From her earliest songs as a curly-haired teenage hopeful trying her luck in Nashville, her lyrics have continually been permeated with heartbreak and longing. Showing a maturity belying her years, she chronicled the ache of first love and betrayal – as well as imagined fairytale endings that were always just out of reach. Through formative albums such as her self-titled debut *Taylor Swift* and follow-ups *Fearless* and *Speak Now*, she amplified the misery of unrequited love and rejection with diary-like intimacy, mapping the messiness of growing up in the relentless glare of the public eye. 'I think that allowing yourself to feel raw, real emotions in public is something I am never going to be afraid to do,' she told *New York* magazine in 2013. 'Hopefully that's the case, if I can remain a real human.'

As the years passed by, Taylor's songwriting grew more intricate and self-referential, yet her central themes and lyrical tendencies consistently circled back to loss, heartache and the never-ending search for a soulmate. Her inner melancholy was laid bare like never before in 2024's *The Tortured Poets Department*, an album which directly followed the demise of her relationship with Joe Alwyn. Songs like 'So Long, London' and 'loml' captured the disillusionment of an all-encompassing love which promised permanence but left only ghosts behind. As a BBC review at the time speculated, 'The singer is bereft and bewildered. Vulnerable in a way we've never heard before. She sings of being so depressed she can't get out of bed, comfort-eating children's cereal, and crying at the gym. You can hear her heart breaking.'

Yet even within the desolate confines of the album, there were small shards of light. A handful of *Tortured Poets* songs – including 'The Alchemy' and 'So High School' – shimmered with the thrill of intoxicating new beginnings, namely her romance with Travis. Taylor herself indicated she was done with all the angst in a social media post coinciding with the album's release. 'This period of the author's life is now over, the chapter closed & boarded up,' she said. 'There is nothing to avenge, no scores to settle once wounds have healed. Once we have spoken our saddest story, we can be free of it.' In that sense, *The Tortured Poets Department* served as a long-overdue farewell to her heartbreak years. Like a bolt from the blue, Travis had upended her world, pursuing her with the kind of old-fashioned romantic bravado she'd long sung about. 'This kinda felt like a 1980s John Hughes movie and he was standing outside my window with a boombox, just being like, "I wanna date you!"' she recalled on the *New Heights* podcast in August 2025. 'This is sort of what I've been writing songs about wanting to happen to me since I was a teenager.' For anyone who had been following the twists and turns in her life since then, that statement spoke volumes.

At the start, few might have picked Travis as a natural match for Taylor. But any doubts that swirled around the world's most articulate songwriter and the 6ft 5in athlete smacked of cultural snobbery, as eloquently expressed by the *Guardian*. 'A new dream man has dropped – the laid-back, confident beefcake,' it said in a comment piece analysing the cult of Kelce. Pointing out that 'women want something quite different now', it added, 'Cartoonish muscles and the ability to bench-press a grizzly bear can make for a partner who wears his masculinity lightly, with an identity that isn't threatened by a successful, independent woman.' But aside from his physical appeal, the lure of Travis ran far deeper for Taylor, and she found in him a rare combination of swagger, kindness and unflinching support. Friends noticed how secure she seemed in his presence, as if she'd finally met someone who understood both the scale of her world and the woman behind it. 'I love the person that I am with because he loves what I do and he loves how much I am fulfilled by making art and making music,' she said on Radio 2's *Scott Mills*

Breakfast Show. 'That's the coolest thing about Travis, like he is so passionate about what he does, that me being passionate about what I do, it connects us.' Another big draw was his unashamed sensitivity. Despite the intimidating shoulder pads and helmet worn when rampaging across the football field each week, his coach once called him 'an emotional guy', and he freely admitted 'I'm a crier' on his podcast. 'This is a man who is not afraid to speak openly about his feelings,' an *Elle* editorial said of Travis. 'Nor is he threatened by the archaic rules of traditional masculinity he'd potentially be breaking by being vulnerable online.'

The biggest love story of a generation began in July 2023, when Travis turned up to Taylor's Eras tour in his hometown of Kansas. His initial attempt to meet her backstage – while bearing a friendship bracelet – failed, and when he admitted on his podcast that he'd been 'butthurt' by the rejection, Taylor's curiosity was piqued, and she agreed to meet him. What could have remained a throwaway anecdote developed into something more, and by the time she began showing up at Chiefs' games and the world realised they were an item, they had, in fact, been quietly dating for months. 'We actually had a significant amount of time that no one knew, which I'm grateful for, because we got to get to know each other,' Taylor later revealed. For fans and media alike, the combination was irresistible: the stadium queen and Super Bowl king, bridging pop music and sport in an enthralling new way. Their status as a modern power couple was undeniable. The NFL credited Taylor's appearances at Chiefs games with generating an estimated $331 million in brand value; and in a twist nobody saw coming, a whole new audience of jersey-wearing football fans began avidly streaming her music. Yet beyond the economic juggernaut they rode in on, the affection between them was pure and unmistakable. Whether embracing on the pitch or sharing a lingering kiss at an afterparty, the chemistry crackled, and they seemed entirely unfazed by the media circus trailing them. 'Whenever I'm with her, it feels like we're just regular people,' Travis told *GQ*. 'When there is not a camera on us, we're just two people that are in love.'

In August 2025, the couple dubbed 'Tay-vis' made it official, announcing their engagement in a joint Instagram reveal that shattered records as one of the most reposted and liked posts in history. In a gesture that would have left teenage Taylor spellbound, Travis transformed the grounds of his Kansas home into an enchanted garden, filling it with thousands of roses. The moment he got down on one knee was caught by a photographer hiding in the bushes, and the post's playful caption – 'Your English teacher and your gym teacher are getting married' – instantly entered pop-culture lexicon.

The ring itself had been custom designed by Travis, and when asked later, Taylor gave his proposal efforts a 'ten out of ten'.

Just weeks after their engagement, Taylor's 12th album, *The Life of a Showgirl*, swept in like a fist-pumping victory lap. Within seven days, it became the fastest-selling album in United States history, shifting over 3.4 million 'pure copies' in its first week, denoting physical and digital sales. In the UK, it also toppled records, scoring the biggest opening-week sales of any international album this century. Almost instantly, she claimed the top three songs in the UK Top 40, too, courtesy of lead single 'The Fate of Ophelia', followed by 'Opalite' and 'Elizabeth Taylor'. Written amid the whirlwind of her Eras tour, when Travis was an ever-present force, the record thrummed with references to the unfiltered joy she had found with him. In the ridiculously catchy 'The Fate of Ophelia', she flipped a tragic myth to become a woman heroically rescued from drowning. In the innuendo-laden 'Wood', she riffed on the idea of superstition, suggesting it was no longer needed with Travis. And 'Opalite' was about emerging from darkness, with his opal birthstone standing as a symbol of serenity after a passing storm.

In interviews, Taylor described *The Life of a Showgirl* as coming from 'the most infectiously joyful, wild, dramatic place', and the visuals, lyrics and tone celebrated love in all its glory. As music critics across the planet noted, the unbridled elation was the polar opposite of the heartbreak that rippled through her earlier albums. '*Showgirl* is everything that *Poets* was not,' said *Business Insider*. 'Was the *Poets* single "Fortnight" too abstract and sombre for you? Did you post on X that Swift should put down the feather quill and make bangers again? Congratulations, she heard you, and now you've got 12 of them.' In a similar vein, *Variety* asked if the world was ready for Taylor the 'untortured poet', calling the light-heartedness of the record 'slightly startling', and stressing that it was 'as close to being an uncomplicated good time as anything she's ever done'. Yet not everyone was quite prepared for this version of her. For a small proportion of fans, the album's sparkle and theatrical abandon felt like a sharp turn away from the aching lyricism and intimacy that defined works like *folklore*, *evermore*, *Midnights* and *The Tortured Poets Department*. Some argued that *The Life of a Showgirl* was verging on overexposure, or even an unnecessary cash grab. But in dividing opinion, it proved Taylor's enduring ability to dictate and reframe the conversation, and to skip just out of reach of all expectations.

Whether the album inspired adulation or lukewarm approval, few could say Taylor hadn't earned the right to the unapologetic happiness it represented. It followed years of trial and error, when her every liaison, near miss and wrong man became an international talking point. Hook-ups and break-ups with celebrities, including Taylor Lautner, Joe

Jonas, John Mayer and Jake Gyllenhaal, were a cultural fixation; her subsequent pain and disappointment were etched on albums like *Fearless* and the shapeshifting *Red*. 'I look back on this as my true break-up album,' she said of the latter in a *Rolling Stone* interview. 'This was an album that I wrote specifically about pure, absolute, to-the-core heartbreak.' But as she sought to find her way, a nasty undercurrent saw Taylor accused of turning every man she dated into a song. 'People would act like [songwriting] was a weapon I was using. Like a cheap dirty trick,' she told *Vogue* in 2019. 'Be careful, bro, she'll write a song about you. Don't stand near her.' Highlighting the double standards implicit in the music industry while appearing on the Australian radio show *Jules, Merrick and Sophie* in 2014, she said, 'You're going to have people who are going to say, "Oh, you know, like, she just writes songs about her ex-boyfriends." And I think frankly that's a very sexist angle to take. No one says that about Ed Sheeran. No one says that about Bruno Mars. They're all writing songs about their exes, their current girlfriends, their love life, and no one raises the red flag there.'

That same year, the release of *1989* – Taylor's first fully fledged pop album – was seen as a symbolic rebirth following her move to New York. Still her bestselling work to date, it catapulted her to new levels of fame that only manifested further obsession with her personal life. Lyrically, the album's story was inextricably linked to her experience of dating one of the world's biggest boyband stars, Harry Styles, leading to much-dissected tracks like 'Style' and 'Out of the Woods'. But it was, perhaps, her long-term partnership with Joe Alwyn that impacted Taylor most profoundly, with later albums *reputation* and *Lover* steeped in giddying love, and subsequent releases *folklore, evermore, Midnights* and *The Tortured Poets Department* conveying contentment, sorrow and resentment in equal measure.

The acres of coverage that shadowed her every relationship often said more about how society viewed women than about Taylor herself. Speaking at a ceremony at New York University in 2022, she said, 'Having the world treat my love life like a spectator sport in which I lose every single game was not a great way to date in my teens and twenties, but it taught me to protect my private life fiercely. Being publicly humiliated over and over again at a young age was excruciatingly painful, but it forced me to devalue the ridiculous notion of minute-by-minute, ever-fluctuating social relevance and likeability.'

In some ways, the perpetual fascination around her love life is a direct consequence of her unique craftsmanship. By writing and singing so honestly about matters of the heart, Taylor has always invited listeners into her innermost thoughts – simultaneously turning them into something millions can relate to. 'I don't talk about my personal life in great detail. I write about it in my songs,' she told *Glamour* in 2012. 'I feel like you can share enough about your life in your music to let people know what you're going through.' In that way, the Swiftie phenomenon has grown beyond fandom into a global community, with connections built not just on music, but also deep emotional investment in her storytelling. Fans don't simply listen to her songs – they inhabit them. It's a symbiosis, and as Taylor once revealingly said at a *Billboard* awards ceremony, 'To the fans who come to the shows, who buy the albums, I just want you to know this one thing – you are the longest and best relationship I have ever had.'

Showing a distinct pride in the way Swifties have so avidly decoded her hidden Easter eggs through her career, Taylor once told *Entertainment Weekly*: 'I've trained them to be that way. I love that they like the cryptic hint-dropping. Because as long as they like it, I'll keep doing it. It's fun. It feels mischievous and playful.' Each single and album release has accordingly brought a new treasure hunt; her lyrics shelling out tiny breadcrumbs that led back to a significant other. 'I let people fill in the blanks on their own,' she told *TIME*. 'If they want to think about their ex, that's fine. If they want to think about maybe who one of my exes is, then that's fine. And it might not be right, because I'm the only one who knows what these songs are really about. It's the one shred of privacy I have in the matter.' But here lies the great paradox bound up in Taylor's work: the more authentic and truthful her song-writing has been, the more blurred the line between art and autobiography. Her efforts to protect what is hers alone have only intensified the scrutiny – and in that context, it is little wonder so many of her romances have previously struggled to go the distance.

But with Travis, things seem altogether different. For once, there has been no tug of war between privacy and performance, and no need to hide one from the other. His bit part on the Wembley stage felt like the perfect metaphor for that shift, and after years of translating her love life into imagery and metaphor, Taylor no longer had to disguise the real thing. With Travis, she has simply been able to live it. As she said when promoting *The Life of a Showgirl* on SiriusXM's *Morning Mash Up* in October 2025, 'It's all turned out great. He's one of those people where as soon as you meet him, you know he's the best. And you know there's no one else on the planet that's ever been even remotely similar to him. He's one of one.' All of a sudden, a fleeting comment dropped into her album notes for *Red* seems more apt than ever. 'Real love shines golden like starlight, and doesn't fade or spontaneously combust,' she said. 'Maybe I'll write a whole album about that kind of love if I ever find it.'

With Travis, she finally seems to have done just that.

CHAPTER ONE

With more than 280 million Instagram followers, Taylor Swift commands a digital audience larger than most nations. In 2024 alone, her music was streamed over 26 billion times on Spotify; she was crowned the world's bestselling recording artist for a record-breaking fifth time and her Eras tour became the highest-grossing tour in history, surpassing the 2-billion-dollar mark and solidifying her status as the most powerful entertainer on the planet. Yet amid the towering statistics, it's easy to forget where it all began. How she was once just a teenage girl with a guitar, turning the random scribbles in her school notebooks into stories and songs that would soundtrack an entire generation.

Nearly two decades before meeting NFL star Travis Kelce, she sat in a seventh-grade maths class, her mind drifting aimlessly past equations and algebra. A simple melody began forming in her head, soft enough to hum under her breath. It was shaped by her first experience of heartbreak – and would become the breakthrough that set her extraordinary career in motion. 'The concept for this song hit me because I was dating a guy who moved away, and it was going to be over for us,' she later recalled. 'I started thinking of things that I knew would remind him of me.' After school finished for the day in Hendersonville, Tennessee, Taylor sat down at the piano with Liz Rose, the professional songwriter paired with Taylor, who would go on to become her long-term writing partner, and it took the pair just a quarter of an hour to compose the track 'Tim McGraw'. 'It may be the best 15 minutes I've ever experienced,' Taylor said. The curious title was inspired by the name of one of her favourite country artists, who she had listened to on loop with the boy in question, who had now left town for college. Nursing the sting of their break-up, she told *SongwriterUniverse* magazine, 'The song is based on true events – it happened in real life ... After the break-up, I wanted him to be reminded of me.' Though it's hard to grasp the speed at which she wrote the song, it has never been Taylor's style to agonise over her work. 'I didn't have time to complicate it or overthink it. I just wrote it,' she told the *LA Times*.

Several months later, in June 2006, 'Tim McGraw' was chosen as her debut single, and it's fair to say it changed the trajectory of her life. Peaking at No. 40 on America's *Billboard* Hot 100, the mid-tempo ballad hit No. 3 on the Hot Country Songs chart and went on to sell over 1.6 million copies in America. The song not only introduced listeners to Taylor's acoustic harmonies and lilting vocals, but also showcased a deeply personal, confessional style of songwriting that would characterise her career. 'I like to write songs about boys. I like to write songs about relationships,' she once told E! 'It's really, really fun for me to tell stories that have actually happened.'

Since the beginning, Taylor's music has been anchored in relationships and emotional truths, with her hopes of one day finding the right man an ever-present theme. 'I have always been fascinated with fairytales, and the idea that Prince Charming is just one castle away,' she told *Allure* magazine in 2010. 'And you're gonna run across a field and meet each other in the middle, and have an amazing, perfect movie kiss. And it's gonna be happily ever after.' Years later, she quite literally found herself running across a field toward Kansas City Chiefs star Travis. Yet such romantic ideals were formed long before fame came knocking, and even as a toddler she could recite all the words to the Righteous Brothers' classic 'Unchained Melody'. As her father Scott Swift told the student newspaper *UDaily* in 2009, 'She was always singing music when she was three, five, six, seven years old.'

With her quest for the definitive happy ending permeating her music, Taylor's journey has often felt like a shared experience, creating an unbreakable bond with millions across the world. 'There is an element to my fanbase where we feel like we grew up together,' she said in her 2020 *Miss Americana* documentary on Netflix. 'I'll be going through something, write the album about it and then it'll come out, and sometimes it'll just coincide with what they're going through. Kind of like they're reading my diary.'

That precedent was firmly set by 'Tim McGraw', with its wistful memories widely thought to have referred to Drew Dunlap, a freshman from school who was Taylor's first love. The track saw her reflect on a month's worth of tears as she lamented the end of the relationship, although in a fashion that would continue throughout her career, Taylor chose not to publicly confirm his identity. As *Vanity Fair* once stated, 'Swift writes songs about the guys she dates and then sends her fans on scavenger hunts to find out who they are.' Offering up a few more clues to listeners, she did tell the music channel Great American Country, 'The guy I wrote "Tim McGraw" about, I dated him for about a year and we are still friends, but we don't talk that much because his new girlfriend isn't too much of a fan. He really thought it was cool that, even though we weren't going out anymore, I remembered our relationship nicely.' It was a classic Swiftian strategy: presenting the bare bones of a real-life love story, but keeping it shrouded in mystery.

Music critics were instantly drawn to 'Tim McGraw', with *PopMatters* declaring that its 'suitably twangy and atmospheric' qualities were on a par with 'some of the best country singles of recent years'. As *Pitchfork* also championed the fresh-faced 16-year-old who had 'crash-landed into this land-scape', Taylor's arrival certainly seemed like a blast of fresh air in the mid-2000s, when the country scene was heavily dominated by older male artists who stuck to well-established formulas. But while she incorporated traditional instruments like the banjo, mandolin, fiddle and guitar into her songs, cowboy-boot wearing Taylor embellished them with a glossy pop sheen, so they transcended genres and brought a whole new audience to country. No wonder, then, that the *New York Times* called her both 'revolutionary' and 'the most remarkable country music breakthrough artist of the decade'.

Hot on the heels of 'Tim McGraw', her self-titled debut album *Taylor Swift* was released in October 2006. Co-produced by musician Nathan Chapman – a key figure in the early stages of Taylor's career – it received widespread acclaim and shot to No. 1 in the US country album charts. It also reached No. 5 on the *Billboard* 200 and spent a total of 157 weeks on the chart – the longest for any album in the 2000s. Adapted from the restless doodles that filled her notebooks, the album's 11 songs navigated adolescent desire and heartache, enticing fans to try to unearth the concealed Easter eggs. The track 'Should've Said No' was a case in point, coming in response to a betrayal by a school crush called Sam. In the lyrics, Taylor repeatedly capitalised the letters S, A and M, later admitting to *Women's Health*: 'I like to encode capital letters in the printed lyrics, so they spell out phrases. I encoded the "Should've Said No" guy's name over and over. It was only his first name, but everyone figured it out. I'd get texts from him. He was scared out of his mind I'd crucify him on a talk show. All I could think was, "Well, you should've said no. That's what the song is about."'

The album's second single, 'Teardrops on My Guitar', was another tale of romantic angst, dealing with Taylor's unrequited feelings for an unnamed classmate. '[He] would sit there every day talking to me about ... another girl: how beautiful she was, how nice and smart and perfect she was,' she wrote on her website at the time. 'And I sat there and listened, never meaning it any of the times I said, "Oh, I'm so happy for you."' Unafraid to wear her heart on her sleeve from day one, she added, 'I guess this is a good example of how I let my feelings out in songs, and sometimes no other way.' Divulging the cathartic nature of her songwriting back in 2007, Taylor told *Unrated Magazine*, 'If it's a heartbreak song or something like it, it usually helps me get through it, and I've actually gotten a few missed calls from Mr. Teardrops on My Guitar. And I'm not going back, because he's still got a girlfriend.' Despite its less-than-cheery sentiment, the song fared even better than her debut single, peaking at No. 2 in the Hot Country Songs chart and reaching No. 13 on the *Billboard* Hot 100, too. Then came her third single, 'Our Song', which she originally wrote on a napkin for a high-school talent show. 'The song was finished in like 20 minutes,' she told music channel Great American Country. 'I wrote it about this guy I was dating, and how we didn't have a song. So I went ahead and wrote us one.' It led to her first Hot Country Songs No. 1, occupying the top spot for six weeks, and made her, at just 17, the youngest person to write and sing a chart-topping country hit. Slowly but surely, she was beginning to carve out a name for herself in mainstream music circles, too, and she was nominated for her first ever Grammy in February 2008. In the end, the Best New Artist award went to Amy Winehouse, but it signalled the start of a long and productive Grammy association for Taylor.

With her career now firing on all cylinders, 'Picture to Burn', the fourth single from her album, landed the same month. 'She's a genius, coming in with ideas and a melody,' said Liz Rose, who co-wrote the track with Taylor. 'She'd come in and write with this old lady, and I never second-guessed her.' 'Picture to Burn' showed Taylor's gutsier side, dissing a boyfriend for dumping her and plotting a revenge that included setting fire to old photos and, amusingly, dating his friends. Rumour has it that during one of their after-school songwriting sessions, Taylor told Liz: 'I hate his stupid truck that he doesn't let me drive. He's such a redneck! Oh my God!' It was said the subject of her wrath was a boy called Jordan Alford, who was in her year group at Hendersonville

High School. Though they briefly went out, he ended up with her friend Chelsea, whom he later married. Speaking in 2014, Chelsea told the *Daily Mail* they were both tickled after ending up in one of Taylor's songs. '[Jordan] was like, "I'm not a redneck! She makes me look like some redneck!" but other than that we just thought it was kind of funny.'

Regardless of what went on, the spiky lyrics in 'Picture to Burn' showed how Taylor could vent her relationship frustrations while channelling them creatively. 'A lot of my writing on my album is just honest,' she told the *LA Times* in 2007. 'For me it's always been about keeping it as real as possible. Because I felt that people can identify with that.' That desire to tell her truth has never faltered, and in a piece she wrote for *Elle* in 2019, she explained that music is the most effective way of documenting her life: 'I love writing songs because I love preserving memories, like putting a picture frame around a feeling you once had,' she said. 'I like to be able to remember the extremely good and extremely bad times. I want to remember the colour of the sweater, the temperature of the air, the creak of the floorboards, the time on the clock when your heart was stolen or shattered or healed or claimed forever.'

In lighter moments, the album celebrated pure, harmless lust, too – as seen in the track 'Stay Beautiful'. The song was about admiring a good-looking boy from afar. Taylor explained, 'I was standing in the hallway at school and this guy walked past. And I was like, "Wow, he's really hot". And so I went home and I wrote a song about it.' While you might imagine that today's Taylor harbours a few regrets over professing her innermost adolescent thoughts in such a way, she in fact recalls the era with immense pride. 'I look back on the record I made when I was 16, and I'm so happy I made it,' she told MTV years later in 2011. 'I got to immortalise those emotions that when you're so angry, you hate everything. It's like recording your diary over the years, and that's a gift.'

The success of her first album and its flurry of singles served as the ultimate reward for several years of persistence and crushing rejection. From the age of just 11, she had set her sights on launching a career in Nashville, known as Music City. 'I began relentlessly nagging, begging, and pleading with my parents to take me on a trip there,' Taylor told *TIME* magazine in 2014. Eventually, mum Andrea relented, and during a spring-break visit they arrived with recordings of karaoke-style covers of the likes of the Dixie Chicks and Dolly Parton. 'She would wait in the car as I scampered into record labels one by one, handing my demo CD to the receptionists,' Taylor told *TIME*. Walking up and down the city's famous Music Row, she would boldly announce herself: 'Hey, I'm Taylor, I'm 11, and I want a record deal. Call me.' Unsurprisingly, the less-than-subtle pitch fell on deaf ears, and she later admitted, 'I went back home after that trip. And I realised that everyone in that town wanted to do what I wanted to do. So, I kept thinking to myself, I need to figure out a way to be different. I need to have something to really bring to that town.' Back on the farm she grew up on in Pennsylvania, Taylor doubled down, pouring her heart into her songwriting and learning the 12-string guitar. 'Don't ever say never or can't do to Taylor,' Andrea told *Entertainment Weekly*. 'She started playing it four hours a day – six on the weekends. She would get calluses on her fingers and they would crack and bleed, and we would tape them up and she'd just keep on playing.'

Spending so much time working on music rather than hanging out with friends did leave Taylor isolated, however. 'A lot of girls thought I was weird. Actually, the word they liked to use was *annoying*,' she told *Women's Health*. 'I'd sit down at their lunch table, and they'd move to a different one.' But she was nothing if not resilient, and she told *Vogue* in 2012, 'It never mattered to me that people in school didn't think that country music was cool, and they made fun of me for it.' Being less fashion-savvy than her peer group did not sit quite so comfortably, but as she stressed, 'I was just like, "I like wearing sundresses and cowboy boots".'

Though being an outsider is tough for any teen, Taylor learned to articulate her feelings through her music. 'It's my way of coping,' she said. 'I write when I'm frustrated, angry or confused.' Songwriting gave her a voice, and as she once told the *Sunday Times Magazine*, 'I could say things in songs that I wasn't brave enough to say in person ... because I couldn't tell that guy in the English class I thought he was cute, and I couldn't tell that group of popular girls it really hurt my feelings that they didn't invite me to that sleepover. I could turn that into a metaphor, into a chorus, and then, for some reason, those emotions made more sense to me.'

One track that explored her loneliness was 'A Place in This World', written while she was travelling back and forth to Nashville. 'I knew where I wanted to be, but I just didn't know how to get there,' she said of the song, which she later included on her debut album. Down in Tennessee, her youth and inexperience continued to be a stumbling block. 'Having label executives in Nashville tell me that only 35-year-old housewives listen to country music and there was no place for a 13-year-old on their roster made me cry in the car on the way home,' she said during a speech at New York University in 2022. Never disheartened for too long, though, Taylor realised that one way of getting noticed was to perform at sporting events. 'I started singing the National Anthem anywhere I possibly could – 76ers' games, the US Open, and I would just send my tapes out everywhere,' she told *Rolling Stone*. 'I would sing the National Anthem at garden club meetings. I didn't care.'

In a twist of fate, one of her renditions was spotted by New York-based talent manager Dan Dymtrow, who was already working with Britney Spears. Impressed by her vocal range, he duly took Taylor under his wing, landing her a slot in a 'Rising Star' campaign, which saw her posing on the pages of *Vanity Fair* with her trusty guitar. Introducing herself in the magazine in August 2004, Taylor said, 'I sometimes write about teenage love, but I am presently a 14-year-old girl without a boyfriend. Sometimes I worry that I must be wearing some kind of guy repellent, but then I realise that I'm just discovering who I am as a person.' More significantly, Dan then helped her secure what she had dreamed of for so long: an artist-development deal with RCA Records. It essentially provided her with sponsorship and mentoring – though it turned out to be more like a holding arrangement than a fully fledged recording contract. 'A development deal is an in-between record deal,' Taylor told NBC. 'It's like a guy saying that he wants to date you but not to be your boyfriend.'

But with the deal putting Taylor in a much more favourable position, the Swift family decided to up sticks from Pennsylvania and relocate to Hendersonville, just outside Nashville. It must have seemed like a rash move to many, but Andrea and Scott Swift had extensive knowledge of the music business thanks to Taylor's maternal grandmother, Marjorie, once having been a professional opera singer, and it made perfect sense to the family. 'I knew I was the reason they were moving,' Taylor later told *Self.* 'But they tried to put no pressure on me. They were like, "Well, we need a change of scenery, anyway," and "I love how friendly the people in Tennessee are".' Aware it was a huge sacrifice for them both, as well as her younger brother Austin, Taylor has often expressed her gratitude to them. 'My parents were unbelievable – I will never forget how they did that,' she told CBS in 2019. 'And my brother is a real bro for doing that.' As her biggest supporter, Andrea was never in any doubt about Taylor's motivations either. 'It was never about, "I want to be famous". Taylor never uttered those words,' she said. 'It was about moving to a place where she could write with people she could learn from.' Taylor has never lost sight of all that Andrea gave up for her, and on winning one of her first big newcomer trophies at the Academy of Country Music Awards in Las Vegas in 2008, she memorably said, 'There are so many people that deserve to be thanked for this, but I'm just gonna thank one – and that's the person that used to love to go to lunch with her friends and cook dinner for her family and sleep in her bed every night, and she gave that all away and left it all behind to go on the road with her 16-year-old daughter. Then she was sleeping in rental cars and in airplanes with her mouth hanging wide open 'cause she was so tired. And so, Mom, thank you so much. I love you. This is for you.'

As the family settled into Nashville life, a pivotal acoustic performance at the legendary Bluebird Café in November 2004 led Taylor to music exec Scott Borchetta. The timing could not have been better, as he was in the process of founding Big Machine Records and actively searching for new talent. Within two weeks he had signed her to the fledgling label, on the strict proviso she would write all her own songs – which was music to Taylor's ears. 'I fell in love with her,' Scott told the business magazine *Fast Company*. 'It's really that simple.' Inevitably, many within the staunchly traditional country sector saw the signing as risky, but Scott was unfazed. 'True talent is ageless,' he said in a *Billboard* interview years later. 'It was a lightning bolt for me.' And when Taylor played him 'Tim McGraw', he knew it should be her first single. 'She finished the song and I said, "Do you realise what you have just written? Do you have any idea?"' Scott told NBC. But at the start, Big Machine only had ten employees, so Taylor had to get involved at the most rudimentary level. 'When they were releasing my first single, my mom and I came in to help stuff the CD singles into envelopes to send to radio,' she later told *Entertainment Weekly*. 'We sat out on the floor and did it because there wasn't furniture at the label yet.' Though her partnership with Scott soured over the controversial sale of her master recordings in future years, Taylor recognised in the beginning that his backing was the key to unlocking her career. In a long list of thanks accompanying her debut release, she singled him out 'for believing in me and actually DOING something about it'. Crucially, Scott championed her candid style of songwriting from the outset. 'She had that teen angst in those songs that is really at the heart of great rock 'n' roll,' he told *Billboard*. 'There's such a beautiful sadness to many of those things she wrote. Such a great heartbreak to her voice, you can't just create that.'

As her partnership with Scott and Big Machine Records flourished, Taylor began work on a second album, *Fearless*. As before, her personal experiences directly shaped its production, with what she called 'cataclysmic crushes and brushes with heartache' smouldering in the background. Comprising 13 tracks, all of which she either wrote or co-wrote, she said the album was 'full of magic and curiosity', and that she intended it to be 'the diary of the adventures and explorations of a teenage girl who was learning tiny lessons with every new crack in the façade of the fairytale ending she'd been shown in the movies'. Released in November 2008 in America and four months later elsewhere, *Fearless* debuted at No. 1 on the *Billboard* 200 chart, where it spent 11 weeks – the longest chart-run for any female country musician. It was also the bestselling album in the US in 2009, and in the UK, it reached No. 5, with Taylor later calling it 'the breakthrough moment I'd always dreamed of, one that catapulted my career to new realms of success'.

However, she admitted her newfound stardom brought with it 'a tidal wave of pressures and pitfalls and growing pains', and despite its commercial success, *Fearless* was not well received by everyone. Dedicated country afficionados found it too pop-heavy, while *Pitchfork* was unmoved by what it called Taylor's 'faux-country accent'. Some critics also voiced ambivalence to the record's themes, which they said bordered on juvenile or were too repetitive. *Q* magazine was especially scathing, saying, 'Her giggly peers will find she speaks their language, while grown-ups will prefer her to keep quiet.'

Nevertheless, Taylor had the last laugh, and the album's lead single 'Love Story', released in September 2008, was largely seen as the track that transported her from Nashville prodigy to global phenomenon. It became one of the bestselling country singles of all time, with Taylor saying it 'turned into something I never expected it to be. Our first number-one worldwide hit.' The song documented a troubled romance based on Shakespeare's *Romeo and Juliet* – although the star-crossed lovers ended up marrying instead of suffering one of the most devastating denouements in literary history. 'I feel like they had such promise and they were so crazy for each other. And if that had just gone a little bit differently, it could have been the best love story ever told,' Taylor said in a

2008 interview with the *LA Times*. In her album notes, she tellingly said, 'It's the ending that I want. You want a guy who doesn't care what anyone thinks, what anyone says. He just says, "Marry me, Juliet, I love you."'

The happily-ever-after energy of 'Love Story' cemented Taylor's reputation as a voice of authenticity when it came to young love. Rooted in real life, the track concerned a potential boyfriend she had been advised to avoid at all costs. 'When I introduced him to my family and my friends, they all said they didn't like him. All of them,' Taylor said in a Q&A with *TIME*. 'For the first time, I could relate to that Romeo-and-Juliet situation where the only people who wanted them to be together were them.' She once called 'Love Story' 'the most romantic song I've written', and it was partly born out of the misty-eyed reveries of her lost youth. 'I never got to have a normal college experience, per se,' she said during a talk with students in New York in 2022. 'I went to public high school until tenth grade and then finished my education doing homeschool work on the floors of airport terminals. As a kid, I always thought I would go away to college, imagining the posters I would hang on the wall of my freshman dorm. I even set the ending of my music video for my song "Love Story" at my fantasy imaginary college, where I meet a male model reading a book on the grass, and with one single glance, we realise we had been in love in our past lives.'

Fast forward to February 2021 and Taylor chose 'Love Story' as the first single from her re-recorded album *Fearless (Taylor's Version)*. The reworking was the result of a £237 million sale of Big Machine Records in June 2019 to music manager Scooter Braun, who, without Taylor's knowledge, sold the master recordings of her first six albums to a company called Shamrock Holdings. She later said the sale 'ripped my heart out of my chest', and it became her life's mission to claw back ownership of her songs by re-recording all six albums. After signing a new deal with Republic Records, she kickstarted the process with *Fearless (Taylor's Version)*, and the more mature vocals and slicker production heard on 'Love Story (Taylor's Version)' served as a striking metaphor for a teenage fairytale that had evolved into a message of resilience and empowerment. The song was a global smash hit all over again, and Taylor told *Good Morning America*, 'It's been the most fun doing "Love Story" because [in] the older music, my voice was so teenaged and sometimes, when I hear my older music and my older young teenage voice, it makes me feel like I'm a different singer now.' When *Fearless (Taylor's Version)* subsequently arrived in April 2021, the album also topped the charts worldwide and, reflecting on what it meant to take back what was rightfully hers, she said on Instagram, 'This process has been more fulfilling and emotional than I could've imagined and has made me even more determined to re-record all of my music.'

The original version of *Fearless* spawned five official singles overall, with 'White Horse' portraying a fairytale gone wrong. 'In the song "White Horse", you put everything you have into love and you get your heart broken,' Taylor told *The Boot*. 'More people have been able to relate to those songs; the ones that I wrote when I was really going through something terrible.' The song hit No. 2 on the US Hot Country Songs chart, but a truer measure of its impact came when it triumphed at the 2010 Grammys, scooping Best Country Song and Best Female Country Vocal Performance. 'This is my first Grammy, you guys!' a jubilant Taylor said as she made her debut acceptance speech. 'I'm so happy! Thank you so much.' The evening also saw her become the youngest person ever, aged just 20, to win the coveted Album of the Year Grammy for *Fearless* – a record she held until 2020 when she was eclipsed by an 18-year-old Billie Eilish. 'This is for my dad,' Taylor said, as she collected the trophy. 'This is for all those times that you said I could do whatever I wanted in life. And my mom, you're my best friend. This is the story all of us when we're 80 years old and we are telling the same stories over and over again to our grandkids and they're so annoyed with us, this is the story we're going to be telling over and over again in 2010 that we got to win Album of the Year at the Grammys.' After once describing Dad, Scott, as 'a big teddy bear who tells me everything I do is perfect', Taylor also wrote *Fearless* song 'The

Best Day' as a surprise for her mum, Andrea. 'When I got the track, I synced up all of these home videos from when I was a little kid to go along with the song like a music video, and played it for her on Christmas Eve and she was crying her eyes out,' she told *Taste of Country*. Calling Andrea 'my only friend when I was 13', she added, 'My mom was my escape in a lot of ways.' Eventually, Taylor had to stop playing 'The Best Day' live, though, because it was too emotional for them both.

As well as earning her a clutch of golden Grammys, *Fearless* brought Taylor her first ever MTV Video Music Award, courtesy of third single 'You Belong With Me', which won Best Female Video in 2009. The song, which had stormed to No. 2 on the *Billboard* Hot 100 and broken the UK Top 30, was a tale of unrequited love inspired by Taylor overhearing a band member getting a hard time from his girlfriend on the phone. 'She was just yelling at him! I felt so bad for him at that moment,' she explained. 'I ran that into the story line that I'm in love with him and he should be with me instead of her.' The award-winning video cast Taylor in a high-school romcom, where she played both 'the nerd, who is pining away for this guy that she can't have', as well as 'the popular girl'. The guy in question was played by *Hannah Montana* actor Lucas Till, whom Taylor had met the year before when she landed a small cameo in the film. After reconnecting on the video shoot for 'You Belong With Me', they went on a few innocuous dates. However, Lucas later told MTV it didn't progress, adding that there was 'no friction' between them. 'With us, I really just liked her as a friend. That's the only reason that didn't work out.'

While Taylor's night of victory at the VMAs should have been one of the most glorious of her life, it was remembered for all the wrong reasons when Kanye West famously interrupted her 'You Belong With Me' acceptance speech at the star-studded ceremony. 'Yo, Taylor, I'm really happy for you, I'mma let you finish, but Beyoncé had one of the best videos of all time,' he interjected, leaving Taylor utterly speechless on stage. He believed Beyoncé should have won the gong for 'Single Ladies (Put a Ring on It)' instead, but the incident, known as 'Kanye-gate', drew international condemnation and even prompted the US president of the time, Barack Obama, to brand the rapper a 'jackass'.

As Taylor albums go, few have been more crowded with unfiltered observations on messy relationships than *Fearless*. In a review of the album, the *Boston Globe* noted somewhat drily, 'She's had some seriously bad luck with boys', while *Blender* went a step further, snarking: 'Since she's only 18 and has been a hard-working full-time country megastar for the past two years, it's a marvel she has so much romantic roadkill under her wheels. As for her boys – oh,

the carnage. She makes mincemeat out of these hapless crit-
ters.' One such track was 'Forever & Always', written in the
aftermath of Taylor's split from the musician and actor Joe
Jonas. The song only narrowly made it on to *Fearless*, after
she booked a last-minute studio session and laid down the
track with just a day to spare. Her relationship with the Jonas
Brothers singer was complicated – not least because it was
her first with another big-name celebrity – but there's little
doubt it left an indelible mark on her.

They first met in the summer of 2008 when she joined
Joe and his brother Nick on stage during their Burnin' Up
tour. But when asked, amid a deluge of rumours, if she and
Joe were an item, Taylor coyly told *People*, 'He's an amazing
guy and anybody would be lucky to be dating him.' As if they
were sharing the same PR playbook, Joe was equally vague,
telling TV host Ryan Seacrest, 'She's a great girl ... I think
anybody would love to go on a date with her.' Speculation
went into overdrive when they sat together at the MTV Video
Music Awards that September, and the pair were known to
enjoy cosy double dates with Nick and his then girlfriend,
Selena Gomez – still one of Taylor's BFFs. But within weeks,
it was all over for her and Joe. 'It's been tough,' a dejected
Taylor told LA's KIIS-FM. 'You just have to try to realise someday you'll find someone that's right for you.' Soon after, there
was an awkward encounter during a pre-booked televised

New Year's Eve concert in New York, when she and Joe were spotted standing at opposite ends of the stage as the famous ball dropped at midnight.

Far from offering a nostalgia-soaked reflection of their brief time together, the song 'Forever & Always' conveyed nothing but anger and confusion. As Taylor told *People*, it was 'about watching somebody fade away in a relationship and wondering what you did wrong'. Clearly a woman scorned, she added, 'This song starts with this pretty melody that's easy to sing along with, then in the end ... I'm basically screaming it because I'm so mad.'

Adding salt to her wounds, she claimed on *The Ellen DeGeneres Show* in late 2008 that Joe finished with her on the phone. 'When I find that person who is right for me, he'll be wonderful, and when I look at that person, I'm not even gonna be able to remember the boy who broke up with me over the phone in 25 seconds when I was 18,' she said. Clearly scarred by the incident, she also referred to it when hosting *Saturday Night Live* for the first time in 2009. In a musical monologue that showed a glimpse of her sharp self-awareness, she sang, 'This is my musical monologue/You might think I'd bring up Joe/That guy who broke up with me on the phone/But I'm not gonna mention him.' With their demise airing so publicly, Joe himself hit back at separate claims he had strayed, writing in an online letter, 'Several things I will state with all my heart. I never cheated on a girlfriend. It might make someone feel better to assume or imply I have been unfaithful but it is simply not true. Maybe there were reasons for a break-up. Maybe the heart moved on. Perhaps feelings changed.' He also implied that it was Tayor who cut short their infamous telephone conversation, adding, 'I called to discuss feelings with the other person. Those feelings were obviously not well received. I did not end the conversation. Someone else did. Phone calls can only last as long as the person on the other end of the line is willing to talk.' Later, when asked about his megastar ex during a chat on SiriusXM, Joe paid his respects to Taylor's 'incredible' talent, before cattily quipping, 'But yeah, the girl likes to date.'

Whatever the reason for the souring between them, Taylor found it hard to let go, and she once called 'Last Kiss' on her later album *Speak Now* from 2010 the 'the saddest song I've ever written'. Composed in the wake of her split from Joe, she explained on her website: 'The song "Last Kiss" is sort of like a letter to somebody. Going through a break-up you feel all of these different things. You feel anger, and you feel confusion, and frustration. Then there is the absolute sadness. The sadness of losing this person, losing all the memories, and the hopes you had for the future ... When I was in one of those moments I wrote this song.' Aside from her sorrow, Taylor felt humiliated, too, and 'Better Than Revenge' on *Speak Now* evoked the tricky situation in a different way, disparaging an actress who allegedly stole Joe away. However, with the benefit of a few more years' experience, she later distanced herself from that response, telling the *Guardian* in 2014, 'I was 18 when I wrote that. That's the age you are when you think someone can actually take your boyfriend. Then you grow up and realise no one can take someone from you if they don't want to leave.'

She also showed a mellowing over the situation on the song 'Holy Ground', which appeared on her 2012 album *Red*. Instead of conjuring up old fury, the track gave a more positive spin on her union with Joe, with the album's notes also mentioning a *Speak Now* gig in San Diego he attended in 2011. Once asked how he felt about repeatedly cropping up in Taylor's songs, Joe told *Access Hollywood*, 'That's part of being a musician, I guess. You write songs about each other.' Insisting things were amicable, he added, 'She's great ... Obviously, it's tough to be friends with people that are always constantly travelling, but yeah, we're cool.'

Later that year, Taylor invited Joe to one of her famous Fourth of July parties at her Rhode Island home, along with his brother Nick. And in 2019, during a return appearance on *The Ellen DeGeneres Show*, she spoke of her regret over shaming Joe. Asked by Ellen what was the most rebellious thing she did as a teenager, Taylor replied, 'Probably when I, like, put Joe Jonas on blast on your show. That was too much. Yeah, that was too much. I was 18. We laugh about it now, but that was mouthy ... just teenage stuff there.'

Despite so much water under the bridge, her enduring disappointment seemed to rear its head once again in the spring of 2021. The song 'Mr Perfectly Fine' appeared on the reworked *Fearless (Taylor's Version)*, telling of an ex who had once seemed like Mr Right – assumed to be Joe – who had turned out to be only okay, or 'perfectly fine'. When the song dropped, Joe's then wife, *Game of Thrones* star Sophie Turner, showed her liking for the song, posting on Instagram, 'It's not NOT a bop.' And shortly before they announced their divorce, she shared a photo of herself wearing a friendship bracelet bearing the words 'Mr Perfectly Fine'.

Other songs giving wayward boys short shrift on *Fearless* include the barbed track 'Tell Me Why' – a generic observation on a partner's unreliability. It was written rapidly after Taylor's co-writer Liz Rose asked what she'd like to tell a former beau who had let her down. 'I would say to him, "I'm sick and tired of your attitude, I feel like I don't even know you,"' Taylor told Associated Press. 'I just started rambling, and she was writing down everything that I was saying, and so we turned it into a song.' 'You're Not Sorry' belted out similar views on a disappointing love interest. 'It turned out Prince Charming had a lot of secrets that he didn't tell me about,' said Taylor. 'I wrote this when I was at the breaking point of: "You know what? Don't even think that you can keep on hurting me".' Rather less dramatically, the fourth single, 'Fifteen', recounted Taylor's and best friend Abigail Anderson's teenage dalliances at Hendersonville High. 'I just decided I really wanted to tell that story about our first year of high school because I felt in my freshman year, I grew up more than any year in my life so far,' she said. As the album's final single in January 2010, the title track, 'Fearless', encapsulated the album's broader theme of being true to yourself. 'Fearless doesn't mean you're completely unafraid and it doesn't mean that you're bulletproof,' she told MTV News. 'It means that you have a lot of fears, but you jump anyway.' She added: 'This is a song about the fearlessness of falling in love. No matter how many break-up songs you write, no matter how many times you get hurt, you will always fall in love again.'

CHAPTER TWO

Long before she became synonymous with billion-dollar world tours, Taylor had to learn how to command the attention of tens of thousands of fans in packed-out arenas. Her Fearless tour, in 2009–10, was her first outing as a headliner, with more than 100 shows playing out across five continents. Signifying a key point in her artistic evolution, the ambitious staging incorporated theatrical elements such as a fairytale castle and flying butterflies, while Taylor channelled her inner Juliet for 'Love Story', wearing a floaty white wedding dress as she sang. The tour also brought an important new observation to eagle-eyed fans: before each concert, she scrawled the number 13 on the back of her hand with eyeliner. 'I paint this on my hand before every show because 13 is my lucky number,' she told MTV News. 'It's really weird.' A small but telling ritual, it hinted at Taylor's increasingly mystical streak and belief in finding meaning in patterns. 'I was born on the 13th. I turned 13 on Friday the 13th,' she added. 'My first album went gold in 13 weeks. My first No. 1

song had a 13-second intro. Every time I've won an award, I've been seated in either the 13th seat, the 13th row, the 13th section or row M, which is the 13th letter. Basically, whenever a 13 comes up in my life, it's a good thing.'

As her long-standing lucky charm, the number 13 has continued to make its presence felt, even cropping up in her relationship with Travis Kelce, who wears the number 87 jersey for Kansas City Chiefs. 'Thirteen plus 87 equals 100 – that's numerology,' Taylor quipped several years later in his *New Heights* podcast. 'We always keep it 100,' agreed Travis.

Time and again, Taylor's prized number has crept into her work – and in ever more sophisticated ways. Several albums have comprised 13 tracks; she repeats words or phrases 13 times in certain songs, and her videos have been stuffed with imagery relating to it. Turning her lucky number into a secret language with her fans, she even weaves it into her release schedule, timing announcements and launches to fall on the 13th, or choosing dates where the individual digits add up to it.

During the long, often lonely hours spent on the road during the Fearless tour, Taylor composed her third album, *Speak Now*. It served as a true career landmark because she wrote each song entirely by herself. 'I'd get my best ideas at 3am in Arkansas, and I didn't have a co-writer around, so I would just finish it. That would happen again in New York and then again in Boston and that would happen again in Nashville,' she told *SongwriterUniverse*. Released in October 2010, the record was inspired by 'situations that pop up and people that come into your life', she explained. 'Sometimes you don't get to tell them what you wish you would have told them. This album is my opportunity to do that track-by-track. Each song is a different confession to a different person.' In a clear departure from the early teen sentiments on *Fearless*, the album displayed a more mature and confrontational approach, which was seen as a move to silence growing noise from critics who found fault with her lyrics and vocals. She threw her all into *Speak Now*'s production, and in a heartfelt note accompanying the vinyl edition, she even revealed she had taken singing lessons. 'I wanted to get better, to challenge myself, and to build on my skills as a writer, an artist, and a performer,' she wrote. 'I underwent extensive vocal training and made a decision that would completely define this album.' She also confessed how hard she had found the lukewarm reception to *Fearless* in certain quarters, adding, 'I was trying to create a follow-up to the most awarded country album in history while staring directly into the face of intense criticism. I had been widely and publicly slammed for my singing voice and was first encountering the infuriating question that is unfortunately still lobbed at me to this day: does she really write her songs? Spoiler alert: I really, really do.'

Another motivation for *Speak Now* was a below-par performance at the Grammys in January 2010, when Taylor's duet with Stevie Nicks resulted in an intense media backlash. Though she won an astounding four awards on the night – including Best Album for *Fearless* – the evening was sullied by a rendition of Fleetwood Mac's track 'Rhiannon' and Taylor's song 'You Belong With Me'. Writing afterwards, the *New York Times* branded Taylor 'pitch-challenged' and the *LA Times* called her 'strikingly bad', while the *Washington Post* unkindly accused her of 'off-key caterwauling'. One music critic who took her down, Bob Lefsetz, called her performance 'dreadful', cruelly adding that 'Taylor Swift can't sing', and that she was 'young and dumb'. It hurt her badly, and speaking in a *60 Minutes* TV interview afterwards she said, 'The things that were said about me by this dude floored me and levelled me. I don't have thick skin. I hate reading criticisms. You never really get past things hurting you.' But she hit back in the best way she knew: through a song on *Speak Now* called 'Mean', which called him out for using his words as 'weapons'. Released as the album's third single, the song became known as an anti-bullying anthem and, satisfyingly for Taylor, it later went on to win two Grammys in 2012. 'There's really no feeling quite like writing a song about someone who's really mean to you and someone who completely hates you and makes your life miserable and then winning a Grammy for it,' she said on the night. Explaining the meaning behind the banjo-flecked track on her website, she said, 'There is constructive criticism. There's professional criticism. And then, there's just being mean. There's a line that you cross when you just start to attack everything about a person, and there's one guy who just crossed the line over and over again.'

Speak Now debuted at No. 1 on the *Billboard* 200, notching up over a million sales in the US in its first week and breaking a Guinness World Record as the fastest-selling album by a female country artist. It peaked at No. 6 in the UK chart, although *Speak Now (Taylor's Version)*, her third re-recorded album in July 2023, shot straight to No. 1 on both sides of the Atlantic and shattered world records in the process. Upon its original release, *Speak Now* was praised for a new level of maturity, and Taylor told on Instagram how it was conceived amid 'the whims, fantasies, heartaches, dramas and tragedies I lived out as a young woman between 18 and 20'. It held a special place in her heart, and she added, 'I love this album because it tells a tale of growing up, flailing, flying and crashing … and living to speak about it.'

Still drawing on the heady nature of love affairs, her earlier fairytale lens was replaced by a more realistic kind of storytelling, and lead single 'Mine' focused on what she dubbed her 'tendency to run from love'. In an online uStream chat with fans, she said, 'Every really direct example of love that I've had in front of me has ended in goodbye, has ended in break-ups. I think I've developed this pattern of sort of running away.' Stressing that the song was about finding the exception to that rule, she said, 'I'm never, ever going to go past hoping that love can work out. I'm always going to be very hopeful and blindly optimistic when it comes to love.' Speculation simmered that 'Mine' was about the late *Glee* actor Cory Monteith, but there was little evidence of romance to go on – other than the pair both seeming to blush when quizzed separately by chat show host Ellen DeGeneres.

After 'Mine' reached No. 3 in the *Billboard* Hot 100 and narrowly scraped into the UK Top 30, Taylor followed up with a second single 'Back to December'. Another US Top 10 hit, it offered a different take on the break-up trope, with Taylor calling the song a much-needed apology to an old flame. 'I write songs about people who deserve to have songs written about them, and whatever they need to hear – whatever is the right thing to say to that person – ends up being said,' she told MTV News. 'I've never felt the need to apologise in a song before. But in the last two years I've experienced a lot ... And sometimes you learn a lesson too late and at that point you need to apologise because you were careless.' It turns out the peace offering was intended for *Twilight* actor Taylor Lautner, whom she dated late in 2009 after starring with him in the romantic comedy *Valentine's Day*. They played high-school sweethearts in the film, and leaked shots from the set showed them wearing matching athletic outfits and kissing passionately while in role. During filming, Taylor's hunky co-star was notably seen wearing a vest with the 13 on the back, while she had the same number written on her hand, as was her habit. Later that year, when he presented Taylor with her VMA for 'You Belong With Me', the two shared a tight hug on stage, and he was also seen at two of her Fearless tour shows. Dinner dates and a trip to a hockey match followed, and it wasn't long before fans cutely dubbed them both 'Taylor Squared' and 'Tay-Tay'. She also addressed their relationship in her humorous *Saturday Night Live* monologue in November 2009. 'If you're wondering if I might be dating the werewolf from *Twilight*, I'm not going to mention that,' she jokingly sang, before mouthing 'Hi Taylor' at the camera, and blowing a kiss. Further confirmation of their status came when she told *InStyle* they had 'gotten really close' since making the movie together, and when the magazine contacted the actor for his own comment, he said, 'Taylor is hilarious. It was definitely not hard to play her love interest.'

But with a distance of more than 2,000 miles between Tennessee and LA, it proved hard to keep the momentum going, and soon after she received a surprise visit from Taylor on her 20th birthday in Nashville, the romance seemed to fizzle out. It was commonly acknowledged that 'Back to

December' was about the movie hunk, with Taylor's lyrics expressing how much she missed his tanned skin and sweet smile; and he admitted as much during a Facebook Live chat in 2016. Years later, chatting on the *Call Her Daddy* podcast in December 2023, he explained how they had managed to keep things amicable. 'I think when you respect somebody, for who they are in their soul, it allows you to move on, forgive and continue that love in a different way,' he said. 'And thankfully, we had that.' Showing the extent of their connection, he added, 'I would say one of the greater things to happen in my life over the last year is the rekindling of our friendship because she just is ... just a wonderful human. And she's pretty great to have in your life.' That same year, when Taylor recorded the spicy track 'I Can See You' for her *Speak Now (Taylor's Version)* album, she cast her ex in the action-packed video. Introducing him for its live video premiere during an Eras tour show in Missouri in July 2023, she said of Taylor, 'He was a very positive force in my life when I was making the *Speak Now* album, and I want to say he did every single stunt that you saw in that music video.' Taylor himself gave a heartfelt speech while on stage, saying, 'I respect you so much. Not just for the singer you are, the song-writer, the performer – but truly for the human you are. You are gracious, humble, kind and I'm honoured to know you.'

While the two Taylors gave a textbook example of post-split civility, that was not quite the case with singer John Mayer, with whom she embarked on a romance after guesting on his single 'Half of My Heart' in 2009. He first suggested they work together in a tweet earlier that year, saying, 'Waking up to this song idea that won't leave my head. 3 days straight now. That means it's good enough to finish. It's called "Half of My Heart" and I want to sing it with Taylor Swift.' She enthusiastically agreed, telling *Elle*, 'I freaked out when I heard, because I've been such a big fan of John for such a long time.' It's believed they became romantically involved for a few months before the song hit the airwaves, and both looked smitten when performing the track at the December 2009 Jingle Ball in New York. 'Taylor is the world's biggest star who doesn't know she's a star ... Which I think is totally sweet,' John told *Access Hollywood*. 'I think she's a really remarkable person.' They were also seen having dinner together in Nashville, and a few days later, Taylor and her mum, Andrea, were spotted in the audience as John filmed an episode of the Country Music Television show *Crossroads*.

But it wasn't long until cracks in the relationship were filling the pages of news sites, and by February 2010, it was said to be over. Much was made of the fact that Taylor was aged only 19 at the time, while John was 32, which she seemed keen to reiterate over the ensuing months. Though neither ever spoke about what went wrong, it undoubtedly left a bad taste, and the pair went on to use their music to wage a back-and-forth battle of attrition. Taylor hurled the first grenade with two songs on *Speak Now*, including its fourth single 'The Story of Us'. The up-tempo track was thought to have been inspired by an awkward encounter with John at an awards bash, when they were apparently mortified to find themselves sitting near each other. 'Afterward, I just felt so empty, like we were both fighting this silent war of pretending we didn't care that the other was there,' Taylor told MTV. 'And I went home, and I wrote this song about it.' Even more overt was 'Dear John', a letter-style track which suggested deep regret over their rumoured involvement, and seemingly accusatory lines about their age gap. John was furious about the song, saying he 'didn't deserve' such a public dressing-down. 'It made me feel terrible. It was a really lousy thing to do,' he told *Rolling Stone*. 'I never got an email. I never got a phone call. I was really caught off guard.' He also called it 'cheap songwriting', but Taylor was adamant John had been presumptuous in publicly stating the song was about him. 'I never disclose who my songs are about,' she told *Glamour*, before pointing out that her lyrics had resonated with many women. 'I think that song really hit home with a lot of girls who had been through toxic relationships and had found their way to the other side of it,' she said. 'I've never looked out while singing a song during a concert to see so many girls crying.'

John appeared to retaliate in his own 2013 song 'Paper Doll', which cast the blame of a break-up back on to the woman in question, repeatedly hinting at her fragility. Yet he later denied the song was about Taylor, saying in an Instagram Live in 2016, 'When "Paper Doll" came out, 100 per cent of the people believed it was about somebody ... But the song is not about that person.' He refused to specify further, arguing, 'I would be breaking my rule that songwriters don't say who the songs are about or not.' In any case, the thinly veiled bitterness played out for years, and even on Taylor's birthday in 2016, John posted a tweet which said, 'Tuesday, December 13, may be the lamest day of the year, conceptually'. He quickly deleted it, insisting he cast 'absolutely no shade'. But as the tit-for-tat continued, their ill-fated relationship was raked over again when Taylor recorded 'Would've, Could've, Should've' for her 2022 *Midnights* album. The song again focused on a problematic age gap, as well as apparent regrets over lost girlhood.

However, suggesting a softening of the tone in 2023, she implored fans not to unleash a fresh attack on John as she prepared to release *Speak Now (Taylor's Version)*. Before a rare live performance of 'Dear John' during an Eras tour show in Minneapolis, she urged the Mayer-bashers to refrain from an online pile-on – especially as he previously admitted to receiving abhorrent threats from over-zealous Taylor devotees. Pleading for the re-release to be met with only 'kindness' and 'gentleness', she told the audience: 'I'm 33 years old, I don't care about anything that happened to me when I was 19 except the songs I wrote. So what I'm trying to tell you is that I am not putting this album out so you should feel the need to defend me on the internet against someone you think I wrote a song about 14 million years ago.' While such a moment highlighted Taylor's innate desire to play fair and to treat others with the respect she herself deserves, it also appeared to signal a truce – and a much-needed sign-off on a traumatic chapter of her life.

Elsewhere on *Speak Now*, the title track was written about a close friend who was going through her own heartache. 'The guy she had been in love with since childhood was marrying this other girl,' Taylor told Yahoo Music, 'and my first inclination was to say, "Well, are you gonna speak now?" And then I started thinking about what I would do if I was still in love with someone who was marrying someone who they shouldn't be marrying. And so I wrote this song about exactly what my game plan would be.' The album's fifth single, 'Sparks Fly', was first written when she was 16, but a more mature reworking showed she had not forgotten the lure of a rose-tinted pop hook, with its lyrics revolving around a kiss with a green-eyed boy in the pouring rain. The track secured Taylor a fifth Hot Country Songs No. 1 and went on to spend 21 weeks on the chart. The album's final single and bonus track, 'Ours', was also a Hot Country Songs No. 1, serving as a love letter, which *Taste of Country* called 'cheesy and delicious'. Taylor explained it was about 'a guy nobody thought I should be with', telling *VH1 Storytellers*, 'I wrote this song specifically just to play it for him, just to show him, "I don't care what anyone says. I don't care that you have tattoos. I don't care that you have a gap between your teeth. I love you for who you are."'

Another song, 'Enchanted', told of the dizzying moment Taylor was left 'wonderstruck' by a guy she met in New York. Laying some of her customary Easter eggs in the song's notes, she appeared to tease his true identity when she capitalised the letters 'A-D-A-M' – and gratifyingly, Owl City singer Adam Young then confirmed the song was about him. 'I'm so tremendously honoured that Taylor would write such an elegant song and thereby offer a gracious nod in my direction,' he wrote on his band's blog. 'Needless to say, I was lost for words and utterly smitten. I couldn't stop smiling.' In contrast to *Speak Now*'s more romantic musings, 'Never Grow Up' served as the album's most introspective and thought-provoking segue. The song flicked back in time, beginning with an array of childhood memories before fast-forwarding to Taylor leaving her parents' home and settling into her first condo in Nashville. 'I walked into this apartment after I bought it and thought, "Oh man, this is real now,"' she told *60 Minutes Overtime* on CBS News. 'We're all getting older, and soon my parents are going to be older, and then I have to think about grown-up things.'

I n the wake of *Speak Now*, Taylor found herself at a curious crossroads. She had proved she could write a critically acclaimed record without outside help, and on its supporting tour, more than 1.5 million fans flocked to over 100 shows spanning four continents. It was everything she could ever have dreamed of, but at the same time, her musical horizons were widening. Outgrowing her country-pop roots, the call of bigger, bolder sounds beckoned, giving rise to her fourth album, *Red*. As it germinated over a lengthy two-year spell, she began experimenting with new collaborators – including Swedish duo Max Martin and Shellback and British superstar Ed Sheeran. Keen to take herself out of her comfort zone to create a more expansive sonic experience that incorporated electronic and rock influences, she told *TIME*, 'I really wanted to push myself. I called the people that I've always wanted to work with – my production, songwriting, artist heroes – and said, "Hey, do you want to get in the studio and work together and make something different?"' Writing the album over an extended spell rather than in a concentrated burst enriched *Red*, while also reflecting the turbulence of Taylor's early 20s. Dispensing with the more wholesome good-girl image that had defined her earlier recordings, *Red* combined a range of different moods during its 24-month inception. The result was finally unveiled in October 2012, with a vast pool of songs being carefully pared down to a final cut of 16. 'I wrote so many songs for this album,' she told CBS. 'I wrote about 30 songs that I had to choose from. It becomes absolute gridlock, trying to figure out which ones you're going to have to cut from the record.'

In the spirit of her earlier work, the album's primary theme was, of course, love, but this time it was of the more chaotic kind, chronicling intoxicating and frequently destructive feelings. As Taylor later reflected, '*Red* resembled a heartbroken person. It was all over the place, a fractured mosaic of feelings that somehow all fit together in the end. Happy, free, confused, lonely, devastated, euphoric, wild, and tortured by memories past.' She also maintained that the name of both the album and title track perfectly represented what it is to be human. 'Red is such an interesting colour to correlate with emotion, because it's on both ends of the spectrum. On one end you have happiness, falling in love, infatuation with someone, passion, all that. On the other end, you've got obsession, jealousy, danger, fear, anger and frustration. It's an interesting colour to correlate with all the really intense parts of a relationship, whether they're good or bad.' Fans later noted how Taylor's colour palette softened, and where this album was immersed in burning shades of volatile red, future songs were often marked out by calmer, golden hues – particularly those which corresponded to periods of stability with both Joe Alwyn and Travis Kelce.

Enticingly, even as *Red* was still being finished, Taylor told *Vogue* that its songs would revolve around one her most painful relationships yet. 'There's just been this earth-shattering, not recent, but absolute crash-and-burn heartbreak,' she said. 'And that will turn out to be what the next album is about.' The end result was heralded by the celebrated lead single 'We Are Never Ever Getting Back Together', which landed in August 2012 and resulted in Taylor's first ever *Billboard* Hot 100 No. 1. It fared similarly well around the world, hitting No. 4 in the UK.

Deliriously infectious though it was, 'We Are Never Ever Getting Back Together' had a darker meaning than its frothy chorus suggested. On the day the song fell into shape, Taylor was in the studio in Nashville with Max Martin and Shellback when the friend of an ex-boyfriend turned up. 'At this point we'd broken up an embarrassing amount of times,' Taylor told iHeartRadio. When the friend suggested a reconciliation could be on the cards, she was stunned. 'Immediately after he left, I just looked at Max and was like, "You know it's weird, it's like we are never getting back together. Like ever, ever, ever. Ever. We are never getting back together." And I just kind of went on this rant, and he was like, "We need to write that song actually."' Taylor picked up her guitar and they completed the song in just 25 minutes. 'It just happened so fast. It was so much fun,' she recalled.

Memorably, the song's sarcastic lyrics dismissed an ex who had been unsupportive of her work, aligning himself with edgier rock groups. 'It was a relationship where I felt very critiqued and subpar,' Taylor told the *Guardian*. 'He'd listen to this music that nobody had heard of ... but as soon as anyone else liked these bands, he'd drop them. I felt that was a strange way to be a music fan. And I couldn't understand why he would never say anything nice about the songs I wrote or the music I made.' It didn't take long for sleuthing Swifties to deduce that the song was about actor Jake Gyllenhaal, who was known to be a fan of indie acts. He had first been linked to Taylor after they met backstage at *Saturday Night Live* in late 2010 and were seen out for brunch in New York the following day, as well as strolling around a park in Brooklyn.

Over three intense months, the pair became Hollywood's hottest couple, and on one occasion the *Brokeback Mountain* star was said to have splashed six figures on a private jet so Taylor could join him in London for a 48-hour reunion. They reportedly stayed in a plush suite at the Dorchester Hotel on Park Lane, and while in the capital they also went for dinner at the home of Gwyneth Paltrow and Chris Martin. As the press fed on paparazzi sightings and titbits from inside sources, it was claimed Jake plied Taylor with gifts, including a rare Fender vintage guitar and a diamond bracelet worth thousands of dollars. Taylor then spent Thanksgiving with Jake and his family that November, and the pair were seen holding hands when out with his sister – actress Maggie Gyllenhaal – and her children.

Though he was nine years older, it seemed to be going swimmingly between them, and another *Red* song, 'State of Grace', touched on their shared fire signs and matching blue eyes, as well as the euphoria of falling head over heels. But when Taylor threw a party for her 21st birthday in December 2010, Jake was suddenly nowhere to be seen. Rumours swirled that he hated being in the paparazzi's firing line, and abruptly chose to end it before it got too serious. Taylor was evidently distraught, but rather than mourn a lost happy ending, as earlier tracks might have done, 'We Are Never Ever Getting Back Together' was an altogether ballsier response which refused to shoulder any of the blame. As MTV stated, this was a 'defiant, liberated' Taylor, who had learned a vital lesson that 'she's not only better off alone, she's *fine* with that'.

That wasn't the end of it where Jake was concerned, though, and another *Red* song, 'All Too Well', picked up the baton, painting vivid details of their romance, such as autumn drives, family dinners, laughter and eventual crushing silence. One of the lyrics, about dancing around the kitchen in the glow cast from the refrigerator was almost unbearably poignant. Memorably, Taylor gave a spine-tingling performance of the song at the Grammys in 2014, earning a standing ovation in the process. 'Her performance was fierce and focused,' raved the *Guardian*. 'When she finished, she turned from the piano and faced the audience with an intent gaze of defiance and held it for several seconds. The message was clear: no more the victim.' 'All Too Well' saw Taylor reunite with old writing partner Liz Rose, but Taylor described it as the album's hardest song to write, telling *Good Morning America* it took a long time 'to filter through everything she wanted to say'. She also revealed to *Rolling Stone* that prior to its recording she was 'a broken human, walking into rehearsal just feeling terrible about what was going on in my personal life'. As a result, the original version ran to ten minutes, which, as she said, 'you can't put on an album'.

Conveying a haunting sense of affection that had long since disintegrated, the most striking motif of 'All Too Well' was a forgotten red scarf, which, the lyrics noted, was stashed in a drawer 'at your sister's house'. Such a specific reference led fans to assume the scarf's final resting place was Maggie Gyllenhaal's home, and when she was asked if it was still there in a 2017 interview, she replied, 'It's totally possible. I don't know.' As a brilliantly simple metaphor, the scarf was not only a misplaced accessory, but a stand-in for a past intimacy and trust that was then carelessly lost. Over time, it became cultural shorthand for heartbreak itself, and was woven into TV sketches, fan fiction and even literary analysis by leading academics. Though Taylor never confirmed its literal truth, she amusingly sold $45 scarves on her website for a time. Then, when she released *Red (Taylor's Version)* in November 2021, featuring the previously unheard full-length version of 'All Too Well', an accompanying short film included a chunky red scarf, prompting a resurgence of interest in its whereabouts. Headlines like 'Where the Hell Is Taylor Swift's Scarf?' were rampant, and even music legend Dionne Warwick urged Jake to give it back. 'If that young man has Taylor's scarf he should return it,' she tweeted. 'It does not belong to you. Box it up and I will pay the cost of postage, Jake.'

Throughout all the drama, Jake never publicly broke ranks, but in 2021 he did speak to *Esquire* about the song. 'It has nothing to do with me,' he said. 'It's about her relationship with her fans. It is her expression. Artists tap into personal experiences for inspiration, and I don't begrudge anyone that.' The renewed interest in 'Jakegate' did wonders for the unabridged ten-minute incarnation of 'All Too Well' in 2021, and it debuted at No. 1 on the *Billboard* Hot 100 and broke a Guinness World Record as the longest-running song ever to top the chart. It was also the lengthiest song to reach the UK Top Five in chart history, and for Taylor, the track became a symbol of the relationship between her and her fans. 'It has a story that is so sacred to me because … it was my favourite song on the record,' she said in a release put out by her record label. 'And what was so crazy is that when it went out into the world, the fans just among themselves decided it was their favourite, too.' Hawk-eyed observers were quick to pin other tracks from *Red (Taylor's Version)* on Jake as well. 'I Bet You Think About Me' was seemingly littered with digs at the actor's plush Beverly Hills lifestyle and evenings spent at cool gigs, and though she never confirmed as much, it was certainly one of Taylor's more embittered offerings. 'We wanted this song to be like a comedic, tongue-in-cheek, funny, not caring what anyone thinks about you sort of break-up song,' she told radio station Country 102.5. 'There are a lot of different types of heartbreak songs on *Red* – some of them are very sincere, some of them very stoic and heartbreaking and sad – we wanted this to be the moment where you're like, "I don't care about anything".'

But of course, she cared very deeply about what had happened at the time, and post-Gyllenhaal, she was happy to remain resolutely single for several months. Asked by *Vogue* in January 2012 if she was dating, she replied, 'I got nothing going on! I just don't really feel like dating. I really have this great life right now, and I'm not sad and I'm not crying this Christmas, so I am really stoked about that.' On her own, she could at least get a breather from the media reports that she felt continually chided and belittled her. 'I know that one of my spins is: "Oh, Taylor's heartbroken. Oh, Taylor fell in love and the guy broke her heart. She's sad all the time, and lonely,"' she later said in *New York* magazine, while stressing that her emotions were never anything but genuine. 'Those are real feelings that every single person goes through. I think it's okay to be mad at someone who hurt you. This isn't about, like, the pageantry of trying to seem like nothing affects you. I'm a songwriter. Everything affects me.'

However, within a couple of months of revelling in her singledom, she was linked to another megastar – Harry Styles, the floppy-haired One Direction heartthrob who was propelled to superstar status following the 2010 series of *The X Factor*. They met in LA in March 2012 at the Kids' Choice Awards, an annual Nickelodeon event celebrating the biggest names in children's entertainment. Taylor, then 22, attended with her friend Selena Gomez, who was there with her boyfriend at the time, Justin Bieber. As One Direction performed their smash hit 'What Makes You Beautiful', Taylor was seen dancing and singing along with Selena, and the band's 18-year-old lead singer was said to have caught her eye. Rumours she had a crush on Harry were then fuelled by Justin. 'I already know one of the biggest artists in the world thinks Harry is so hot, but I have been sworn to secrecy,' he told the *Mirror* newspaper. Although he refused to name the artist, the timing – just days after the awards – made it reasonably easy to guess who he meant. Meanwhile, Harry was said to have been struck by Taylor, too, and in an interview with *Seventeen*, he said, 'Honestly, she couldn't be a sweeter person. She's a great girl and she's extremely talented. Some people you meet and they are not as nice as you make them out to be, but she's one of those people who's really just amazing.'

What happened between them after their initial introduction has always been shrouded in uncertainty, but the *Mirror* later claimed the two had a brief fling before going their separate ways. According to the paper, Taylor was hurt after Harry was photographed kissing an American model in New Zealand. A few weeks later, in June, perhaps still feeling bruised, she wrote the explosive track 'I Knew You Were Trouble', which subsequently appeared on *Red*. A feisty collab with producers Max Martin and Shellback, peppered with themes of betrayal and regret, it was released as the album's second single and stormed the charts worldwide. The song was about recognising the warning signs of a toxic relationship, and, in hindsight, the haunting spoken-word introduction of its video felt like a pointed reflection about being scorched by Harry's flame. 'I knew his world moved too fast and burned too bright,' Taylor said in the clip. 'But I just thought, how can the devil be pulling you toward someone who looks so much like an angel when he smiles at you?'

Though 'I Knew You Were Trouble' has long been linked to her romance with Harry, when it was first released, few realised they had been an item. It wasn't until Taylor spoke to the *Sunday Times Magazine* years later that she confirmed the song was about him, recalling her 2013 Brit Awards performance of it while Harry looked on from the audience. 'It's not hard to access that emotion when the person the song is directed at is standing by the side of the stage watching,' she admitted. Back when it was first released, she referred to the alarm bells that had inspired the track, telling *Taste of Country*, 'It's bold sonically because it sounds like that chaotic feeling of just feeling like you got tricked ... It talks about that feeling of, not shame on you, you broke my heart – shame on *me* you broke my heart. I knew. I saw you and saw red flags. So, it's kind of an emotion I hadn't dealt with before.' Yet, as history would show when she and Harry were reunited months afterwards, recognising the signs didn't mean she was done with them.

In the interim, the summer of 2012 promised a smoother chapter. Taylor began dating Conor Kennedy, the grandson of the late Robert F. Kennedy, after meeting him at a Fourth of July party at the family's estate in Massachusetts. Soon after, the couple were photographed together on the beach and, in a more sombre moment, visiting the grave of Conor's mother,

Mary, who had died earlier that year. They also attracted headlines after attending the wedding of Conor's cousin Kyle together. According to *Vanity Fair,* Taylor even snapped up a nearby mansion in Hyannis Port on Cape Cod. But the romance was said to have run its course by September of that year, with Taylor reportedly selling her house for a $1 million profit just months later. Still, it is widely believed that the *Red* track 'Begin Again' is about her time with Conor, and the lyrics refer to embarking on a new start after heartbreak.

Shortly after the split, Taylor spoke to US news presenter Katie Couric about the hardships of dating in the public eye. 'I don't know how to have a normal relationship because I try to act normal, love from a normal place and live a normal life, but there is sort of an abnormal magnifying glass, like telescope lens, on everything that happens between me and anybody else,' she said with unusual candour. 'I don't really know that much about love, it turns out.'

Having made a big impression on her, the Kennedy family also inspired the song 'Starlight' on *Red*. It came about after Taylor had discovered an old picture of Conor's grandparents Ethel and Robert F. Kennedy as teenagers in the 1960s. 'It immediately made me think of, like, how much fun they must have had that night,' she told the *Wall Street Journal*. 'So I just kind of wrote that song from that place, not really knowing how they met or anything like that.' Taylor and Ethel struck up a close bond in the short time she was with Conor, and when asked whether she would welcome Taylor as a 'granddaughter-in-law', Ethel said, 'We should be so lucky.'

Although Taylor would have to wait a couple more years before releasing her most successful album ever, the masterpiece that was *1989*, many considered *Red* to be a seminal work that captured her artistic coming-of-age. For *Rolling Stone*, it sealed her status as 'the supreme pop songwriter of her generation', while *Billboard* labelled it her 'first adult pop album'. The record hit No. 1 in more than 40 countries, and at long last resulted in her first chart-topping album in the UK. Crucially, singles like 'The Last Time' with Snow Patrol's Gary Lightbody and 'Everything Has Changed', featuring Ed Sheeran, also broadened her reach within the British market. Speaking of her long-running friendship with singer Ed when promoting her 2025 album *The Life of a Showgirl* on Hits Radio, Taylor said there is a 'really sort of strange mind-melt thing that happens between us two'. She added, 'We've always had it, we always will.' And when host Fleur East cheekily asked if Ed would perform at Taylor's wedding to Travis Kelce, she diplomatically replied, 'Oh, it would be hard to keep him from it, I think! He knows what people want, and he wants to give people what they want.'

Overall, *Red* has shifted over 8 million copies worldwide, and in the US, more than a million were sold in its first week alone. The record also made her the first artist since The Beatles – and the only female artist ever – to have three consecutive albums spend at least six weeks at No. 1. *Red* went on to earn Album of the Year and Best Country Album nominations at the 2014 Grammys, and her accompanying tour in 2013–14 grossed more than $150 million worldwide, establishing Taylor as one of the world's most commercially powerful performers. Nearly a decade later, *Red (Taylor's Version)* was a critical and commercial sensation, too – debuting at No. 1 in the US *and* UK and breaking Spotify's record for the most-streamed album by a female artist in a single day. Comprising 30 tracks in all, including a collab with one of her heroines, Phoebe Bridgers, Taylor spoke of the joy of returning to the album so many years on. 'I would never have thought it was possible to go back and remake my previous work, uncovering lost art and forgotten gems along the way,' she posted on her social feeds ahead of the release. '*Red* is about to be mine again, but it has always been ours. Now we begin again ...'

CHAPTER THREE

With Taylor still basking in the glow of her *Red* era, fate led her back into the arms of Harry Styles. It was claimed he had been pleading for another chance ever since their initial liaison faltered, and after both performed at the MTV Video Music Awards in September 2012, the embers were rekindled. News of them dating leaked that November – with most people, of course, oblivious to their earlier fling. 'There's someone I like,' Harry told that month's issue of *Cosmopolitan*. 'But this girl ... isn't my "type". It's more about the person. How they act, their body language, if they can laugh at themselves.' When he was spotted visiting the set of the US version of *The X Factor*, where Taylor was rehearsing for a live performance, they made little attempt to hide their flirtation. 'He was smiling at her while she rehearsed,' *People* magazine was informed by a show insider. 'When she was done, he jumped up on stage, picked her up, put her over his shoulder and carried her off. The whole crew was really surprised.' Later, the show's anchor, Mario Lopez, told his radio show listeners that he saw the two walking 'hand in hand' on set.

Just over two weeks later, the pair were photographed strolling around New York's Central Park, where they giggled like teenagers and later met up with friends. They were spotted again at a late-night karaoke session and then, a third time that week, at a birthday party at the Crosby Street Hotel, where witnesses said they 'definitely looked like a couple'. Christened 'Haylor' by their respective fanbases, they set the internet ablaze – but while some were delighted by their union, a contingent of hardcore Directioners bristled, posting sinister online threats towards Taylor, as well as ludicrous messages like, 'She will not date my Harry'. As a lightning rod for the tabloid press, any chances of pop's most talked-about duo keeping it low-key were scuppered from the outset. Their every move was pored over, and the British tabloids could hardly believe their luck when they flew to England to celebrate Taylor's birthday that December. Staying with Harry's mum, Anne Twist, at her home in Holmes Chapel in Cheshire, they were seen out and about holding hands, sharing cosy pub meals and then on a trip to the Lake District. Harry even surprised Taylor with a box of 23 cupcakes in honour of her 23rd birthday. A ski trip to Utah followed, where they were joined by pals Selena Gomez and Justin Bieber, and a New Year's Eve kiss in Times Square confirmed them as the showbiz couple of dreams. But although their romance grabbed the public's imagination, it was short-lived, crashing and burning almost as quickly as it began. On a New Year holiday in the British Virgin Islands in 2013, onlookers reported an 'almighty row', and Taylor was photographed on a boat as she left the island alone. Harry, who stayed behind as she flew back to Nashville, then turned up at Richard Branson's Necker Island mansion, where he was photographed in a hot tub with other guests, apparently 'letting off steam'. By 7 January, sources confirmed what fans already suspected: the whirlwind romance was over after just a few weeks.

The split was analysed in *Vanity Fair*'s April 2013 edition, with Taylor shrewdly authorising a source to tell the magazine that Harry 'wore her down' and that she had felt the continual strain of him 'looking at every girl'. He refuted all such claims, calling them 'undeniably false'. But with the same article seeing Taylor hit out at the 'ridiculous' tabloid culture that was turning her into a 'fictional character', this was a woman intent on standing her ground and pushing back against the prevailing narrative. Amid the implosion of 'Haylor', she refused to play the role scripted for her or, as she put it in *Vanity Fair*, to be 'some clingy, insane, desperate girlfriend'. It was an unusual approach, given she previously tended to speak out through her songs, rather than comment on her individual relationships. But as we would later discover, this was only the beginning of Taylor turning public judgement into power.

At the same time, she began channelling her pent-up frustrations into lyrics and melodies that would shape her next studio album, *1989*, named after her birth year. Written mostly while on the Red tour – her third global outing, comprising nearly 100 shows over 15 months – *1989* was a musical epiphany. 'I woke up not wanting but needing to make a new style of music,' she later revealed in a global livestream. Her restless instinct coincided with the decision to cut her long hair short on the London leg of the tour. 'I had a secret,' she later said. 'For me, it was more than a change of hairstyle. When I was 24, I decided to completely reinvent myself.' The resulting *1989* took a sharp turn from Nashville's country twang, ushering in a far poppier, synth-heavy era. Released in October 2014, its 1980s-tinged new sound was partly due to the involvement of producer Jack Antonoff, a figure who would prove instrumental in the progression of Taylor's music. 'His excitement and exuberance about writing songs is contagious,' she said of him. 'He's an absolute joy.'

The release of *1989* brought a new level of intimacy and trust with her growing brigade of Swifties. Introducing her legendary 'Secret Sessions', she held a series of album-listening parties in her homes – from LA and London to Nashville and New York – where she handpicked devoted fans from social media and invited them to hear her music. By baking them cookies, posing for photos and giving away generous goody bags, it proved that Taylor didn't just see her loyal supporters as consumers, but as active participants in her journey. 'I wanted it to be this whole secret society gathering in living rooms,' she told American TV journalist Barbara Walters. 'And so I decided to have them in my houses.' In such a ruthless industry that had become defined by money, sales and chart stats, her willingness to open her doors to fans reflected the authenticity and emotional transparency that have always been at the heart of her success.

When it came to *1989*'s content, she decided to leave out any score-settling tracks that dissed her exes, telling *Billboard*, 'It's not about revenge or break-ups. It's about what my life looks like now.' Instead, several tracks were widely interpreted as nostalgically reminiscing on her time with Harry. In 'Out of the Woods', one verse referenced December, the month they had been blissfully happy, while another part mentioned matching paper-plane necklaces they had both worn. Capturing the essence of their fraught relationship, the song's dramatic video saw Taylor being chased through dark woodland and pursued by wolves, and fans noted a reference to her favourite number as she tripped and fell 13 times before breaking free. In the same track, Taylor also referred to an accident that had happened during her ski trip with Harry,

when sudden sharp braking on a snowmobile left him needing urgent medical treatment. The same incident cropped up
in her 2023 No. 1 hit 'Is It Over Now?', released as part of *1989
(Taylor's Version)*, with a reference to blood dripping on to the
snow. In a 2014 radio interview with NPR, Taylor spoke of
the double meaning of 'Out of the Woods'. 'Hit the brakes too
soon could mean the literal sense of, we got in an accident and
we had to deal with the aftermath. But also, the relationship
ended sooner than it should've because there was a lot of fear
involved. And that song touches on a huge sense of anxiety
that was, kind of, coursing through that particular relationship, because we really felt the heat of every single person in
the media thinking they could draw up the narrative of what
we were going through and debate and speculate.'

To mark the first anniversary of *1989*'s release, Taylor
unveiled an acoustic rendition of 'Out of the Woods', recorded
at LA's Grammy Museum. In a message she released with it,
she again appeared to draw on her relationship with Harry.
'The number-one feeling I felt in the whole relationship was
anxiety, because it felt very fragile. It felt very tentative,' she
said, adding that such emotion in no way devalued the experience. 'It doesn't mean that it's not special and extraordinary
just to have a relationship that's fragile and somehow meaningful in that fragility.' In another interview with Grammy
Pro, she divulged more about the inspiration behind the

song. 'Everybody was watching, everybody was commenting,' she said. 'You're constantly just feeling like, "Are we out of the woods yet? What's the next thing gonna be? What's the next hurdle we're gonna have to jump over? Are we gonna make it to next week?"'

'I Know Places', another 1989 track, co-written with OneRepublic's Ryan Tedder, explored Taylor's struggles with life in the spotlight and her wish to simply escape. 'I kind of was in a place where I was like, "No one is gonna sign up for this,"' she said in the Grammy Pro interview. 'There are just too many cameras pointed at me. There are too many ridiculous elaborations on my life. It's just not ever gonna work ... So I wrote this song called "I Know Places" about, like, "Hey, I know places we can hide. We could outrun them."' Again, the lyrics seemed to point directly to Harry with mention of her protagonist's striking green eyes – often described as one of his most distinctive features. Elsewhere, the 1989 song 'Style' seemed like a cheeky spin on his name, with the plotline aptly concerning a couple trapped in a doomed relationship. The lyrics seemed to neatly allude to their fateful appearance at the 2012 MTV VMAs, including a nod to Harry's white T-shirt and slicked-back long hair and her bright red lips. But with 1989 written and recorded over a timeframe of more than a year, it covered a vast spectrum of emotion, and end track, 'Clean', suggested Taylor finally had closure over him. The track was written in London where she used to meet Harry, and as she told *Elle* in 2015: '"Clean" I wrote as I was walking out of Liberty in London. Someone I used to date – it hit me that I'd been in the same city as him for two weeks and I hadn't thought about it. When it did hit me, it was like, "Oh, I hope he's doing well." And nothing else ... The first thought that came to my mind was, I'm finally clean.'

In the years after their split, Harry himself was continually besieged with questions about Taylor. When asked by *Rolling Stone* in 2017 how he felt about songs like 'Out of the Woods' and 'Style' being about him, he carefully sidestepped the issue. 'I write from my experiences; everyone does that,' he replied diplomatically. 'I'm lucky if everything [we went through] helped create those songs.' But he did address the difficulties of dating so publicly, saying, 'Relationships are hard, at any age. And adding in that you don't really understand exactly how it works when you're 18, trying to navigate all that stuff didn't make it easier.' With only kind words to say about Taylor, he was keen to show appreciation for their time together, adding, 'Meeting someone new, sharing those experiences, it's the best sh*t ever. So thank you.' Later, in a 2020 interview on *The Howard Stern Show*, he was even more complimentary about the songs Taylor had penned about him. 'I think about what it means to me to write a song about somebody else and for somebody else to do that, it's flattering. Even if the song isn't that flattering, you still spent time on it and ultimately, using Taylor as an example, she's a great songwriter. So at least they're good songs.' With so much water under the bridge, the pair have been on friendly terms whenever their paths have crossed in the years since, and Taylor has later insisted she has no regrets about Harry – or any former boyfriend. 'I wouldn't change anything because I think being a songwriter, every experience you have ... shapes your work. So even the times where I've felt terrible emotions like regret or humiliation or embarrassment or failure, I took those emotions and kind of turned them into the next batch of songs,' she told *Pop Crush*. 'It leaves you in this place where you wouldn't really give yourself any advice to help yourself out, because even your struggles kind of got you to where you wanted to be.'

Aside from the lasting hues of Harry, the upbeat tempo that lit up *1989* was the ideal way to soundtrack Taylor's life-changing move to New York, which took place in April 2014. 'I dreamed about moving to New York. I obsessed about moving to New York and then I did it,' she told *Good Morning America*. 'The inspiration that I found in that city is kind of hard to describe and hard to compare to any other force of inspiration I've ever experienced in my life.' Calling it 'a place of endless potential and possibilities', she used her mounting wealth to buy a $19 million penthouse in Manhattan's trendy Tribeca neighbourhood, which directly influenced songs like album opener 'Welcome to New York' in its celebration of fresh beginnings. Life in the Big Apple suited Taylor's desire to live as below-radar as she could, and she told *Billboard,* 'I'm not going to stop grocery shopping just because it tends to be a very hectic situation.'

As well as being a time for nesting, Taylor's new domestic set-up meant she could enjoy life as a singleton. 'I found a place in my life that feels really great and I'm not willing to compromise that for just anyone,' she told *E! News* that October. 'I'm really happy about the fact that being single doesn't feel like being alone. I have love in my life, I just don't have a relationship, and that feels really natural right now.' It was also a time in which she could concentrate on her being with her closest girlfriends – including the likes of model Gigi Hadid and actress Lena Dunham (the latter having first got acquainted with Taylor after DMing her to tell her how many heartbreaks her songs had helped her through). 'I have friends around me all the time,' Taylor told *Rolling Stone.* 'I've started painting more. I've been working out a lot. I've started to really take pride in being strong.'

Against this backdrop of autonomy, one of Taylor's most prolific hits was born: the anthemic 'Shake It Off'. It was the obvious choice for *1989*'s lead single, and after release in

August 2014 it shot to No. 1 in multiple countries and became her biggest-selling song in Britain ever. 'I really wanted it to be a song that made people want to get up and dance at a wedding reception from the first drum beat,' she said. One of seven collaborations with Max Martin and Shellback that gave 1989 its rocket fuel, the ballsy track was also a show of defiance which put haters squarely in their place. Speaking about the song's comedic video which showed her clumsily attempting dance moves alongside a host of surefooted professionals, she told *Rolling Stone*, 'I'm being embarrassingly bad at it. It shows you to keep doing you, keep being you, keep trying to figure out where you fit in in the world, and eventually you will.' But aside from the humorous visuals and girl-power overtones, 'Shake It Off' carried a far weightier meaning. In April 2015, Taylor opened up to *Glamour* about the public policing of her love life and relentless criticism that inspired the song. 'I do feel jaded about relationships, to be honest,' she admitted. 'The media has sent me a really unfair message over the past couple of years, which is that I'm not allowed to date for excitement, or fun, or new experiences or learning lessons. I'm only allowed to date if it's for a lasting, multiple-year relationship. Otherwise, I'm a, quote, "serial dater". Or, quote, "boy crazy".' She also compared her day-to-day experiences to preparing for battle. 'You take something very fragile, like trying to get to know someone, and it feels like walking out into the middle of a gladiator arena with someone you've just met.'

Even in supposedly friendly media spaces, Taylor's personal life had become a recurring punchline, frequently reduced to throwaway jibes. On a popular US talk show, one commentator said flippantly, 'She's going through guys like a train,' and on the red carpet at the Grammys in 2015, an *Entertainment Tonight* reporter told Taylor, 'You're going to walk home with more than maybe just a trophy tonight ... I think lots of men.' Looking momentarily stunned, she replied coolly, 'I'm not going to go home with any men. I'm going to hang out with my friends, then I'm going to go home to the cats.'

The more famous Taylor became, the more ludicrous the headlines, and one daft story suggested she had a treasure chest of ex-boyfriends' belongings which she had to touch in order to write a song. 'I read that, and it creeped. Me. Out,' she told the *Sunday Times Magazine*. 'When I click on one of those blogs, it makes me feel as if the next article is going to say that I also have a coffin and conduct nightly séances. Like, it creeps me out that people would write that, and that a proportion of them would believe it.'

For Taylor, the continued barbs and tittle-tattle must have been draining, and yet at that point in her career, she did not have the confidence or clout to put her foot down and say, 'Enough'. That was painfully clear during a questionable segment on an earlier episode of *The Ellen DeGeneres Show*. In the clip from 2013, which later resurfaced, the host introduced a buzzer game to determine which of Taylor's famous exes was the subject of 'We Are Never Ever Getting Back Together'. 'I don't know if I'm going to do this,' Taylor protested. 'This is the one thing that I have; it's like the one shred of dignity that I have.' As photos of celebrities flashed up on the screen – some former partners, others absurd decoys like Danny DeVito – her discomfort was acutely obvious. When an image of her ex John Mayer popped up, Ellen told her, 'You're supposed to ring,' to which Taylor replied, 'I don't want to!' And when Ellen began ringing the buzzer herself, a visibly upset Taylor pleaded, 'Stop it. Stop it. Stop.' She added, 'It makes me feel so bad about myself; every time I come up here you put like a different dude up there on the screen, and it just makes me really question what I stand for as a human being.'

The excruciating exchange crystallised the impossible double standard Taylor confronted on a daily basis: a young woman mocked over who she dated and simultaneously condemned for singing about it. It showed how deeply embedded the 'boy-crazy' caricature had become, and explains why, by the time she wrote 'Shake It Off', her frustration had boiled over. An interview in the *Guardian* shed further light on her situation, as she said, 'In the last couple of years I've had to come to terms with the fact that anyone can say anything about me and call TMZ or Radar Online or something, and it will be an international headline.' But she also recognised that since it was a path she had chosen, she had to dust herself down and plough on. 'You can either go crazy and let it make you bitter and make you not trust people, and become really secluded or rebellious against the whole system. Or you can just shake it off and figure that as long as you're having more fun than anyone else, what does it matter what anyone else thinks? Because I've wanted this life since I was a kid.'

Another 1989 song that highlighted her plight was 'Blank Space', released as the album's second single. It stole the No. 1 slot from 'Shake It Off' on the *Billboard* Hot 100, making Taylor the first woman to replace herself at the chart's summit. Satirising the perception of her being a man-eating heart-breaker, she said it portrayed a woman who 'jet sets around the world collecting men ... but she's so clingy that they leave and she cries.' Speaking to a live audience at a Grammy event, she added, 'She gets another one in her web and she traps them and locks them in her mansion and then she's crying in her marble bathtub surrounded by pearls.' In playing such a bitterly ironic version of herself, Taylor effectively took back control of the joke, and the song's biting self-awareness led to rave reviews. As her second bestselling song in the UK ever, 'Blank Space' was even declared her greatest single by the

Guardian in 2019. 'The melody sounds effortless,' it said. 'The lyrics are sharp and funny and self-deprecating, the end result is a pop song so strong it has withstood covers by everyone from Imagine Dragons to Ryan Adams to Father John Misty.' Taylor opened the Brit Awards in February 2015 with a thumping performance of 'Blank Space', while she also won her first Brit for International Female Solo Artist – beating Beyoncé, Lana Del Ray, Sia and St Vincent to the prize. 'Oh my god!' Taylor said. 'I've been coming to England and playing shows for eight years and this is my first Brit Award – I'm so happy.'

Interestingly for trivia-loving Swifties, Travis Kelce went on to name the bouncy 'Blank Space' as his all-time favourite Taylor track, calling it 'a song I'll always listen to forever' on his *New Heights* podcast. 'It's just unbelievable – everything about it,' he said. Sharing the same birth year as Taylor, he also told *Access Hollywood* that 1989 was the first of her albums to grab his attention and convert him to the Swiftiesphere.

With so many standout singles, 1989 was one of the most influential albums of the decade. 'Without a doubt this is the best thing I've ever done,' Taylor told *Good Morning America* when she was on the promo circuit. Critics agreed, with *The Times* calling it 'the best pop album of the century so far' and *Billboard* later saying it represented a seismic moment in music history. 'With 1989, Taylor Swift moved beyond love songs,' it said. 'The album spoke to a generation of millennials living through uncertain times, looking for stability as young adults. Taylor's songs offer no easy answers, but endless emotional generosity.'

A commercial triumph, 1989 has sold 14 million copies to date, with over a million of those shifted in the US in seven days. That feat made Taylor Swift the first artist to hit the million-in-a-week milestone three times. Yet just days after its release, she made headlines for a very different reason after pulling her entire back catalogue from Spotify. Taking a stand against the way in which she felt business models were devaluing music, she had previously raised the issue in the *Wall Street Journal*. 'Music is art, and art is important and rare,' she said. 'Important, rare things are valuable. Valuable things should be paid for. It's my opinion that music should not be free.' In an unusually bold show of defiance against the streaming giants, she said in another interview with Yahoo Music: 'I'm not willing to contribute my life's work to an experiment that I don't feel fairly compensates the writers, producers, artists, and creators of this music.' In response, Spotify was adamant it did treat musicians fairly, hitting back: 'We believe fans should be able to listen to music wherever and whenever they want, and that artists have an absolute right to be paid for their work and protected from piracy. That's why we pay nearly 70 per cent of our revenue back to the music community.' The platform then compiled two playlists for fans mourning her music, one of which was called 'What to Play While Taylor's Away'. Only two and a half years later, in 2017, did Taylor end her boycott and return her music to Spotify, saying it was a 'thank you' to fans who had helped *1989* sell 10 million copies.

Regardless of the streaming saga, the 1989 world tour became the world's highest-grossing tour of 2015, with Taylor playing to more than 2.28 million people globally and taking over $250 million at the box office. Featuring her most ambitious shows yet, the tour became renowned for its stellar line-up of special guests, with the likes of Justin Timberlake, Selena Gomez, Julia Roberts, Ellie Goulding, Nick Jonas, Keith Urban, Leona Lewis, Little Mix and Avril Lavigne all appearing with her. Members of her so-called 'squad' – including Kendall Jenner, Karlie Kloss, Lena Dunham, Gigi Hadid and Cara Delevingne – also joined her at various intervals.

Taylor's achievements with both the tour and the album were all the more remarkable given label execs had begged her not to jump headfirst into pop. 'I went to Scott Borchetta and said, "I have to be honest with you: I did not make a country album. I did not make any semblance of a country album,"' she told *Billboard*. 'And of course he went into a state of semi-panic and went through all the stages of grief – the pleading, the denial. "Can you give me three country songs? Can we put a fiddle on 'Shake It Off'?" And all my answers were a very firm "no".' Despite being told the album would be her 'biggest mistake' by those around her, she told *GQ* in 2015: 'To me, the safest thing I could do was take the biggest risk.' It was a gamble that paid off, and *1989* went on to win three of the seven Grammys it was nominated for in 2016, including Album of the Year – making her the first woman to win the top honour a second time. Overcome as she accepted the monumental award, Taylor said, 'As the first woman to win Album of the Year at the Grammys twice, I want to say to all the young women out there, there are going to be people along the way who will try to undercut your success or take credit for your accomplishments or your fame. But if you just focus on the work and you don't let those people sidetrack you, someday when you get where you're going, you'll look around and you will know that it was you and the people who love you who put you there, and that will be the greatest feeling in the world.'

Taylor's astonishing Grammy sweep also saw her pick up the Best Pop Vocal Album gong, and Best Music Video prize for 'Bad Blood', featuring Kendrick Lamar. Echoing her star-studded tour, the no-expense-spared video brought together an entourage of Taylor's squad, lining up beside her as she played a machine gun-toting action heroine. As *1989*'s fourth single and one of its most talked-about tracks, the acerbic 'Bad Blood' was initially thought to have been about an ex-love, but Taylor later told *Rolling Stone* that it concerned a rift with another female artist who 'did something so horrible ... I was like, "Oh, we're just straight-up enemies".' She claimed the musician had 'tried to sabotage an entire arena tour' by hiring 'a bunch of people out from under me', and it was later claimed the offender was singer Katy Perry, who supposedly poached some of her Red world tour dancers for her own California Dreams tour. Though the feud rumbled on, it seemed to have been resolved by the time Katy appeared as a hamburger in Taylor's 2019 'You Need to Calm Down' video, along with the caption 'This meal is BEEF-free'.

As the fourth of her re-recordings, *1989 (Taylor's Version)* dropped in October 2023, nine years to the day after the original. It heralded a new wave of appreciation for the album, with the BBC calling it a 'pop music masterpiece' and *NME* saying, '*1989 (Taylor's Version)* feels more symbolic than her previous re-releases. Not only is it another step closer to having a full back catalogue of albums that she will own, but it's also a celebration of the moment Swift really took ownership of her pop sound.' Its success outstripped all expectations; in the UK, its first-week sales were more than double those of the original, and it became the fastest-selling record of 2023 overall. Taylor also broke her own record for the most single-day Spotify streams, and in America the reworked album became her sixth to sell a million copies in a week. Critics were particularly taken with a batch of five previously unreleased 'From the Vault' tracks, including 'Slut!' – a critique of the misogynistic double standards that had surrounded Taylor for over a decade. In a letter to fans that came with *1989 (Taylor's Version)*, she reminisced about the original record with retrospective clarity. 'The voices that had begun to shame me in new ways for dating like a normal young woman? I wanted to silence them,' she wrote. 'You see – in the years preceding this, I had become the target of slut shaming – the intensity and relentlessness of which would be criticised and called out if it happened today. The jokes about my amount of boyfriends. The trivialisation of my songwriting as if it were a predatory act of a boy-crazy psychopath. The media co-signing of this narrative. I had to make it stop because it was starting to really hurt.' Pointing out that she had been treated 'with the harsh moral codes of the Victorian era', she added: 'It became clear to me that for me there was no such thing as casual dating, or even having a male friend who you platonically hang out with. If I was seen with him, it was assumed I was sleeping with him.' Her reaction at the time was to stop dating full-stop, and focus on time with her girlfriends because 'people couldn't sensationalise or sexualise that – right?' But as she found out, people could – and they did. For many years, a subgroup of fans, known as 'Gaylors', clung to the conviction that Taylor was secretly gay or queer, analysing her music, lyrics and public appearances for evidence that supported their theory – including her friendships with other female celebrities and even her clothing choices.

Staunchly single for two years in the time she wrote and released *1989*, it wasn't until February 2015 that Taylor felt ready to date again. When her good friend Ellie Goulding introduced her to Scottish DJ Calvin Harris at the *Elle* Style Awards in London, the two hit it off instantly. The next night, they were spotted together after her performance at the Brit Awards, and the following month they got together in Nashville where they attended a Kenny Chesney concert. That April, Calvin made it Instagram official when he posted a photo of Taylor's beloved cats, Meredith and Olivia. During a gap in her 1989 world tour in December, the pair took a winter break in Colorado, with Taylor posting an Instagram photo of a snowman they had built. Then, on her momentous night of triple Grammy glory in February 2016, Calvin wrote on Twitter, 'Congratulations to my beautiful girlfriend'.

Though they kept things under wraps as much as possible, both shared social media shots of a Caribbean holiday that coincided with their one-year anniversary that March, with a since-deleted shot showing them kissing on the beach. The following month, Taylor warmly acknowledged Calvin – whose real name is Adam Wiles – at the 2016 iHeartRadio

Music Awards, where she won the Tour of the Year award. 'For the first time, I had the most amazing person to come home to when the spotlight went out and when the crowds were all gone,' she said. 'So I'd like to thank my boyfriend, Adam, for that.' She also told *Vogue*: 'I'm in a magical relationship right now. I want it to be ours and low key. This is the one thing that's been mine about my personal life.'

However, just weeks later, it was all over between music's hottest power couple. The parting was said to have been Calvin's decision, and in an interview with *GQ* that September he said, 'For both of us it was the wrong situation. It clearly wasn't right, so it ended.' Speaking of the difficulties of dating in the glare of the paparazzi, he added, 'I'm not good at being a celebrity.' Although the split seemed amicable at the time, their one and only musical collaboration – 'This Is What You Came For', which Calvin sang with Rihanna – led to a strange turn of events. Taylor had used the pseudonym Nils Sjöberg to co-write the song, to avoid it being overshadowed by their relationship. But after its release in April, Calvin bluntly dismissed the idea of ever working with her. 'I can't see it happening,' he told an interviewer. Later, when Taylor's team confirmed persistent rumours of her secret co-authorship, Calvin reacted defensively in a series of aggressive tweets, with one saying, 'Hurtful to me at this point that her and her team would go so far out of their way to try and make ME look bad at this stage.' And while he admitted Taylor did contribute to the song, he claimed he did most of the work, saying, 'I wrote the music, produced the song, arranged it and cut the vocals.' He also took a personal swipe at Taylor who had been romantically linked with actor Tom Hiddleston in the wake of their split. 'I figure if you're happy in your new relationship you should focus on that instead of trying to tear your ex bf down for something to do.' Taylor maintained a dignified silence in the face of the onslaught, and Calvin later deleted the tweets, telling *GQ,* 'It was completely the wrong instinct. I was protecting what I see as my one talent in the world being belittled. It felt like things were piling on top of me and that was when I snapped.'

With Taylor no doubt smarting over her break-up from Calvin, her whirlwind romance with British star Tom in the summer of 2016 was surely just the tonic she needed. They were first seen dancing together to T.I. hit 'Bring Em Out' in video footage recorded at New York's Met Gala in May 2016, and they also leapt to their feet as The Weeknd performed. Speaking afterwards, Tom told Radio 1 Breakfast Show host Nick Grimshaw: 'She said, "If they play 'I Can't Feel My Face' we have to get up and dance as an encore." I said, "I'm in, of course, let's go. Absolutely." We just jumped up and started dancing – and everybody else started dancing – which was great.' Within a fortnight of her break-up from Calvin, Taylor and Tom (then riding high from his stint in *The Night Manager*) were photographed kissing near her Rhode Island home. 'Tinker Taylor snogs a spy,' blazed an exclusive in the *Sun*. And with that, #Hiddleswift was officially born.

Yet the rapid pace and visibility of the relationship led many to question its authenticity, with conspiracy theorists falsely suggesting they only hooked up to plug an imminent music video. Even highbrow broadsheet the *Observer* jumped in, asking, 'Tom Hiddleston and Taylor Swift: match made in heaven or a PR stunt?' Analysing the timing of the viral photo opp, the piece ruminated, 'The images do indeed look as if a team of PR consultants and fashion stylists had just stepped out of the shot, rather than as though they were captured by a lucky lurking snapper.' But opting for a less cynical verdict, it added, 'Forget the photos and enjoy the story, which comes with such a strong aroma of invention that it can only be true.' When Tom was then snapped at Taylor's star-studded Fourth of July party on Rhode Island, wearing the now infamous 'I ♥ T.S.' tank top and sporting a faux heart tattoo on his arm, British TV show *This Morning* launched a debate scrutinising the couple's behaviour. 'Tom, have you really lost your senses that much?' asked body-language expert Deidre Sanders. 'It's that vest that did for me ... he is a wonderful Shakespearean actor, what *is* he doing?'

Over those hazy summer months, the pair were spotted meeting each other's parents in both Suffolk and Nashville, touring the Colosseum and Vatican in Rome and even having dinner on Australia's Gold Coast where Tom was filming *Thor: Ragnarok*. In an interview with the *Hollywood Reporter*, the actor was keen to set the record straight on speculation that it was a 'fauxmance': 'The truth is that Taylor Swift and I are together, and we're very happy. Thanks for asking,' he said. 'That's the truth. It's not a publicity stunt.'

But as the sheen began to fade, the romance quietly ended that September. Reports suggested Taylor wanted to keep things strictly off grid, while Tom's happiness for them to be more visible made her uncomfortable. However, he did hit back at those who doubted Hiddleswift, telling *GQ* in 2017, 'She's generous and kind and lovely, and we had the best time … Of course it was real.' He also retaliated over the much-maligned tank top, saying: 'The truth is, it was the Fourth of July and a public holiday and we were playing a game and I slipped and hurt my back. And I wanted to protect the graze from the sun and said, "Does anyone have a T-shirt?" And one of her friends said, "I've got this" … We all laughed about it.'

For Taylor, what might have been a genuine connection was smothered by the weight of fame, once again leaving her stranded between private need and public perception. Although she chose not to discuss Tom directly, fans have long speculated that he shaped her 2017 song 'Getaway Car'. Co-written with Jack Antonoff, it saw Taylor liken herself to someone using a rebound relationship as an escape route – interpreted as a memory of her moving on from Calvin and towards Tom. Its lyrics described a love that was thrilling but doomed; a glamorous distraction that could never last. But whatever its true meaning, 'Getaway Car' captured the speed, drama and inevitable crash of that heady summer – while also hinting at an exhaustion so extreme that Taylor eventually stepped out of the spotlight altogether.

CHAPTER FOUR

Not only did Taylor have to navigate two highly public break-ups in 2016, but it was also the year she effectively found herself cancelled. In what was the darkest juncture of her career, her age-old feud with Kanye West and Kim Kardashian re-erupted that summer over a controversial lyric from his song 'Famous', in which he referred to Taylor as a 'b*tch' he made famous. Her team denied she had approved it, condemning it as 'misogynistic'. But when Kanye and Kim both claimed she had given her blessing, the internet quickly turned on her, branding her manipulative and deceitful. The vicious firestorm resulted in snake emojis and spiteful memes, and the hashtag #TaylorSwiftIsOverParty became the top worldwide trend on Twitter. 'You know how many people have to be tweeting that they hate you for that to happen?' Taylor said in her 2020 Netflix documentary, *Miss Americana*. For someone who had built her career on authenticity and connection, the backlash was shattering, and it resulted in her withdrawal from public life over the ensuing months. 'When people fall out of love with you, there's nothing you can do to make them change their mind,' she said in the documentary. 'I just wanted to disappear. Nobody physically saw me for a year, and that was what I thought they wanted. When people decided I was wicked and evil and conniving and not a good person, that was the one that I couldn't really bounce back from because my whole life was centred around it.'

Lifting the lid on her inner turmoil with unusual candour, *Miss Americana* also focused on sensitive subjects that Taylor had always tended to avoid in interviews, such as her past struggles with body dysmorphia and an eating disorder. Revealing how she once became 'triggered' by photos where 'my tummy was too big or someone said I looked pregnant', she said she would 'starve a little bit. Just stop eating.' She also told how she thought she was 'supposed to feel like I was going to pass out at the end of a show or in the middle of it'. With Andrea Swift appearing by Taylor's side throughout the Netflix film, she additionally touched on her mother's ordeal with cancer, first diagnosed in 2015. 'That has been really hard for me because she is my favourite person,' she said. 'It woke me up from this life where I used to sweat all these things, but, like, do you really care if the internet doesn't like you today if your mom's sick from her chemo?'

With the cracks in her polished pop exterior deepening, it was unsurprising that Taylor was finding the strain hard to bear. As she said in the film, 'I've been doing this for 15 years and I'm tired ... It feels like it's more than music now. Most days I'm okay, but ... it just gets loud sometimes.' Reflecting in a *Vogue* interview in 2019 on the toll of being cancelled, she said, 'When you say someone is cancelled, it's not a TV show. It's a human being. You're sending mass amounts of messaging to this person to either shut up, disappear or it could also be perceived as "Kill yourself".'

In 2020, a leaked phone call showed Taylor *had* been telling the truth during the Kanye/Kim spat, but by then, the damage was done. 'You have a fully manufactured frame job, in an illegally recorded phone call, which Kim Kardashian edited and then put out to say to everyone that I was a liar,' she told *TIME* in 2023. 'That took me down psychologically to a place I've never been before. I moved to a foreign country. I didn't leave a rental house for a year. I was afraid to get on phone calls. I pushed away most people in my life because I didn't trust anyone anymore. I went down really, really hard.' With her anger still palpable after so many years, Taylor added, 'Make no mistake – my career was taken away from me.' However, rather than retreat permanently, she did what she always did in moments of crisis, turning to songwriting as a form of refuge. 'I knew immediately I needed to make music about it because I knew it was the only way I could survive it,' she said in her *Vogue* interview. 'It was the only way

I could preserve my mental health and also tell the story of what it's like to go through something so humiliating.'

That creative burst gave rise to one of the most powerful rebirths in modern music: Taylor's sixth album, *reputation*, which came out in 2017. Written largely during the time she spent lying low in London, it saw her turn her villain-ous persona on its head, charting her journey from fury and disillusionment to hope and renewal. With Jack Antonoff returning as her closest collaborator alongside Max Martin and Shellback, its pulsating synths and distorted vocals led the *Daily Telegraph* to call it 'a big, brash, all-guns-blazing blast of weaponised pop', while *Variety* duly named it 'pop album of the year'. In the first sign of what was to come, Taylor mass-deleted posts and pictures across her social media accounts in August 2017, before breaking her silence with a cryptic video of a snake slithering across a black background. When lead single 'Look What You Made Me Do' landed soon after, its razor-sharp lyrics and hip-hop-infused beats perfectly captured the mood. As *NME* put it: 'In short: no more Mrs Nice Gal'. Her first UK No. 1 single and fifth chart-topper in America, 'Look What You Made Me Do' saw Taylor confront a very public 'death' – presumably that of her career follow-ing the Kanye/Kim scandal – promising sweet revenge on all those who had wronged her. When its video – one of the most expensive ever made – dropped at the MTV VMAs, it drew

43 million YouTube views in a mere 24 hours, crashing Adele's record for 'Hello'. Wearing some spectacular zombie-style prosthetics, the video saw Taylor climb out of her own grave before going on the rampage, wielding a baseball bat and chainsaw as venomous snakes squirmed in the background. Astute fans picked up on a blink-and-you-miss-it Easter egg in the video, where Taylor lay in a diamond-filled bathtub with a single dollar bill next to her. It was a deft symbol of the token $1 she was awarded in a sexual-assault case against former radio DJ David Mueller, who had groped her as she posed for photos during the Red tour in June 2013. He had initially tried to sue Taylor, saying her claims cost him his job, but she countersued for a dollar. And after a jury finally found in her favour in the summer of 2017, she said the fight was never about money, but rather 'to help those whose voices should also be heard'. The case affected her profoundly, though, and speaking 12 months later on tour in Florida she told fans, 'A year ago I was not playing in a stadium in Tampa; I was in a courtroom in Denver, Colorado. This is the day the jury sided in my favour and said that they believed me.' As her voice trembled with emotion, she added, 'I guess I just think about all the people that weren't believed and the people who haven't been believed and the people who are afraid to speak up because they think they won't be believed.' Referencing her victory in 'Look What You Made Me Do' in that small but

potent way was a striking reminder that beneath the satire and million-dollar-budget shoots, Taylor was determined to own every aspect of her story.

A similarly seething standout on *reputation* was the track 'I Did Something Bad', in which she turned accusations of manipulation back on those who made them, with faux gunshots echoing in the background. Many thought the track was aimed at Calvin Harris, but its veiled attack on untrustworthy narcissists also led to suggestions it was a Kanye diss-track. In spite of the album's rage-flecked opening, *reputation* gradually softened into something far more intimate and tender. The shift seemed intentional, because where the first half focused on reclaiming power, its second act was about surrendering to new love. Partway through the record's inception, British actor Joe Alwyn had stepped gently into Taylor's world; not as a brash headline but as a vessel of safety amid stormy seas. As she told fans at a gig in Chicago in 2018, *reputation* was 'about finding love throughout all the noise', and in that sense, it was understandable she described it as her 'most cathartic' album to date. 'When it first came out everyone thought it was just going to be angry; upon listening to the whole thing they realised it's actually about love and friendship, and finding out what your priorities are,' she told *Entertainment Weekly*.

It's thought that she and Joe first crossed paths at the 2016 Met Gala, but they were not reported to be an item until many months later. In October that year, both attended a Kings of Leon concert in New York before heading to an afterparty at the Bowery Hotel. Then, in November, she was on the guest list at the premiere of Joe's film, *Billy Lynn's Long Halftime Walk*, along with her mum and several of her girlfriends. Somehow, they managed to keep their early encounters entirely secret, and a diary entry dated January 2017 that accompanied her album *Lover* told of the efforts Taylor had gone to. 'I'm essentially based in London, hiding out trying to protect us from the nasty world that just wants to ruin things. We have been together and no one has found out for three months now.' Speaking in *Miss Americana*, she told how she had fallen for 'someone who had a really wonderfully normal, balanced, grounded life', and at one point she mouthed 'I love you' to Joe, as he filmed her playing her guitar at home. Another scene in the documentary saw her running off stage and jumping into his arms after a performance.

Initially staying with Joe in his north London apartment, Taylor threw a ring of steel around their life together, wearing hats and scarves to avoid detection, travelling in blacked-out cars and flying in and out of remote UK airports. She and the *Conversations with Friends* star were then said to have moved into a £7 million townhouse in Primrose Hill, an area popular with a host of British celebrities, including Jude Law, Kate Moss and the Gallagher brothers. One of their favourite local spots was said to be the Spaniard's Inn pub in nearby Hampstead and, according to insiders, Taylor would some-times wear a black wig so she could enjoy a drink with Joe in peace. The cloak-and-dagger approach was part of her plan to keep what they had for themselves, and in an interview with the *Guardian* in 2019, she explained why she chose not to talk about Joe. 'I've learned that if I do, people think it's up for discussion, and our relationship isn't up for discussion,' she said. Meanwhile, in his own interview with *Mr Porter*, Joe voiced similar sentiments: 'I don't think anyone you meet on the streets would just spill their guts out to you, therefore why should I?' he said. 'And then that is defined as being "strangely private". Fine. But I don't think it is. I think it's normal.'

Eventually, though, Taylor began leaving small, subtle traces for fans to devour, as seen in May 2018 – almost a year after their relationship was first reported – when she and Joe shared separate Instagram shots in which they stood next to a giant cactus in the desert. While Taylor's caption was about her Reputation tour kicking off, Joe simply included a cactus emoji in his. On the opening night of the tour in Arizona that same week, Joe was then spotted in the audience wearing a baseball cap, and fans claimed Taylor pointed straight at him as she sang 'Gorgeous' from the album. Months earlier, during a *reputation* listening party, she had apparently admit-ted that 'Gorgeous' – with its references to hypnotic blue eyes

– was about him, with the 300 lucky Swifties in attendance claiming that she seemed happy for the world to know.

Through this track and other similarly gentle offerings on *reputation*, listeners were given a glimpse into the couple's early days, and the cautious joy Taylor had allowed back into her heart. Second single and album opener '...Ready for It?' was about the excitement and infatuation of a new fling, set against vivid imagery of bank robbers and heists. 'King of My Heart' saw her celebrate finding someone who saw her through the chaos, and the hesitant 'Delicate' captured the fragility of a relationship formed in high-pressure circumstances. The sexually charged 'Dress', alluded to her bleached blonde hair and the buzzcut Joe had when they met, and 'Call It What You Want' was about learning to trust again. Especially poignant was piano-led closing track 'New Year's Day', which explored her yearning for something more meaningful amid life's fleeting highs. 'I was thinking about how everybody talks and thinks about who you kiss at midnight. And I think that is very romantic,' she said during an iHeartRadio release party for *reputation*. 'But I think there's something even more romantic about who's gonna deal with you on New Year's Day. Who's willing to give you Advil and clean up the house? I think that states more of a permanence.'

On its release in November 2017, critics were impressed by what the *New York Times* dubbed the 'bombastic, unexpected, sneakily potent' force of *reputation*. The *LA Times* called it 'her most focused, most cohesive album yet', while *USA Today* said it was 'a fully formed snapshot of a singer in love'. It also credited Taylor with being 'predator, the person holding all the control, the gatekeeper to her own heart, flipping the script'. However, the album did prove divisive, with a BBC critic saying, 'She is handy with a pen, but Bob Dylan she is not.' *Pitchfork* was also less than complimentary, saying *reputation* was 'sadly conventional' and that Taylor herself seemed 'beleaguered and defensive, a figure fighting back from public relations problems she largely could've avoided'. Such criticism certainly left a mark, and she later said of the album, 'It just got thrown into a fire ... blown to bits.' Speaking on KRBE Radio in Texas, she added that despite it being one of her favourite records, it 'didn't really get a fair swing'.

Regardless, on a commercial level *reputation* easily matched the success of her previous five efforts, becoming her fourth consecutive album to sell over a million copies in a week in the US. Holding the top spot on the *Billboard* 200 for four weeks, it was her third UK No. 1 and it received a nomination for Best Pop Vocal Album at the 2019 Grammys. But interestingly, she decided against releasing a *Taylor's Version* of *reputation*, saying in a letter to fans that it felt too 'specific to that time in my life', and that she 'kept hitting a stopping point when I tried to remake it'. She added, 'To be perfectly honest, it's the one album in those first six that I thought couldn't be improved upon by redoing it.'

In the aftermath of *reputation*, Taylor enjoyed one of the most relaxed phases of her life. Having spent years feeling under siege, there was a stillness with Joe she had seldom experienced before. Dividing their time between London and her homes in Nashville and New York, they were able to live relatively anonymously, enjoying quiet trips to cafés and pubs, as well as taking surreptitious walks in the countryside. There were blissful trips to the Maldives and the Caribbean, and as Taylor said in *Miss Americana*, 'It was happiness without anyone else's input.' At music and movie events, they avoided walking the red carpet together, but would attend afterparties hand in hand, fully on their own terms. Together, they shared an understanding: Joe recognised the impossible weight of fame she carried, and she saw in him a rare, uncompromising steadiness. With the relationship becoming Taylor's longest to date, she had found a rhythm and grounding that had so long been missing from her world.

By late 2018, that contentment had begun to filter through to her songwriting, and after completing her six-month Reputation stadium tour – her first to play only stadiums – she began recording a seventh album, *Lover*. Released in August 2019 and marking her debut with Republic Records (following the expiry of her contract with Big Machine Records), it again brought right-hand man Jack Antonoff front and centre. A lyrical portrait of Taylor's domestic happiness, the album displayed a new sense of fun and confidence; the sound of someone in love without fear. 'When I started writing, I couldn't stop,' she told *Vogue* in 2019. 'There are so many ways in which this album feels like a new beginning. This album is really a love letter to love, in all of its maddening, passionate, exciting, enchanting, horrific, tragic, wonderful glory.'

Leaving behind *reputation*'s darker tones, *Lover* brought back a more diaristic and internalised kind of writing, as well as 1980s-style synth-pop and even shades of country. The first clues around the album's playful aesthetic arrived at the iHeartRadio Awards in March 2019, when Taylor wore a pastel-coloured playsuit and butterflies on her shoes. At the event, she won the Tour of the Year award for Reputation – which had sold over 2 million tickets in America to become the highest-grossing tour ever by an artist in the US.

The following month, she launched a mysterious countdown on her social media platforms and website, with pink hearts and glittery images building anticipation. Later in April, she unveiled 'ME!', the first single from *Lover*, a collaboration with Panic! at the Disco frontman, Brendon Urie. The song was about self-love and acceptance, and despite being a touch saccharine for some, plenty of critics were sold. 'Swift once again proves her mastery of the infectious pop hook in one of the most drastic reinventions of her career to date,' said the *Independent*. Explaining the song on *Good Morning America*, Taylor said, '"ME!" is a song about embracing your individuality and really celebrating it and owning it. I think that with a pop song we have the ability to get a melody stuck in people's heads, and I just want it to be one that makes them feel better about themselves, not worse.' As comebacks go, it was a rampant success, breaking streaming records, winning an MTV Video Music Award and earning a Guinness World Record for the most YouTube views by a solo artist in 24 hours. It was no wonder the camped-up video attracted so much attention. Co-directed by Taylor, it saw her dancing under rainbow skies at a Pride parade, dripping in paint, before seemingly rejecting a man's advances – in favour of a kitten. It was also no coincidence that 'ME!' dropped on 26 April, Lesbian Visibility Day, for Taylor was entering a new era in which she began to more openly champion equality and inclusivity. Despite being viewed as apolitical earlier in her career, she told *Vogue* how she felt she had no choice but to make a stand. 'Rights are being stripped from basically everyone who isn't a straight, white, cisgender male,' she said. 'I didn't realise until recently that I could advocate for a community that I'm not a part of.'

Second single, 'You Need to Calm Down', in June 2019, cranked up the idea further, sending a full-throttle message to bullies and haters. 'I wrote this song about the energy and effort that some people put into spreading negativity,' she said in her Spotify song notes. 'With all of the trolling, cancel culture, telling people how to live their lives, or pitting women against each other ... you're being too loud. This is a song where I'm just saying, "You Need to Calm Down". Go outside, it's the summer.' Released to coincide with Pride Month, the song was seen as a rallying call for the LGBTQ+ community, and its gloriously technicolour video featured cameos from celebrities, activists and queer icons, including RuPaul, Laverne Cox and the cast of *Queer Eye*. At the end of the video, Taylor urged fans to sign a petition she had started to encourage the passing of the US Equality Act through the Senate. 'The fact that, legally, some people are completely at the mercy of the hatred and bigotry of others is disgusting and unacceptable,' she wrote in a letter in support of the petition. 'Let's show our pride by demanding that, on a national level, our laws truly treat all of our citizens equally.'

At the MTV Video Music Awards that August, where she won Video of the Year for 'You Need to Calm Down', Taylor bravely used her moment of glory to call out the Trump administration for not responding to her appeal. 'I want to thank everyone who signed that petition because it now has half a million signatures, which is five times the amount that it would need to warrant a response from the White House,' she said on stage. Taylor then glanced at her wrist, tapping an imaginary watch as if to signal it was time for the administration to act. Such a stance represented a major shift in Taylor's career, and the act of solidarity cemented *Lover* as her most openly progressive album, fusing personal joy with a social conscience.

The album's title track was released as the third single – one of three tracks Taylor wrote alone. Evoking a timeless, committed monogamy, it was seen as a reflection of her bond with Joe and the simple joys of life together, including leaving the Christmas decorations up until the new year. 'In my head I had like, just the last two people on a dance floor at 3am swaying. Whatever that would sound like,' she told the *New York Times*. Part of the song was structured like a set of wedding vows, with Taylor even asking listeners to stand. 'There's a line in the song that I'm really proud of,' she said at a select NPR radio gathering. 'And the line says, "With every guitar string scar in my hand, I take this magnetic force of a man to be my lover", and that line is really special to me because I've spent quite a bit of time writing break-up songs.'

In the track 'London Boy', Joe's British roots were celebrated, with the lyrics homing in on Camden market, Soho, Brixton, Shoreditch and the West End, as well as the tradition of high tea and watching rugby in the pub with his friends. So much attention could have been anathema to ultra-discreet Joe, but when asked by the *Sunday Times* if he minded being Taylor's muse in so many songs, he insisted, 'No, not at all. No. It's flattering.'

Another song, 'Afterglow', seemed to be a plea for forgiveness from Taylor after rows caused by her deep-seated insecurities, and the giddy lyrics of 'I Think He Knows', 'Cornelia Street' and 'Paper Rings' all signposted listeners straight to her love for Joe. But on a more serious note, one of *Lover*'s most resonant songs was 'Soon You'll Get Better' featuring The Chicks, which addressed Andrea Swift's ongoing struggle with cancer. Taylor understandably described it as one of the hardest things she had ever written, and despite the Swifts being very private, she said on YouTube: 'We as a family decided to put this on the album. It's something I'm so proud of. I can't sing it. It's hard to emotionally deal with that song.' She also told *Variety* how Andrea was 'the guiding force' in her life, saying, 'Almost every decision I make, I talk to her about it first. So obviously it was a really big deal to ever speak about her illness.'

With *Lover* essentially serving as a reset for Taylor following the antagonistic *reputation*, the album debuted at No. 1 in both the UK and America, and by the end of 2019 it was the bestselling record by a solo artist globally. It also earned three Grammy nominations in 2020, although Taylor found herself eclipsed by that year's big winner, Billie Eilish. But while the pandemic meant that Taylor's planned Lover Fest tour was scrapped, there was still unfinished business, and 'Cruel Summer', another of the album's songs, was released as the final single years later in June 2023. It came about due to a resurgence in popularity when it formed part of Taylor's Eras tour setlist, and performing one night, she said, 'What's happening right now, thanks to you – and honestly no one understands why this is happening – [is that] you guys have streamed "Cruel Summer" so much right now in 2023 that it's, like, rising on the streaming charts so crazy. My label just decided to just make it the next single.' The decision was vindicated, and the track she called her 'pride and joy' became *Lover*'s first and only No. 1 single in the US, and its highest-charting track in the UK, reaching No. 2.

While 'Cruel Summer' was assumed to be about Taylor and Joe's passionate, top-secret beginnings, it took on a whole new meaning when she later began her relationship with Travis. He was spotted singing and dancing along to the track during her Eras tour shows, and, speaking on the *Bussin' with the Boys* podcast in June 2024, he even admitted it ranked among his all-time favourite Taylor tunes. '"Cruel Summer" is one of the ones she opens with at her show, and when she comes out, it's electric,' he said. 'I was fired up when that happened the first show I was ever at.' Similarly, a viral clip of her performing

Lover's title track at Wembley in 2024 saw Travis pointing at Taylor on stage and then back to himself as he joined in, word for word. In that sense, *Lover* had found new life – no longer just an album from her past, but a bridge between 2019's version of herself and the unguarded, self-assured woman she had become with Travis. Then, when he got down on one knee in the summer of 2025, fans breathlessly noted that the garden he proposed in looked uncannily like *Lover*'s cover art, awash in soft pastels and blooming with near-identical flowers. 'The *Lover* era prophecy fulfilled,' one fan declared online, as if the moment was scripted years in advance. 'Proof that manifestation is real,' concluded another.

Three years before Travis entered Taylor's life, the spring of 2020 brought the world and everything in it to a standstill. Taylor had only just turned 30 and was preparing for her Lover Fest shows, while she had also been booked to headline Glastonbury that June for the first time. But as Covid-19 took hold, everything she'd planned came to an abrupt halt and she was forced into a rare period of stillness. Locked away in isolation with Joe in London, she turned inward, and began writing a new and unplanned record – which would be her eighth. 'I wasn't expecting to make an album,' she told *Entertainment Weekly*. 'The only people who knew were the people I was making it with, my boyfriend, my family and a small management team.' Composed and recorded in secret over three months, the result was *folklore*, which was unlike anything she had ever made before. In place of *Lover*'s bold, bombastic pop came the sound of muted pianos, acoustic guitars and strings, with Taylor's voice softer and more hushed. She told how she had 'poured all of my whims, dreams, fears, and musings' into the new songs, and when it arrived, at midnight on 24 July, it did so with less than a day's notice, effectively breaking the internet in the process. 'Most of the things I had planned this summer didn't end up happening. But there is something I hadn't planned on that DID happen,' she announced on social media. 'And that thing is my 8th studio album, folklore. Surprise.'

In her big reveal, Taylor credited a line-up of collaborators she had worked remotely with on *folklore*, including The National's Aaron Dessner, who co-wrote or produced 11 of the 16 tracks. He told how he had been 'excited and honoured' when Taylor first approached him, saying in an online post, 'I've rarely been so inspired by someone and it's still hard to believe this even happened. These songs came together in such a challenging time.' Also pivotal in the album's creation were Justin Vernon of Bon Iver and her longtime ally Jack Antonoff, as well as another mystery contributor – William Bowery. His inclusion left many scratching their heads, and when fans discovered there was no registered songwriter or producer with such a name, suspicions immediately fell on someone closer to home: Joe Alwyn. Only in November 2020 did Taylor confirm they had used an alias for him on the record. 'There's been a lot of discussion about William Bowery and his identity because it's not a real person,' she said in her Disney+ film *folklore: The Long Pond Studio Sessions*. 'William Bowery is Joe, as we know.' Long after the riddle was solved, Joe explained the reasoning behind it. 'We chose to do it so the people first and foremost would listen to the music before dissecting the fact that we did it together,' he said on *The Kelly Clarkson Show*. 'It sounds like a kind of Agatha Christie character that should be wearing a monocle with a big moustache.'

The seemingly random name was an amalgamation of Joe's grandfather William and the area of New York he had once lived in, Bowery. Joe co-wrote two of the album's most compelling songs as William Bowery, showing his musical talents were considerable: the Grammy-nominated 'exile', a haunting duet with Bon Iver about a relationship turned sour, and 'betty', a moving tale of young regret. He also co-produced six songs on the album, but as he told *GQ*, there was nothing gimmicky about his involvement. 'It was really the most accidental thing to happen in lockdown,' he said. 'It wasn't like, "It's three o'clock, it's time to write a song!" It was just messing around on a piano and singing badly and being overheard and then thinking, "You know, what if we tried to get to the end of it together?"' Speaking with Zane Lowe at the Apple Music Awards, held virtually in December 2020, Taylor also told how their joint songwriting venture had happened organically. 'We've always bonded over music,' she said. 'We write the saddest songs. We just really love sad songs. What can I say?'

Among the main drivers of the album were the films Taylor and Joe obsessively watched during lockdown, which led her to think, 'Why have I never created characters and intersecting story lines?' Her creative curiosity culminated in a trio of songs about a teenage love triangle written from different perspectives – 'cardigan', 'august' and 'betty', the song she co-wrote with Joe. 'the last great american dynasty' presented a fictionalised account of heiress Rebekah Harkness, who had once lived in Taylor's Rhode Island home. 'I found myself not only writing my own stories, but also writing about or from the perspective of people I've never met, people I've known, or those I wish I hadn't,' she wrote in her album notes. 'In isolation my imagination has run wild and this album is the result, a collection of songs and stories that flowed like a stream of consciousness. Picking up a pen was my way of escaping into fantasy, history, and memory.' Her decision to give no interviews around *folklore*'s release meant fans were left to fill in the gaps and encouraged to unpick the stories framing each track. 'One thing I did purposely on this album was put the Easter eggs in the lyrics, more than just the videos,' Taylor said in a live Q&A to promote 'cardigan'. 'I created character arcs and recurring themes that map out who is singing about who.'

Despite *folklore* being rich in invented characters and imagined romances, there were still several more autobiographical songs that cast new light on her relationship with Joe. The song 'peace' was a confession of vulnerability in which she acknowledged the threat her fame had on their life together. Discussing the track with Sir Paul McCartney in the November 2020 edition of *Rolling Stone*, Taylor said, 'I cannot control if there are 20 photographers outside in the bushes and what they do and if they follow our car and if they interrupt our lives. I can't control if there's going to be a fake weird headline about us in the news tomorrow.' But she told how she had managed to find 'bits of normalcy' with Joe, adding, 'I think that in knowing him and being in the relationship I am in now, I have definitely made decisions that have made my life feel more like a real life and less like just a storyline to be commented on in tabloids.' Another song, 'invisible string', was about an imperceptible tie that bound her and Joe to one another, while 'the lakes' seemed to be a recollection of their time in the Lake District, where they had spent their third anniversary. Despite the album's mellow tones, there was room for something a little feistier, and 'mad woman' allowed Taylor to have the last word on her long battle with Scooter Braun over the sale of her master recordings. Addressing themes of sexism and power dynamics in the music industry, the song saw Taylor drop the F-bomb for the first time in her recording career, and she told afterwards of how that felt 'f***ing fantastic', and that 'every rule book was thrown out'.

Though it caught the world's media off-guard, *folklore* did receive universal praise from critics. The *Independent* hailed Taylor's 'exquisite, piano-based poetry', *NME* described the album as 'fresh, forward-thinking and, most of all, honest', and in a five-star review, the *Guardian* said the record 'proves that she can thrive away from the noise'. As the lead single, the wistful meditation on love and loss that was 'cardigan' brought instant success, debuting at No. 1 on the *Billboard* Hot 100, where it remained for two months. With *folklore* simultaneously at No. 1, Taylor was now the first artist ever to debut at the top of both charts in the same week – and the first female to have seven albums debut at No. 1 in the US. Further records tumbled when *folklore* achieved 80.6 million streams on Spotify in a single day – the highest-ever tally for a female artist. Five Grammy nominations followed in 2021, and when she took home the all-important Album of the Year award on the night, it made her the first woman in history to win the top honour three times. At the socially distanced ceremony in

LA, Joe didn't appear with her, but he did feature prominently on her thank-you list. 'I had the best time writing songs with you in quarantine,' she said on accepting the award.

L ess than five months after releasing *folklore*, Taylor surprised fans once again with *evermore*, which she called its 'sister record'. It was created in the same lockdown conditions with the same collaborators, also welcoming the Haim sisters, other members of The National and Marcus Mumford into the fold. Released, again, with no warning or promo, Taylor announced the album across social media on 10 December. 'To put it plainly, we just couldn't stop writing songs,' she wrote. 'To try and put it more poetically, it feels like we were standing on the edge of the folklorian woods and had a choice: to turn and go back or to travel further into the forest of this music. We chose to wander deeper in. Ever since I was 13, I've been excited about turning 31 because it's my lucky number backwards, which is why I wanted to surprise you with this now.'

As a companion piece that took on themes like murder, intrigue and ill-fated romance, its tone was more playful and experimental than the earlier work, but it was still rich in delicate piano, lush strings and plucked guitar. As *NME* said, 'If *folklore* is an introspective, romantic older sister, *evermore* is the freewheeling younger sibling.' With the album crammed with more stories and make-believe, Taylor wrote in her album explainer, 'I loved the escapism I found in these imaginary/not imaginary tales. I loved the ways you welcomed the dreamscapes and tragedies and epic tales of love lost and found. So I just kept writing them.' As before, Joe co-wrote three songs as William Bowery: sombre break-up number 'coney island', 'champagne problems' which was about a thwarted proposal and title track 'evermore', a hopeful song about mental healing.

But it was lead single 'willow' that generated most buzz, not least because Taylor appeared in its video wearing an off-white gown by Australian designer Zimmermann. Over-zealous fans were convinced she and Joe had secretly married, with one posting online, 'CAN WE FINALLY ADMIT TAYLOR IS A MARRIED WOMAN??' The theory came just a few months after Taylor appeared to wear a large diamond ring on her left hand in her Netflix documentary *Miss Americana*. Then, another song on the album, 'ivy', threw mention of a 'husband' into the mix, cranking up the excitement further. Despite the unfounded speculation, she and Joe had continually found themselves dogged by wedding and engagement rumours – an irritation Taylor sang about in her *Midnights* song 'Lavender Haze', in which she asked why the world was so desperate to marry her off. In April 2022, Joe voiced his frustrations, too. 'If I had a pound for every time I think I've been told I've been engaged, then I'd have a lot of pound coins,' he quipped to the *Wall Street Journal*. 'I mean, the truth is, if the answer was yes, I wouldn't say, and if the answer was no, I wouldn't say.' As the theories continued to bounce around gossip sites, Taylor's publicist Tree Paine finally hit out in late 2023. 'Enough is enough with these fabricated lies about Taylor,' she wrote on social media. 'There was NEVER a marriage or ceremony of ANY kind.'

All the hearsay did not harm the song's trajectory, however, and the release of 'willow' alongside *evermore* again saw Taylor break records with an album and single debuting at No. 1 simultaneously in the US. The song also helped *evermore* set a new record for vinyl sales, with more than 40,000 copies sold in just three days – the most since 1991. And when *evermore* soared straight to the top of the UK chart, it made Taylor the fastest female ever to score six No. 1 albums in British history. It was hardly a shock, then, when the album received a Grammy nomination in 2022, again for Album of the Year, although, as it turned out, even the high-flying 'T-Swizzle' could not claim music's most esteemed prize two years on the bounce.

Other *evermore* tracks included 'marjorie', an ode to the beloved grandmother she lost in 2003 when she was 13, and 'gold rush', a musing on jealousy and infatuation. The song 'no body, no crime', featuring Haim, was a true-crime-based murder ballad, and 'tolerate it' dealt with a rocky relationship with an older man. The tracks 'dorothea' and 'tis the damn season' developed Taylor's interest in telling a story from different perspectives – in this case, from the point of view of an actress called Dorothea, who rekindled a romance with an ex during holiday season. As critics savoured another round of Taylor's vibrant storytelling, *USA Today* called *evermore* a 'weird and wonderful thing' which, in many ways, was 'even more spellbinding than *folklore*'. *Variety* agreed, saying, 'This particular quarantine bubble? It's one we may not want to pop.'

For Taylor, the acclaim capped an unparallelled creative streak, with two world-class albums delivered in one of the most discombobulating times in modern history. Yet even she seemed uncertain about what might follow. 'I have no idea what comes next,' she wrote on her socials after *evermore*'s release. 'I have no idea about a lot of things these days, and so I've clung to the one thing that keeps me connected to you all. That thing always has and always will be music.'

CHAPTER FIVE

While *evermore* closed the door on Taylor's rush of pandemic-era creativity, her subsequent project was one she believed in above all else. Within the space of seven months in 2021, she released two of her six planned album re-recordings – *Fearless (Taylor's Version)* in April and *Red (Taylor's Version)* in November. Few artists had ever embarked on such an absorbing mission, and for Taylor it was not about repackaging old songs, but about taking a stand over musical ownership and legacy. As we saw earlier, the decision was born out of the despair that hit her when her former manager Scott Borchetta sold his label Big Machine Records – and with it, the master recordings of her first six albums – to music manager Scooter Braun, the record executive and manager who is credited with discovering Justin Bieber and Ariana Grande, among others. In an open letter posted on Tumblr back in June 2019, she said she had only found out about the sale 'as it was announced to the world'. Accusing Scooter of 'incessant, manipulative bullying', she claimed she was offered the chance to 'earn back' her work, one album at a time for every new record she delivered to Big Machine. But feeling that was an unacceptable deal, she walked away. 'I had to make the excruciating choice to leave behind my past,' she wrote. 'Scooter has stripped me of my life's work ... Essentially, my musical legacy is about to lie in the hands of someone who tried to dismantle it.'

She went on to question the motives of Big Machine's founder, too, writing, 'Any time Scott Borchetta has heard the words "Scooter Braun" escape my lips, it was when I was either crying or trying not to. He knew what he was doing; they both did. Controlling a woman who didn't want to be associated with them. In perpetuity. That means forever.' Calling the situation her 'worst-case scenario', she added, 'This is what happens when you sign a deal at 15 to someone for whom the term "loyalty" is clearly just a contractual concept.' She also told of her wish to make others aware of the pitfalls so they would be better equipped to navigate the industry in future. 'Hopefully, young artists or kids with musical dreams will read this and learn about how to better protect themselves in a negotiation. You deserve to own the art you make.' She signed off, 'Sad and grossed out, Taylor'.

In response, Scott Borchetta published his own open letter disputing Taylor's version of events, saying she had been made aware of the sale in advance of the announcement. He also claimed she had declined an opportunity to purchase the master recordings. Scooter Braun initially remained silent, but months later posted a long public message to Taylor on Instagram saying, 'To be frank, I was shocked and disheartened to hear that my presence in the Big Machine deal caused you so much pain as the handful of times we have actually met I have always remembered them being pleasant and respectful.' He told how he had wanted to resolve things amicably, but that his attempts to contact Taylor and her team over the preceding six months were all rejected. Revealing that his family had also received death threats over the ongoing argument, he added, 'It is important that you understand that your words carry a tremendous amount of weight.'

Meanwhile, Taylor's industry peers rushed to support her, with singer Halsey one of the first out of the starting blocks. 'It turns my guts that no matter how much power or success a woman has in this life, you are still susceptible to someone coming along and making you feel powerless out of spite,' she tweeted. 'It speaks volumes to how far we have to come in the music industry.' The 'Without Me' singer added, 'She deserves to own the painstaking labor of her heart.' Taylor's close friend Selena Gomez took to Instagram to voice her allegiance, too. 'My heart is so heavy right now. It makes me sick and extremely angry,' she said. Kelly Clarkson weighed in with some advice that that may have influenced Taylor's later actions. 'U should go in & re-record all the songs that U don't own the masters on,' the 'Stronger' singer tweeted. 'Put brand new art & some kind of incentive so fans will no longer buy the old versions.'

Bizarrely, one of Taylor's most unexpected advocates was none other than her long-time adversary Kanye West, who tweeted, 'I'M GOING TO PERSONALLY SEE TO IT THAT TAYLOR SWIFT GETS HER MASTERS BACK'. His stance coincided with his own crusade in 2020 to 'move the entire music industry into the 21st century' and do 'whatever is necessary so artists own their own copyrights'. However, some musicians, including Justin Bieber, took an opposing view. 'Scooter has had your back since the days you graciously let me open up for you!' he said in an online message to Taylor. 'As the years have passed, we haven't crossed paths and gotten to communicate our differences, hurts or frustrations. So for you to take it to social media and get people to hate on Scooter isn't fair.' And singer Demi Lovato posted on Instagram, 'I have dealt with bad people in the industry and Scooter is not one of them. He's a good man.'

The fallout dominated entertainment headlines for months, but in a statement in November 2020, Taylor finally declared she was bringing her *Taylor's Version* vision to life. 'I have recently begun re-recording my older music and it has already proven to be both exciting and creatively fulfilling,' she said. 'I have plenty of surprises in store. I want to thank you guys for supporting me through this ongoing saga, and I can't wait for you to hear what I've been dreaming up.' As an act of defiance, it not only gave her the last word, but finally allowed her to transform years of pain into both a personal and professional victory. As she had previously said when *Billboard* named her Woman of the Decade in December 2019, 'I do want my music to live on. I do want it to be in movies, I do want it to be in commercials. But I only want that if I own it ... It's going to be fun, because it'll feel like regaining a freedom and taking back what's mine.' Recognising that her unique position as an international superstar gave her a voice in an industry where the odds were stacked against up-and-coming musicians, she added, 'I know that it seems like I'm very loud about this, but it's because someone has to be.'

Though the fight had been undeniably tough, the support of her parents, of Joe – and their little feline family – proved vital in carrying her through. 'I really appreciate my experience, the ups and downs,' she told *Billboard*. 'And maybe that seems ridiculously Zen, but ... I've got my friends, who like me for the right reasons. I've got my family. I've got my boyfriend. I've got my fans. I've got my cats.'

When Taylor was awarded the historic Global Icon award at the Brit Awards in May 2021 in recognition of her three No. 1 albums in less than a year – *folklore*, *evermore* and *Fearless*

(Taylor's Version) – organisers were keen to acknowledge her mind-boggling work rate and efforts to make the world a fairer place. 'Taylor's career is unparalleled and her music and influence have resonated with millions of people all over the world,' a statement said. 'She's used her platform to highlight many issues globally and recently has been applauded for her work promoting acceptance of the LGBTQ community.'

Impressively, Taylor became the first ever female and first non-British artist to receive the Global Icon honour, and it put her on equal footing with previous winners Sir Elton John and the late David Bowie. She was full of emotion as she took to the stage at London's O2 in a sparkly Miu Miu crop top and skirt. 'Thank you, Aaron Dessner, thank you, Jack Antonoff, Joe ...' she said. Extolling the rock-solid foundations her friends and family gave her, she added, 'If there's one thing that I've learned it's that you have to look around you every day and take note of the people who have always believed in you, and never stop appreciating them for it, never take them for granted.' She also gave a shout-out to her beloved British Swifties, and in an oblique reference to her industry struggles, she urged others not to be downtrodden or silenced. 'There might be times when you put your whole heart and soul into something and it is met with cynicism or scepticism. You cannot let that crush you. You have to let it fuel you because we live in a world where anyone has the right to say anything about you at any time, but just please remember that you have the right to prove them wrong.' That night was a major indicator of Taylor's meteoric rise from pop princess to critically revered songwriter, and though Joe was not by her side to celebrate, it seemed appropriate that she received the award in London, now her adopted second home.

Following such a relentless stretch of music-making, the summer of 2021 saw Taylor ease her foot off the gas, as she and Joe took a break in Ireland where he was filming *Conversations with Friends*. The pair had rarely been seen together in months – although naturally, rumours of a possible engagement had once again been swarming. 'They grew closer than ever during quarantine and she really trusts him,' a source told *Entertainment Tonight*. 'They've discussed future plans and Taylor can see herself marrying Joe one day.' Though it was another false lead, fans were increasingly hopeful that she was inching towards the kind of relationship goal with Joe she had always envisaged for herself. During a beach trip in County Donegal, she shared an Instagram snap to announce a new orchestral version of 'The Lakes', timed to commemorate the first anniversary of *folklore*. 'It's been 1 year since we escaped the real world together and imagined ourselves someplace simpler,' said her caption. As she explored the Emerald Isle with Joe, they also visited Wicklow, where Taylor picked up a pebble from a beach. As holiday souvenirs go, it was a simple one, but the memento would later find its way on to her next album, *Midnights* – which, in hindsight, would turn out to be a bittersweet soundtrack to their final days together.

A career milestone for any musician, album number ten was always going to have special meaning. As well as marking a return to a more personal and diaristic subject matter, Taylor developed *Midnights* as a concept album which saw her reminiscing on 13 sleepless nights in her life. Unexpectedly announcing it while collecting MTV's Video of the Year award for 'All Too Well (Taylor's Version)' in August 2022, she told millions of viewers, 'I thought it might be a fun moment to tell you that my brand-new album comes out on October 21. And I will tell you more at midnight.' As the hashtag #MeetMeAtMidnight began trending, details duly emerged, including the album's title, and the fact it would have 13 tracks – in keeping with her magic number. 'This is a collection of music written in the middle of the night,' she said in a social post. 'A journey through terrors and sweet dreams, the floors we pace and the demons we face. For all of us who have tossed and turned and decided to keep the lanterns lit and go searching.'

Just a week before the release of *Midnights*, Taylor stoked up interest when she unveiled three themed playlists on Apple Music, offering a rare glimpse into how she categorised her songs. The personally curated lists were intriguingly named 'Quill Pen', 'Fountain Pen' and 'Glitter Gel Pen'. Admitting she had never talked about it before because it was 'dorky', she said on Apple, 'Most of my lyrics are Fountain Pen lyrics. They're modern personal stories, written like poetry, about those moments you remember all too well where you can see, hear and feel everything in screaming detail.' She explained that her Glitter Gel Pen songs contained words that 'make you want to dance, sing and toss glitter around the room', adding, 'They remind you not to take yourself too seriously, which is something we all need to hear these days.' And she said the lyrics of her Quill Pen songs 'make you feel all old-fashioned, like you're a 19th-century poet crafting your next sonnet by candlelight'.

Together, they helped decode the creative DNA of *Midnights*, which came with a kaleidoscopic mix of diaristic confessions and super-slick pop gloss. Recorded largely in New York, the album got Taylor back into the studio with Jack Antonoff and reawakened her passion for 1980s-influenced synths. As so often with Taylor, there was a raft of bonus tracks, too, and just three hours after the initial release, she dropped a *3am Edition* of the album containing seven additional songs which were co-written and co-produced by Aaron Dessner from The National. Alongside the familiar faces, new collaborators included Taylor's actress friend Zoë Kravitz, who co-wrote and sang backing vocals on the album's opener 'Lavender Haze'. A bass-heavy track inspired by her relationship with Joe, the track was originally unveiled in a 13-part TikTok teaser series called *Midnights Mayhem with Me,* in which Taylor drip-fed the title and order of each track. 'The tension is palpable,' she said as a ping-pong ball announcing 'Lavender Haze' popped out. She told how the name was inspired by watching the TV show *Mad Men.* 'I looked it up because I thought it sounded cool. And it turns out that it's a common phrase used in the '50s, where they would just describe being in love.' Speaking of the song's deeper allusions to Joe, she explained, 'We've had to dodge weird rumours, tabloid stuff, and we just ignore it. And so this song is sort of about the act of ignoring that stuff to protect the real stuff.'

As on *folklore* and *evermore,* Joe used the alias William Bowery to get involved with *Midnights,* and he co-wrote the song 'Sweet Nothing', which conveyed Taylor's gratitude for a partner who wanted nothing but her company in an over-demanding world. It also included a reference to finding joy in small things, such as the pebble they picked off the shoreline when in Ireland together. Another song, the woozy 'Snow on the Beach', was a collaboration with Lana Del Rey that fans read as an evocative ode to Joe. In one of her Instagram reveals, Taylor said it was 'about falling in love with someone at the same time that they're falling in love with you, sort of in this sort of cataclysmic, fated moment where you realise someone feels exactly the same way that you feel'. Similarly, the song 'Mastermind' apparently detailed the moment she first set eyes on Joe at the Met Gala in 2016, saying she knew she would end up with him with the inevitability of a line of dominoes falling into place.

Elsewhere on the album, Taylor confessed to lacing the song 'Bejeweled' with a 'psychotic amount' of Easter eggs, saying a PDF file was needed for its video 'because there are so many that we could not keep track'. The clues and hidden meanings mainly linked back to songs and motifs on her *Speak Now* album, secretly signposting the *Taylor's Version* re-recording that was to arrive in 2023. Taylor called 'Bejeweled' 'a little twist on a Cinderella story', and many believed its lyrics about being woefully underappreciated were a dig at her ex Calvin Harris. The song 'Karma' was about living well as a form of revenge, and it seemed to throw shade at arch-enemies like Scooter Braun and Kanye West. But Taylor told presenter Zane Lowe it was more about the 'polarising emotions when you're up late at night and your brain just spirals'. Speaking on Apple Music's *New Music Daily*, she said, 'You know, we can't just be beating ourselves up all the time. You have to have these moments where you're like, "You know what? Karma is my boyfriend and that's it."'

By a country mile, the album's biggest success was lead single 'Anti-Hero', which Taylor said was one of her all-time favourites. It was intended as a 'guided tour' of feelings of self-hatred and anxiety, and she admitted in an Instagram video, 'I really don't think I've delved this far into my insecurities in this detail before. I struggle a lot with the idea that my life has become unmanageably sized ... I struggle with the idea of not feeling like a person.' Resonating with millions afflicted by the same kind of self-doubt, 'Anti-Hero' became one of her most popular songs of all time. It bagged her a second UK No. 1 single and her ninth *Billboard* Hot 100 No. 1, and even overtook 'Blank Space' with an eight-week hold on the US top spot. Incredibly, 'Anti-Hero' also contributed to a remarkable chart takeover where *Midnights'* tracks occupied the entire *Billboard* Top 10 simultaneously.

When it came to the album's overall performance, it demolished all expectations, becoming the most streamed album in a single day on Spotify, with 184.6 million streams. Skittling through a series of sales records, *Midnights* also became the bestselling album of the year in just a day, and it was Taylor's fifth record to sell over a million first-week copies in the US. It additionally debuted at No. 1 in more than 14 countries worldwide, including the UK, where it stuck firm for five weeks. Amid the torment of her sleepless nights, Taylor had once again shaken up the rules of pop – and the glowing critical praise for *Midnights* further underscored its success. *Entertainment Weekly* called it 'a warm murmur wrapped in

After once calling Andrea Swift 'the guiding force' in her life, a young Taylor celebrated with her mum at the CMT Music Awards in 2007. On the night, she won Breakthrough Video of the Year for her debut single, 'Tim McGraw'.

Taylor caused a stir when she sat with singer boyfriend Joe Jonas at the MTV Video Music Awards in 2008. Not long after, he reportedly broke her heart by ending it on the phone.

For her first outing as a headliner, Taylor performed more than 100 shows on her 2009–10 Fearless tour – which included her Romeo and Juliet-inspired hit 'Love Story' at Madison Square Garden in NYC (*below*).

The infamous moment Kanye West interrupted Taylor's Best Female Video acceptance speech for 'You Belong With Me' at the 2009 MTV Video Music Awards proved an international talking point.

Dubbed 'Taylor Squared' while dating movie hunk Taylor Lautner in late 2009, the paparazzi favourites managed to remain good friends after their brief relationship.

Before their romance soured, Taylor and musician John Mayer performed their collaboration 'Half of My Heart' at the Jingle Ball in New York in 2009.

Winning her first Grammys in 2010, Taylor barely had enough arms to carry her four awards. On the night, she became the youngest person ever to take home Album of the Year – aged just 20 – for *Fearless*.

Taylor shared the love with her beloved Swifties on her Speak Now tour in 2011, which was attended by more than 1.5 million fans.

A showbiz coupling like no other, Taylor's 2012 relationship with former One Direction singer Harry Styles was short-lived, but inspired songs like 'Style' and 'Out of the Woods'.

Performing in 2012, Taylor said her *Red* era was driven by 'crash-and-burn heartbreak', shaping songs like her smash hit 'We Are Never Ever Getting Back Together'.

Hot on the heels of her all-time bestselling album, Taylor's 1989 world tour in 2015 was the year's highest grossing, raking in $250 million.

After opening the 2015 Brit Awards with a pulsating rendition of 'Blank Space', Taylor went on to win her first Brit for International Female Solo Artist.

Cosying up at the *Billboard* Awards in 2015, Taylor and her DJ-producer boyfriend Calvin Harris were big winners on the night, taking home nine trophies between them.

In 2016, Taylor joined a super-elite club as she became the first woman to bag the Album of the Year Grammy twice, on this occasion for *1989*.

Taylor's six-month Reputation stadium tour in 2018 propelled her to a different league as she played only mega-capacity venues worldwide.

As part of her sparkly *Lover*-era reinvention, Taylor performed 'ME!' with Panic! at the Disco frontman Brendon Urie during the *Billboard* Awards in 2019.

Snapped while out for an evening in New York in 2019, Taylor and actor boyfriend Joe Alwyn were notoriously private – despite being together for more than six years.

When a thrilled Taylor won the Global Icon honour at the Brit Awards in 2021, it put her on a par with Sir Elton John and the late David Bowie. The award came after she scooped three No. 1 albums in less than a year.

After Taylor's 2023–24 Eras tour broke seven Guinness World Records and became the most lucrative tour ever, Taylor called it 'the most thrilling chapter of my entire life to date'. Given the scale and astonishing impact of the shows, it seemed the entire world agreed with her.

Unbeknown to millions, Taylor was already dating Travis Kelce by the time she showed up at Arrowhead Stadium for her first Kansas City Chiefs game, alongside his mother Donna, in September 2023.

'I've never been so proud in my life,' Taylor told Travis after he and his Chiefs teammates stormed to Super Bowl victory in Vegas in February 2024.

Loyal Travis showed off an impressive collection of friendship bracelets as he supported Taylor – and sang along – during the Australian leg of her Eras tour in early 2024.

The golden couple – known as 'TNT' – celebrated with a kiss as the Chiefs won the AFC Championship against the Buffalo Bills to secure a spot in the 2025 Super Bowl.

As the pair announced their engagement on Instagram in August 2025 – sparking a global meltdown in the process – it was clear that Taylor had finally found her 'happy ever after' with Travis.

a weighted blanket', and it was deemed an 'instant classic' by *Esquire*. 'Thirteen new tracks, three-quarters of an hour, the pop album of the year. Business as usual,' it said. The ultimate icing on the cake for *Midnights* came in 2024 when Taylor swept to double Grammy victory. First up, she scooped Best Pop Vocal Album, which had its own significance. 'This is my 13th Grammy, which is my lucky number. I don't know if I've ever told you that,' she joked. She then went one better and won Album of the Year for the fourth time, setting a new record for any music artist and even surpassing Frank Sinatra and Stevie Wonder. Dazzling in a white Schiaparelli gown during the LA ceremony, she said, 'I would love to tell you that this is the best moment of my life, but I feel this happy when I finish a song, or when I crack the code to a bridge I love, or when I'm shot-listing a music video, or when I'm rehearsing with my dancers or my band, or getting ready to go to Tokyo to play a show. For me the award is the work. All I wanna do is keep being able to do this. I love it so much, it makes me so happy.'

At this point in 2022, four years had passed since Taylor's Reputation stadium tour, and fans were craving her return to live music. During a *Midnights* promo appearance on *The Tonight Show Starring Jimmy Fallon*, she finally gave them hope. 'I think I should do it,' she teased, before admitting, 'I really miss it ... when you write songs and you're proud of the songs and you have the fans reacting, the most potent way you can see them react is when you're looking into their faces. I miss that a lot. I really miss that connection.' Less than a fortnight later, she made good on her promise, announcing the most pioneering project of her entire career. 'I finally get to tell you I'm going back on tour,' she revealed on *Good Morning America*. 'The tour is called the Eras tour, and it's a journey through all of my musical eras of my career.' In an Instagram post that garnered more than 6 million likes, she also said, 'I can't WAIT to see your gorgeous faces out there. It's been a long time coming.'

The tour was scheduled to start in March 2023, and in the lead-up to its mammoth 149-date itinerary, Taylor underwent a strict training routine that included running at different speeds on a treadmill while singing her entire setlist. 'Fast for fast songs, and a jog or a fast walk for slow songs,' she told *TIME* in her 2023 Person of the Year interview. 'I knew this tour was harder than anything I'd ever done before by a long shot. I finally, for the very first time, physically prepared correctly.' She threw herself into a personalised strength, conditioning and weights programme and took three months of intense dance lessons. 'I wanted to be so over-rehearsed that I could be silly with the fans, and not lose my train of thought,' she said.

But ahead of the tour's long-awaited launch in Glendale, Arizona, it seems other elements of Taylor's life had dramatically shifted. Though she had the world at her feet, behind closed doors her long and seemingly secure relationship with Joe was unravelling. What once offered stability amid the chaos and noise had run its course, and three weeks after the tour's launch, their split was announced.

The first report emerged on 8 April, with *Entertainment Tonight* claiming the news as a world exclusive. 'Taylor Swift and Joe Alwyn Break Up After Six Years of Dating', the shock headline stated. Despite citing the fact Joe had not attended any of the initial US Eras dates, it claimed the split was amicable and 'not dramatic'. Though there was no clear indication of exactly when they had called it quits, the suggestion was that it had happened several weeks earlier. Two days after the initial report, *People* suggested the break-up had been caused by nothing more sinister than 'differences in their personalities'. The outlet also quoted a source saying they 'weren't the right fit for one another', and that the pandemic had taken a toll on their relationship – especially from Joe's side. 'They were locked down together and able to continue growing their relationship in this insulated way. But he didn't really "know" her yet outside of that bubble.' *People*'s unidentified insiders also said the strain of intrusion was a major factor in the decision to part ways. 'Joe has struggled with Taylor's level of fame and the attention,' said one. 'The differences in their personalities have also become harder to ignore after years together. They've grown apart.'

Taylor and Joe never confirmed or commented publicly on the split, but whatever was behind the end of their six-and-a-half-year union, it was a poignant conclusion to a chapter that inspired some of her most audacious and brilliant songwriting.

Pro-Joe Swifties were hugely upset, and in the days after the news broke, some even laid bouquets of flowers outside the doors of Taylor's Manhattan home. One woman filmed a TikTok of herself kneeling on the ground outside the property as if locked in a prayer of mourning, and debate subsequently took off online about the couple's right to privacy. Inevitably, the shock break-up triggered a hunt for flesh on the bones of the story. Scouring the setlists of her inaugural Eras shows, fans noticed that in her 31 March concert, Taylor had swapped the song 'invisible string', based on the tie that bound her to Joe, for 'the 1', which was all about failed romance and regret. Not only that, but the track 'All the Girls You Loved Before', which she dropped out of the blue to celebrate the start of Eras, was suddenly seen in an entirely different light. As a previously unreleased outtake from her *Lover* era, it played out, on first listen, like a joyous celebration of finding true love, but post-break-up, it sounded more like a desperately moving farewell to Joe.

Amid the public grieving, there was also a wide re-appraisal of *Midnights*, with every song deconstructed and mined for fresh clues that foretold the couple's gradual demise. The song 'Midnight Rain' was a classic example, with the revisited lyrics seen as a take on their differing objectives in life, and Taylor ultimately choosing to prioritise her career over settling down. 'Joe and Taylor breaking up is less surprising when you realise that every song on *Midnights* sounds like it's from the perspective of a girl grieving the end of a relationship she's still in,' one fan posited online. Another tweeted, 'Taylor Swift's album *Midnights* is a break-up album in disguise and no one can convince me otherwise.' The song 'Bejeweled' was also analysed anew, with listeners wondering if it had actually expressed growing exasperation and resentment towards Joe, as opposed to Calvin Harris as first mooted.

Adding fuel to the theory that parts of *Midnights* did indeed chart the slow ending between Taylor and Joe, she told an Eras crowd in Tampa, Florida just a week after the split was reported that she felt 'really connected' to the album, because it was 'the most accurate picture' of her life to date. Further 'evidence' was pulled from 'The Great War', one of the *3am Edition* bonus tracks found on *Midnights*. Retrospective study of its lyrics suggested that Taylor may have been singing about mistreating Joe because she misguidedly believed he had 'betrayed' her. It even included an agonising reference to cursing a lover in her sleep and irrationally wanting to punish him for things he didn't do. As *Billboard* ruefully pointed out, 'The Great War' was just one of a whole catalogue of songs that were 'way more heartbreaking' following Taylor and Joe's break-up.

Another tearjerker, 'You're Losing Me', arrived a month after the split was announced, as a promotional 'vault' track on *Midnights (The Late Night Edition)*. Though it had been written several months earlier, Taylor's lyrical reflection on a couple growing apart and their fatally wounded love was immediately likened to her and Joe. *Nylon* called it a 'devastating relationship ender if we've ever heard one', adding, 'Amid the grief and sadness of the song, there's also a feeling of inevitability, of sorrow that nothing more could be done, of pointlessly waiting for action when you know nothing is coming.' A *Bustle* review called 'You're Losing Me' 'the closest Swifties will get to a relationship post-mortem', and in a piece ranking all of Taylor's heartbreak songs to date, the *Independent* called it 'the most devastating of the bunch'.

Taylor never spoke of what happened with Joe and opted only to articulate her feelings through her music, but Joe touched on the aftermath when later quizzed by the *Sunday Times Style Magazine*. 'I would hope that anyone and everyone can empathise and understand the difficulties that come with the end of a long, loving, fully committed relationship of over six-and-a-half years,' he said, with his trademark diplomacy.

'That is a hard thing to navigate.' In the interview, published over a year after the split, he stressed that they had agreed to 'keep the more private details of our relationship private', reiterating his past thoughts on the impossible nature of being one half of such a prominent duo. 'What is unusual and abnormal in this situation is that, one week later, it's suddenly in the public domain and the outside world is able to weigh in,' he said. 'So you have something very real suddenly thrown into a very unreal space: tabloids, social media, press, where it is then dissected, speculated on, pulled out of shape beyond recognition. And the truth is, to that last point, there is always going to be a gap between what is known and what is said. I have made my peace with that.' Joe, who spent the period immediately after the break-up filming Oscar-winning movie *The Brutalist*, also batted away interest in his post-Taylor dating life. 'I'm sure you can appreciate, given the level of noise and scrutiny about my past relationship, why I wouldn't want to just open the door to things like that right now,' he very reasonably said.

Meanwhile, as Taylor dusted herself down as a singleton once more, she sought comfort from her New York girlfriends, including Gigi Hadid and Blake Lively, well before the pair's eventual falling-out. Then, in what were the first paparazzi photos taken of her in a new Joe-less era, she was seen going for dinner with Jack Antonoff and his partner, actress Margaret Qualley, at the cosy Via Carota restaurant in West Village. But during that outing, Taylor's wardrobe choice was of greater interest than her celebrity companions. Photographs showed her donning a black off-the-shoulder top and high-waisted jeans that were embellished with a rhinestone butterfly. To the casual observer, it might have meant little, but razor-focused Swifties recognised a giant potential Easter egg in her outfit: while promoting her *Lover* album back in 2019, she'd told *Entertainment Weekly* that butterflies were an important symbol she regularly turned to in her songs, videos and even her attire. 'Easter eggs can be left on clothing or jewellery,' she said. 'People don't usually find out this one immediately ... A butterfly is kind of just breaking free of that darkness and, you know, fluttering into the light.' Whether it was aimed as an intentional message about her newly unattached status or not, the £500 jeans by Mytheresa sold out instantaneously.

With a jaded heart and the demands of a globetrotting tour to keep her busy, Taylor could have been forgiven for swearing off men for the foreseeable future. And yet, as she began putting the pieces of her life back together, she found herself drawn to a man who offered her something wildly different. Matty Healy, enigmatic frontman of rock band The 1975, was swaggering and unpredictable – and light years away from quiet, introverted Joe. She had first met the showman from Manchester at one of his band's gigs in LA in November 2014, which she attended with Selena Gomez and Ellie Goulding. Speaking later on Australian radio programme *Shazam Top 20*, Matty appeared to have been awestruck by the encounter. 'Bloody hell, what am I going to do, go out with Taylor Swift?' he said. 'She's a sensation. I wouldn't say no.' He also confirmed they had swapped numbers, saying, 'Let's see what happens.' A few days after the gig, Taylor was seen wearing a vest top emblazoned with The 1975, and Matty repaid the compliment by wearing a T-shirt featuring her *1989* cover art when performing in Milwaukee. As public flirtation went, it was hardly subtle; a mutual admiration declared through merchandise, rather than words.

Outspoken and provocative, Matty was known for his flowing dark curls, tattoos and party-loving lifestyle. He had once struggled with drug addiction – and had even taken bites of raw steak on stage. But while Taylor seemed to find his edgy persona disarmingly attractive, his rock-'n'-roll image belied his background. Privately educated and the son of actress Denise Welch (known for TV shows *Coronation Street* and *Loose Women*) and Tim Healy (star of the sitcom *Benidorm*), Matty was just 13 when he and his Cheshire schoolmates formed a band. He started out as the drummer, only stepping up to the mic when their singer quit.

In December 2014, Taylor attended another of The 1975's concerts in New York, this time dancing on a balcony with models Karlie Kloss and Lily Aldridge. That sighting prompted speculation that Taylor and Matty had secretly been dating for two months, but weeks later Matty slammed the rumours. 'It is bloody fake. It's all fake. It's all a farce,' he told *Shazam Top 20*. He continued, 'We met each other. We exchanged numbers in the same way a lot of people in this kind of world do. And we spoke occasionally, and then she's the biggest pop star in the world. I'm in Australia. There's no, like, relationship or anything happening. It's just funny how people really, really buy into that.'

The following month, they were photographed with Nick Grimshaw and Ellie Goulding at a Brit Awards afterparty, but that evening was more notorious as one of the first occasions Taylor met Calvin Harris. In March, Matty again denied anything had happened with her, saying harshly in an interview that it would be 'emasculating' to date the world's biggest pop star. 'The one time I did have a flirtation with a girl, it ends up going everywhere,' he lashed out in *Q*. 'It's not really anything to talk about, because if she wasn't Taylor Swift we wouldn't be talking about her. She wasn't a big impact on my life.' With his snidey comments going down like a lead balloon, Matty attempted to better explain himself. 'I may admit to being an idiot on occasion, but I am not a misogynist,' he tweeted. 'This suggestion makes me really sad.' He stressed that he had found the idea of being immersed in such a high-profile celebrity world 'confusing and scary', and added, 'I had fears of being "somebody's boyfriend" (remember this is all speculation as we never dated!) before even being recognised for my music or presence as a person in my own right.' In his lengthy post – which he subsequently deleted – his irritation was plain to see. 'I didn't even date Taylor, but the media's incessant and brutal obsession with her has meant that even a guy who DIDN'T DATE HER has been so battered by their never-ending questions that he's inevitably said something that can be lifted and moulded into something that resembles "shade". It's really sad.' Taylor, as might have been expected, said nothing in response.

It wasn't until years later, in November 2022, that it became clear they collaborated on some material for *Midnights*, but the songs didn't make the cut. 'It was for reasons that are not to be criticised,' Matty said. 'She's amazing.' And showing their earlier flashpoints had long since been resolved, Taylor was a surprise guest during one of The 1975's London shows in January 2023, powering through her first live performance of 'Anti-Hero' as she geared up for her Eras tour. She also covered the band's song 'The City', a favourite from their debut album, accompanied by her acoustic guitar.

With her split from Joe still fresh in many minds, a bombshell photo taken in May 2023 showed single Taylor holding hands with Matty outside a New York restaurant. They were with Jack Antonoff and Margaret Qualley, and the fan who shared the snap captioned it, 'Matty and Taylor are together – confirmed!!' The shot went viral and within hours, social media was ablaze with disbelief, memes and full-blown grief. 'Why is she putting me through hell again?' one Swiftie posted on Twitter. 'I'm going to cry like for real', said another, and one post even read, 'I'm going to have an aneurysm'.

The same month, Matty flew 17 hours from the Philippines to watch one of Taylor's Eras concerts in Nashville, and when on stage she was reportedly seen mouthing the words, 'This one is about you. You know who you are. I love you.' He had apparently used the exact same words when performing with The 1975 in Manila earlier that week. After the show ended, the pair were seen heading back to Taylor's condo, which seemed to validate claims in the *Sun* just two days earlier. 'She and Matty are madly in love', a source was quoted as saying. 'It's super-early days, but it feels right. They first dated, very briefly, almost ten years ago but timings just didn't work out.' The story continued, 'They are both massively proud and excited about this relationship and, unlike Taylor's last one – which was very much kept out of the spotlight, deliberately – she wants to "own" this romance, and not hide it away.' At a second Nashville concert, Matty appeared on stage in a skeleton suit, playing alongside Taylor's opening act, Phoebe Bridgers. And in Philadelphia, he was seen singing along in a VIP area with her dad, Scott.

Over the coming days, they were seen together in New York on several occasions – including at members' club Zero Bond and over dinner at Casa Cipriani, where a *Page Six* mole clocked them 'cuddling and kissing' in a booth. However, over the course of a messy few weeks in June, it appeared to be off, then on again, then finally over for good. 'They are absolutely not together and aren't even in contact anymore,' an insider told *People*. Though undoubtedly painful for Taylor, the split came as little surprise to those who had viewed with cynicism her brief time with Matty. Many felt it was nothing more than an act of rebellion and a knee-jerk rebound following her miserable break-up from Joe. And however much it stung when she and Matty called it a day, it was at least a reminder to herself and to her fans that she could be impulsive, even reckless. Their hot-blooded relationship had flown in the face of her carefully maintained 'good-girl' image, and that must have been oddly liberating for someone so often judged and defined by her reputation. The fallout, and the creative outburst it unleashed, would later filter into the darker seams of *The Tortured Poets Department*. But before any of that, Taylor had to get back to the somewhat daunting task of completing her game-changing Eras tour.

CHAPTER SIX

The Eras tour was not just a series of concerts – it was a spectacle unlike any the world had ever seen. 'This is the most fun, joyful, exciting, intense, powerful and wonderful tour I have ever done,' Taylor said, although even that was something of an understatement. Taking in 51 cities across five continents in 21 months, the numbers remain almost beyond comprehension. Shattering seven Guinness World Records, Eras was hands-down the most lucrative tour of all time, raking in over $2 billion in revenue – double that of any other tour in history. More than 10 million people turned out to watch the shows, and two nights in Seattle resulted in a so-called 'Swift Quake', where so many fans danced to 'Shake It Off' that seismic activity equivalent to a 2.3 magnitude earthquake was recorded. Similar stirrings were noted in Edinburgh, when the British Geological Survey's monitors picked up vibrations up to 6km away from Murrayfield Stadium – strongest during the songs 'champagne problems', '...Ready For It?' and 'Cruel

Summer'. 'The opportunity to explore a seismic activity created by a different kind of phenomenon has been a thrill,' said seismologist Callum Harrison. 'Clearly Scotland's reputation for providing some of the most enthusiastic audiences remains well intact.'

Across the planet, cities reported economic boosts worth millions of dollars. Hotels sold out for miles around stadiums, airports saw huge spikes in passenger numbers, and the effect became known as the 'Swift Surge', where the production functioned like a travelling economy. In America alone, the US Travel Association likened it to the Super Bowl – but in this case, one that took place 53 times across 20 cities. In the UK, the economic injection was estimated at a cool £1 billion, with each fan said to have splashed an average of £848 on concert tickets, travel, accommodation, merch and outfits. In assessing the tour's colossal impact, the term 'Swiftonomics' was coined by Bloomberg, with Eras giving a badly needed boost to world markets that were still spluttering into life post-pandemic. 'Taylor Swift's fans are a microcosm of the post-Covid consumer economy,' affirmed the finance site. 'They're willing to splurge on what they missed during the pandemic – no matter the cost.' Even after the shows ended, the records kept on toppling, and her concert movie – *Taylor Swift: The Eras Tour* – became the highest-grossing of all time, netting over $267 million in cinema sales. A 256-page collectors' photo book released in the US through Target stores also sold 814,000 copies in just two days.

But in truth, what made the Eras tour so earth-shattering wasn't just the eye-popping sums of money that changed hands. It was the sheer magnitude of Taylor's vision. Rather than blazing through a few of her most recent albums as most artists do, she built a three-and-a-half-hour extravaganza based on her entire career – from the cowboy boots and acoustic jangling of *Speak Now* and *Fearless* to the passionate belters of *Red* and synth-pop bangers of *1989*; from the dark drama of *reputation* and joyful pop of *Lover* to the cottagecore intimacy of *folklore* and *evermore*, right through to the laid-back vibes of *Midnights*. For each 'era', she created a different world, with sprawling backdrops, killer choreography and dazzling lighting and pyrotechnics to match. As the *New York Times* put it, 'The Eras Tour has been a mega-event that elevated the already-super-famous Swift to a new level, making her an epochal symbol of cultural saturation on the level of The Beatles in the 1960s or Michael Jackson in his '80s prime.' *Rolling Stone* agreed with such a viewpoint. 'There's nothing in history to compare,' it said. 'This is her best tour ever, by an absurd margin.'

Taylor herself spoke of her aim to give fans a live music experience like no other. 'They had to work really hard to get the tickets ... I wanted to play a show that was longer than they ever thought it would be, because that makes me feel good leaving the stadium,' she told *TIME*. With a live band and 15 dancers, each show typically included 16 costume changes, with stunning creations from designers like Roberto Cavalli, Oscar de la Renta and Zuhair Murad.

The setlist was built around 44 songs, with at least two acoustic 'surprise' songs per show. Inspired by Broadway, there were three interconnected stages and an interactive LED floor which could rise in the air or change shape at the push of a button. At one point, it even transformed into a glittering swimming pool, complete with digital ripples and the sounds of lapping water. As Taylor took a running jump and swan-dived into the illusion, she disappeared beneath the stage, as if plunging into the pool itself.

Swifties were given LED wristbands that synced with the show's lighting, ensuring they played an active part in the visual feast. There were a few unexpected upgrades, too, and in Melbourne, Taylor's dad, Scott, reportedly handed out $2,000 VIP wristbands to unsuspecting fans stuck in the cheap seats. 'Papa Swift is the best,' said one grateful recipient. Even outside the stadiums, mass parties collectively known as 'Tay-gating' were held, where those without tickets enjoyed raucous singalongs and swapped handmade friendship bracelets – just like those lucky enough to be on the inside.

In a world ravaged by conflict and uncertainty, the sense of unity that Eras nurtured was one of the biggest takeaways of all. Thanks to the *Midnights* song 'You're on Your Own, Kid' and its lyrics about friendship bracelets, they became the tour's official emblem, with fans turning up to stadiums with their arms stacked with beaded messages. As creativity flowed, their wrists bore album titles, lyrics, inside jokes and even the names of Taylor's cats, Meredith, Olivia and Benjamin Button. They weren't just accessories, but a currency, traded between strangers and symbolising something intimate and human amid the corporate machinations of a multibillion-dollar empire. During one of her final shows, Taylor summed it up neatly when she said, 'Making friends and bringing joy to each other – that is, I think, the lasting legacy of this tour ... the fact that you have created such a space of joy and togetherness and love. I couldn't be more proud of you, honestly that is all you.'

And as the world would soon discover, even Travis Kelce was inspired to make his initial move on Taylor with a friendship bracelet; a tiny thread that would connect them in the most fitting way.

Never was the extraordinary nature of Swiftmania more apparent than during the Eras stop-off in Munich in late July 2024, when the practice of Tay-gating reached a whole new level. Over two consecutive nights, Taylor performed to around 74,000 fans in the packed Olympiastadion, but outside the venue each evening, another 50,000 Swifties gathered on Olympic Hill to listen in – without paying a single euro. Festooning the grassy hill overlooking the stadium, they brought friendship bracelets and picnics, and gleefully sang along to every word. Rather than discourage the free viewings, the concert organisers handed out bottles of water and emergency blankets; and on stage, Taylor acknowledged how many extras had come along for the ride. 'We have people in a park outside the stadium, thousands of people listening from out there,' she said. 'It makes us feel so incredibly welcome. We're going to spend all night trying to make it up to you.' Posting on Instagram after the Munich gigs, she called it 'a magical experience' and added, 'I've been watching so many videos of the crowds out there fully participating in the show from afar, all that joy'. The images of tens of thousands of fans colonising an entire hill in such a way showed how the tour had transcended any other music event in living memory. 'Swift and her fans have managed to cultivate a community,' said *NME*, calling Eras 'a marvel of a show that comes with a beating heart'.

As the tour progressed, Swifties even began to project a kind of maternal aura onto Taylor, affectionately dubbing her 'Mother'. The nickname began popping up across social media, and despite baffling those on the periphery, it was essentially a term of endearment which was used to highlight her warm nature. According to *Know Your Meme*, an encyclopaedic compendium of internet subcultures, the term was first adopted when she was pictured hugging a fan in 2014 along with the caption, 'Mother is mothering'. The term stuck, and nowadays any new video clips, outfit reveals or Easter eggs herald amusing comments like, 'Mother has returned', 'Mother fed us again' or 'Mother never misses'. With its roots in the Black and Latino LGBTQ+ ballroom scene, the term found added meaning during the Eras tour because Taylor's ability to 'mother' an entire generation seemed more evident than ever.

Beyond all the camaraderie, the tour required military-level logistics, with hundreds of crew members, 90 trucks laden with heavy equipment and cargo planes to ferry the set across continents. As Eras took over each city, the set-up took roughly two days to build, and then the same to dismantle. But despite the epic scale, Taylor maintained total creative control, approving every element, right down to merchandise and even on-site food options – including not-so-nutritious treats like the 'Karma Dog' and 'Bad Blood Waffle Fries'. She also oversaw a long list of other artists who played at different stages on the tour, with some 19 opening acts in all. They included Sabrina Carpenter, Paramore, Gracie Abrams, Raye and Maisie Peters, plus Beabadoobee, Phoebe Bridgers, Benson Boone and Haim. Then there were special guests who frequently performed with Taylor on stage, from Jack Antonoff to Marcus Mumford, and Aaron Dessner to Hayley Williams.

Taylor's superhuman efforts did not come without cost, though, and in her much-publicised August 2025 appearance on the *New Heights* podcast, hosted by Travis Kelce and his brother, Jason, she opened up about the physical toll of performing night after night. 'It was a lot of physical therapy, and it was a lot of being in a state of perpetual physical discomfort,' she said. 'That's why I did so much more training, so much more endurance training, and cardio, and stuff that doesn't come naturally because I'm not an athlete, so it's like that stuff I have to really force myself to do.' Taylor had to push through pain like blisters and aching feet, and she even performed when ill – in Edinburgh, blowing her nose on stage and in Singapore, coughing between the lines of her songs. 'I know I'm going on that stage whether I'm sick, injured, heartbroken, uncomfortable or stressed,' she told *TIME*. 'That's part of my identity as a human being now. If someone buys a ticket to my show, I'm going to play it, unless we have some sort of force majeure.' After a run of shows, she would insist on 'dead days', shutting herself in her hotel room. 'I do not leave my bed except to get food and take it back to my bed and eat it there,' she said. 'It's a dream scenario. I can barely speak because I've been singing for three shows straight. Every time I take a step my feet go crunch, crunch, crunch from dancing in heels.'

The elements were a force to be reckoned with on occasion, too, and thunderstorms and high winds delayed one of

Taylor's Nashville shows, while evacuation procedures were instigated at Sydney's Accor Stadium after a lightning strike triggered safety warnings. Far more seriously, tragedy struck in Rio de Janeiro in November 2023 when 23-year-old fan Ana Clara Benevides died after collapsing in 39°C heat at the stadium. 'I can't believe I'm writing these words but it is with a shattered heart that I say we lost a fan earlier tonight before my show,' Taylor said on Instagram. 'I can't even tell you how devastated I am by this ... I feel this loss deeply and my broken heart goes out to her family and friends.' Later that month, she invited Ana's family to a show in São Paolo, and made a donation of an undisclosed sum to her parents.

Her genuine sorrow and gesture of sympathy seemed to tally with the kind of tour she had built: one rooted in empathy and compassion. Throughout Eras, Taylor used her platform and enormous profit margins to give back to the communities she visited. In dozens of cities, organisations supporting vulnerable people received sizeable donations, and these reached 1,400 Trussell Trust food banks during her UK leg alone. 'We weren't expecting it, but obviously we were really delighted when we found out,' said Sophie Carre from the Trust. One food bank in Cardiff said it had received the largest individual sum of money ever, with chief executive Rachel Biggs saying, 'The breathing space Taylor's donation has given us will enable us to lift our heads and shift our focus from the food bank to the creation of a sustainable operation supporting people who currently need our help.' During the tour, Taylor also quietly made contributions to disaster-relief efforts, including $1 million to the Tennessee Emergency Response Fund following a series of deadly tornadoes, and $5 million in the wake of hurricanes Helene and Milton. Her response showed exactly what a more ethical kind of super-stardom can look like, and despite attracting criticism for using a private plane during the tour, her team claimed she bought double the amount of carbon credits needed to offset her flights.

By the time Eras had concluded, Taylor Swift had distrib-uted bonuses of more than $197 million to those who worked for her – including riggers, drivers, caterers, security staff, technical crew, hair, make-up and wardrobe, plus her band and dancers. Mike Scherkenbach, who runs a concert trans-portation company, told *Rolling Stone*, 'She's giving a sum of money that is life-changing for these people. A lot of these drivers are not homeowners, and a lump sum like this gives you the ability to put a down payment on a home ... That generosity is a game changer for these people.' And such acts weren't incidental; they became part of the very fabric of the tour. So when Bloomberg confirmed in October 2023 that Eras had officially made Taylor a billionaire, it wasn't just an acknowledgement of her economic power, but also the way in which she wielded her wealth. As the first artist in history to achieve billionaire status solely through music and touring (without relying on additional side hustles like beauty and fashion ranges), she still recognised the people at the core of her operation and chose to share her success with them.

Given Taylor had put every fibre of her being into Eras, it was no wonder the finale was a tearful affair. The curtain came down in Vancouver on 8 December 2024, and Taylor told the audience, 'I want to thank every single one of you for being a part of the most thrilling chapter of my entire life to date – my beloved Eras your.' But peculiarly, instead of leaving the stage through the middle of the floor, as she had done night after night, on this occasion Taylor chose to walk through an orange door at the back of the stage. Although nobody realised it at the time, it was a gigantic Easter egg, which would become patently clear a few months later when she announced the release of her new album, *The Life of a Showgirl*.

A few days after the tour ended, Taylor's opening act, Gracie Abrams, spoke of the last day they had together, telling *Nylon*, 'Everyone had been crying all day. It felt like the last day of school backstage.' One of Taylor's dancers, Kameron Saunders, was especially moved by the culmination, writing on Instagram, 'Taylor! My girl! You have steered the HELL out of this ship. So gracefully!! With poise, confidence, heart, passion, kindness, utter bravery and love!' His post continued,

'It has been the honour of my life to have been at your side night after night! ... I love you!'

Four months after it ended, Eras was named Tour of the Century at the iHeartRadio Music Awards, and it seemed like the most rightful accolade. 'This tour was absolutely the most challenging thing I've ever done in my life,' Taylor said on receiving the award. 'Three-and-a-half-hour shows, more shows than I've ever done on a tour, and it really was the most gratifying thing I've ever done.' Speaking via video link, she added, 'I think about that tour constantly. I'm so proud of it ... I'm never going to stop being grateful for it, and I appreciate this more than you know.'

In October 2023, the world had the chance to relive the phenomenon all over again with the release of her record-breaking Eras concert film. Focusing on the tour's LA shows, it caught the movie world off-guard because rather than going down the traditional studio-release route, Taylor and her team struck a direct partnership with cinema and theatre chains, shaking up the established film-distribution model. Such a move meant she could wield more artistic control over her work and, as the *Telegraph* pointed out, it proved once more that she was simply 'the greatest tactician in showbusiness'. Explaining the decision to *TIME*, she said, 'We met with all the studios, and we met with all the streamers, and we sized up how it was perceived and valued, and if they had high hopes and dreams for it. Ultimately, I did what I tend to do more and more often these days, which is to bet on myself.' Upon release, the almost three-hour cinematic event not only broke box-office records, but also proved to be an uplifting exercise in communal celebration, with audiences encouraged to take part as if they were inside a full-to-capacity stadium. 'Audience members sang along and danced in the aisle and cheered so loudly I often couldn't tell where the roar of the crowd onscreen ended and the roar of the crowd in the theatre began,' said a critic from the *Hollywood Reporter*. 'What a concert it is – and what an experience it makes.'

Although the Eras tour was designed as a retrospective that allowed Taylor to celebrate every past iteration of herself, somewhere down the line the focus shifted in a way she would never have dared to imagine. What started as a journey into her past opened a door to something new, and from out of nowhere, her future found her.

It was Saturday, 8 July 2023, night two of the tour at Arrowhead Stadium, the home ground of the Kansas City Chiefs. Footballing hero Travis Kelce was watching the show from a VIP box, along with his brother, Jason, and sister-in-law, Kylie, but his quest to meet Taylor did not go quite according to plan. As he later revealed, he was armed with a collection of friendship bracelets, including one bearing his phone number that he hoped to give her after schmoozing his way backstage. But as he admitted on his *New Heights* podcast a couple of weeks later, 'I was disappointed that she doesn't talk before or after her shows because she has to save her voice for the 44 songs that she sings. So I was a little butthurt I didn't get to hand her one of the bracelets I made for her.' Confiding in his co-host, Jason, he added, 'She doesn't meet anybody, or at least she didn't want to meet me, so I took it personal ... She's up there for three hours straight, so I get it, but I was disappointed I didn't get to talk to her.' Thankfully, the rejection didn't spoil his night. 'Everybody was dressed in pink and purple, going crazy for her,' he said. 'It was wild. It was a wild show.' Travis also told how Taylor's performance had 'captivated' him, and it transpired that his teammate and best friend, Patrick Mahomes, had a small hand in him being in the audience in the first place. During an appearance on *The Pat McAfee Show* in May 2024, Patrick said, 'I like to take some of the credit. I was the one who invited Travis to the first Taylor concert ... I was like, "Dude, you should go for it. Just go for it."'

Joining Travis on *New Heights* two years later, in August 2025, Taylor explained why he had gone about his friendship bracelet mission all wrong. 'He didn't even reach out to our management,' she said. 'He thought because he knew the elevator lady, that he could talk to her about just getting down.' Commenting on Travis's reaction to the rebuttal, she joked, 'He threw a tantrum. He threw a man tantrum, it's so funny. This dude didn't get a meet and greet and he's making it everyone's problem, that's what I thought at first.'

But Taylor also told how she found it amusing that Travis used the broadcast as his 'personal dating app', and that she was grateful he did because it 'got me a boyfriend'. Showing her appreciation of the gesture again in *TIME*, she said the fact Travis 'adorably put me on blast on his podcast' was 'metal as hell'. Owning up so publicly to the rejection on *New Heights* was the best thing Travis could ever have done, because the clip went viral, and soon afterwards, the two were finally put in touch. 'We started hanging out right after that,' Taylor said. It emerged that members of her camp had been 'playing Cupid' to help them along, and speaking to the *Wall Street Journal*, Travis said, 'There were definitely people she knew that knew who I was, in her corner. She told me exactly what was going on.' Taylor was receiving some encouragement closer to home, too. 'My relatives, my cousins, were like, "Please, please, please, he's amazing." There were friends that were like, "He's actually an amazing guy. He's so great." There was a lot of people whispering in my ear.' On Travis's side, FOX Sports commentators Erin Andrews and Charissa Thompson, two old friends of his, even issued a public plea on their podcast. 'Taylor, I don't know what you're doing in your life right now besides rocking the world,' Erin said on *Calm Down with Erin and Charissa.* 'Please, try our friend Travis. He is fantastic. I know we're not the best of friends, we're not even friends, but I consider you one. Take us up on this. Go on a date with this guy.' Charissa agreed, and hoping that Taylor was listening, she said, 'Do it for yourself, do it for us. And do it for the people. Because there is no one who would give you a better time than this guy.' Responding to their appeal on social media, Travis wrote, 'You two are something else!! I owe you big time!!'

When at last Travis met Taylor, sparks flew. 'It was just the easiest conversation I ever had ... it just knocked my socks off,' he told her as the pair revisited their early days on *New Heights.* Fortunately, the feeling was mutual and she replied, 'I felt the same exact way.' She also expanded on her all-important first impressions, saying she was not put off by his dogged pursuit of her. 'I knew he wasn't crazy the first couple of times that we talked. He's truly getting to know me in a way that's very natural, very pure, very normal.' She was instantly drawn to his offbeat sense of humour. 'The way he could make me laugh so immediately about normal things,' she recalled. 'Travis is just a vibe booster in everyone's life that he's in. He's like a human exclamation point.'

One of their first outings was a dinner date in Manhattan. 'When I met her in New York, we had already kind of been talking, so I knew we could have a nice dinner and, like, a conversation, and what goes from there will go from there,' Travis said. It was still secret – top secret – at that point, but when Taylor was first seen in a VIP suite at Arrowhead Stadium in late September 2023, wearing the Chiefs' bright red, the romance was well under way. 'By the time I went to that first game, we were a couple,' she told *TIME*. 'I think some people think that they saw our first date at that game … We would never be psychotic enough to hard launch a first date.' The match was between the Chiefs and Chicago Bears, and Travis revealed the line he had used to invite Taylor along. 'I've seen you rock the stage at Arrowhead,' he told her. 'You might have to come see me rock the stage at Arrowhead and see which one's a little more lit.' Taylor's companion for the game was Travis's mum, Donna Kelce, who must have found the sudden exposure hugely intimidating. When she appeared on the TV show *Today* a couple of weeks later, she told the cameras, 'It's really morphed into something that I could never, ever have expected … I feel like I'm in some kind of alternate universe.' On being asked about her son's status with Taylor, she was understandably guarded, saying, 'It's fairly new, so I don't like to talk about it.' She also explained why she was reluctant to discuss either of her sons' relation-ships. 'I'll talk about my life and when the kids were little and I was with them, but they're men now,' she said. 'They've got their own lives and there isn't a man alive that's going to talk to their mom about their personal life. It's just not gonna happen.' But as the presenters probed further about what it was like to share the VIP box with Taylor, Donna said hesitantly, 'It was okay.' No doubt an understatement caused by nerves, it was a moment of reticence that led many to assume she was not exactly a fan. However, 'Mama Kelce' cleared up her feelings on the matter a few weeks later when she told the *Wall Street Journal* that Taylor had stirred up Travis's life in the best possible way. 'He's happier than I've seen him in a long time,' she said. 'God bless him. He shot for the stars!'

Taylor's first trip to see the Chiefs not only kickstarted a media storm but also caused a stir in the home side's locker room. 'Taylor Swift here – for real? With Travis?' Chiefs player Chris Jones said afterwards. 'We're like, "Oh my God, Travis pulled Taylor Swift!"'

Although the new coupling was a showbiz marvel in itself, the spotlight was very nearly stolen by a humble plate of fried chicken. It was one of those unfathomably hilarious social media moments, activated by a picture of Taylor posing for a selfie with a fan at the stadium while tucking into some fast food. A tweet with the fan's photo read, 'Taylor Swift was eating a piece of chicken with ketchup and seemingly ranch!' and it took off like wildfire, racking up 32 million views. As the peculiar phrase 'seemingly ranch' went viral, food brands speedily muscled in on the joke, with Heinz releasing a limited-edition 'Ketchup and Seemingly Ranch' bottle. Even the Empire State Building was lit up in red and white after the incident, with a tweet on its official account saying, 'Ketchup and seemingly ranch'.

After the game, Travis and Taylor were seen leaving the stadium in a convertible car, reportedly paying for everyone's meals in order to clear out a Kansas City diner so they could eat undisturbed. Speaking about it on his podcast a couple of days later, Travis told how they had snuck away in a 'getaway car', neatly referencing her 2017 song. Saying he 'sure as hell enjoyed this weekend', he added, 'Shout-out to Taylor for pulling up. That was pretty ballsy … I just thought it awesome that everybody in the suite had nothing but great things to say about her. She looked amazing. Everybody was talking about her in a great light.' He also enjoyed seeing footage of Taylor celebrating the Chiefs' win with Donna. 'To see the slow-motion chest bumps, the high-fives with Mom and how Chiefs Kingdom was excited that she was there, that sh*t was absolutely hysterical,' he said. 'It was definitely a game I'll remember, that's for damn sure.'

Perhaps unsurprisingly, the outside world could not get enough of the world's hottest new pairing, and on the *Bussin' with the Boys* podcast months later, Travis revealed how Taylor's confidence at her inaugural match had been a turning point for him. 'The first game she came to against the Bears, I was like, "Okay, so, I could probably set you up with everything." And she just walked right through the front door,' he recalled. 'She was just like, "I just want to be around the family and friends, and experience this with everybody." She got beaucoup points for that. I was like, "Damn, she's in the madness. She wants to be a part of it. She wants to support me and do things like that." She really won me over with that one.' He also spoke of her giving him the chance to revel in his own spotlight. 'She's very self-aware,' he said. 'She understands situations like that. I think that's why I started to really fall for her.' Caught between a desire to share their romance with the world, while also keeping it under lock and key, he added, 'You want to keep things private, but at the same time, I'm not here to hide anything, you know? That's my girl. That's my lady,' he said. 'So, it's like, I'm proud of that.' Even though it was still early days, Travis had already begun to experience the side effects of dating Taylor, with the paparazzi staking out his house round the clock. He acknowledged the sudden interest was partly his own doing, however. 'I know I brought all this attention to me, right?' he said on *New Heights*. 'I'm the one that did the whole friend-ship bracelet thing and told everybody how butthurt I was that I didn't get to meet Taylor. What's real is that, you know, it is my personal life. I want to respect both of our lives ... So everything moving forward, I think me talking about sports will have to be kind of where I keep it.'

In the beginning, Taylor knew little about American football, but it didn't matter. 'You were so non-judgemental that I knew nothing about the world that you're in,' she told Travis on the podcast. 'I didn't know what a tight end was.' She soon learned, and began to demonstrate immense pride in showing up to support him in his role – which was essentially about protecting the quarterback, blocking defensive lines and receiving the ball in attacking positions. 'My friends are like, "Who body snatched you?"' Taylor said as her knowledge and interest in NFL rocketed.

Another game that generated fevered press coverage came in October 2023, when Taylor was snapped at New Jersey's MetLife Stadium with a host of A-list pals. Among those cheering by her side as the Chiefs took on the New York Jets were actor Ryan Reynolds and his wife, Blake Lively, as well as Sabrina Carpenter, *Game of Thrones* star Sophie Turner and *Wolverine* actor Hugh Jackman. 'This Swifties/ NFL crossover has suddenly become the biggest storyline in the most popular sport in America,' observed the BBC.

Yet not everyone welcomed the Taylor-made attention. Among NFL purists, there were escalating grumbles that the game was being turned into a celebrity circus. Critics complained every time the camera cut to her in a VIP suite, and some accused the league of exploiting her presence for ratings. Yet as Taylor herself later told *TIME*, 'There's a camera, like, a half mile away, and you don't know where it is, and you have no idea when the camera is putting you in the broadcast, so I don't know if I'm being shown 17 times or once.' She added, 'I'm just there to support Travis. I have no awareness of if I'm being shown too much and pissing off a few dads, Brads and Chads.' But whether sports fans loved or loathed it, nobody could deny the effect Taylor was having, or – as suggested by the 'TNT' nickname she and Travis had been given – the fact that they were becoming pure box-office dynamite.

With the early days of their romance unfolding like an addictive soap opera, it was easy to see why Taylor had fallen so hard and so fast for Travis. Those who know him best have often spoken of him in glowing terms, insisting that despite his fame and majestic sporting achievements, he has remained thoroughly down to earth. 'Travis has grown up to be a leader, to have a kind heart, to have fun,' his one-time high-school football coach Jeff Rotsky told *The Times*. Meanwhile, his former Chiefs teammate Alex Smith has said, 'Some people are so magnetic and you love being around them, and Travis is one of those guys.'

Growing up in Cleveland Heights in Ohio, sport became a way of life for Travis and brother Jason, who is two years older and played for the Philadelphia Eagles until retiring in

2024. As children, both were highly gifted athletes and thick as thieves, and they would spend hours practising their ball skills in the family's backyard. However, the rivalry was always fierce, and appearing on the *Today* show their mum recalled breaking up 'a lot of fights' when they were boys. 'Everything was a competition,' she said. 'It was a competition to see who could get to the table first, who could get to the front seat of the car ... They egged each other on.' Although no longer married to their dad, Ed Kelce, Donna has told how close they remain as a family unit. 'We're very, very small. We're tight knit. We stay together and try to help each other as much as we can.' Travis has often spoken of his parents being his role models, telling reporters at a training event in June 2024, 'I think over the course of my life, I've found that being kind and being genuine and being who I am and true to that, it's the right way to live. My mom and my dad are the reason I'm always a friendly guy.' He has also drawn direct comparisons between Donna and Taylor, highlighting their 'kindness, their genuineness, their ability to say hello to everyone in the room'. Ed believes both his sons have remained fully grounded, too. 'My boys know where they're from,' he has said. 'They fully understand that how you treat people is what's important in this world.' The siblings have remained extremely close, as was made apparent at a golfing event in the summer of 2025. 'We talk to each other more than we ever have. We loved each other growing up. We still love each other,' Jason told a reporter. 'He's my best friend on the planet.'

Travis initially played as a quarterback, but his burgeoning confidence got him into trouble, and after joining the University of Cincinnati Bearcats, he was suspended for a season in 2010 when he failed a marijuana drug test. Several years later, he confessed that the mistake had been 'a punch in the face' and that it forced him to grow up. Jason, who was playing for the same team, bailed him out. 'I was in his room, his house. Kind of like two brothers growing up living in the same room,' Travis later recalled. 'In terms of rent, I wasn't paying it. In terms of food, he was helping me with that. I was literally living off him for quite a while. He was my lifeline.' Thanks to Jason's intervention, the Bearcats agreed to give Travis another chance, and on his return to the game, he switched positions to tight end – never looking back. Several years later, in February 2023, the Kelces became the first brothers to ever compete on opposing sides in a Super Bowl: Jason playing for the Eagles and Travis for the Chiefs. Although it was dubbed the 'Kelce Bowl', they were never actually on the field at the same time, as their attacking roles meant taking turns on the pitch, rather than facing each other directly. That vital technical detail caught Taylor out in the beginning, when she asked Travis what it had been like to square up against his brother. 'I now know what an insane question that was,' she said sheepishly on *New Heights*. 'I thought everyone was on the field at the same time.' Memorably, on the day of the historic Super Bowl clash, proud mum Donna proved a viral sensation when she wore a custom-made half-Chiefs/half-Eagles jersey in the family's box. Guesting on the brothers' podcast, she called it 'the best day ever ... except for when you were born, when both you guys were born, it can't get any better'. The Chiefs narrowly won the contest, with an emotional Travis paying tribute to Jason afterwards. 'There's nothing really I can say to him other than I love him and he played a hell of a year, a hell of a season.'

Having also clinched Super Bowl victory back in 2020, Travis had far more in common with Taylor than first met the eye. Just like her, his career was studded with multiple record-crunching moments – only his were for catching the ball more times, across more yards and in more high-pressure moments than anyone else. In each other, they had evidently found a rare balance. Both were at the top of their professional game, they each understood the demands of performance and fame, and yet neither ever tried to outshine the other. Their worlds couldn't have been more different, but they spoke the same language. After years of secrecy, scrutiny and heartbreak that had left her feeling vulnerable and exposed, Taylor had finally met someone who was not only on her wavelength, but who also treated her as an equal.

y the end of 2023, Taylor Swift seemed happier than she had been in a long time. Yet beneath the surface, there remained an urge to settle old scores, and to draw a line under what had gone before. As always, that act of closure took shape in Taylor's songwriting, and it became the very heartbeat of her 11th album, *The Tortured Poets Department*. Nobody was expecting new work, since she had been buried in a non-stop cycle of performing and travelling for months on end. The voracious appetite of the Swiftdom had also been satiated by the release of *Speak Now (Taylor's Version)* in July 2023, followed by *1989 (Taylor's Version)* that October. But receiving her Best Pop Vocal Album Grammy for *Midnights* in LA in February 2024, Taylor raised the stakes in spectacular fashion. 'I want to say thank you to the fans by telling you a secret I've been keeping from you for the last two years,' she said. 'Which is that my brand-new album comes out April 19. It's called *The Tortured Poets Department.*' She then headed backstage and posted the cover art for the album on her social media. It featured a black-and-white image of her lying on a bed with her arms wrapped protectively around her body. She included a poetic note with it, which instantly cast light on what the album was going to be about. 'And so I enter into evidence my tarnished coat of arms, my muses, acquired like bruises, my talismans and charms,' she wrote. 'All's fair in love and poetry,' she added, before signing off, 'Sincerely, The Chairman of The Tortured Poets Department'.

Unsurprisingly, the note caused pandemonium, especially as the only suspicion fans had had was that she might announce a future *Taylor's Version* re-recording of *reputation*. Later in the evening she shared the full track listing, which revealed tempting collaborations with Post Malone on opener 'Fortnight', and with Florence + The Machine on 'Florida!!!' As a forensic internet drill-down commenced, it took fans no time at all to decide that the album's title had a direct and intentional link to Joe Alwyn, her ex. In 2022, he and *Normal People* actor Paul Mescal had revealed in an interview with *Variety* that they had a WhatsApp group with *Fleabag* star Andrew Scott, which was called the 'Tortured Man Club'. The name was inspired by brooding characters all three had played on screen, but it evidently stuck firm in Taylor's head – and, as it turned out, a large chunk of the album was shaped in the shadow of her break-up with Joe. Days later, she posted more artwork, one with the words 'I love you. It's ruining my life' typed over it. As excitement built and theories around the song titles gathered momentum, fans were convinced the album would simultaneously delve through the wreckage of her relationship with Matty Healy. And they would not have to wait long to find out they were absolutely right.

Quite how Taylor had managed to work on *Tortured Poets* during her Eras schedule *and* keep it so hush-hush was baffling. Written largely in hotel rooms and between flights, the recording took place mainly in America as she checked into studios in LA, New York, New Orleans, Portland, Nashville and New Jersey. 'I needed to make it. It was really a lifeline for me,' Taylor said during an Eras show in Melbourne two weeks after her big Grammy announcement. 'It sort of reminded me of why songwriting is something that actually gets me through life, and I've never had an album where I've needed songwriting more than I needed it on Tortured Poets.' Once more, the album saw her team up with co-writers Jack Antonoff and Aaron Dessner, and its contemplative tempo was awash with muted piano, soft percussion and frank lyricism. When the album landed as promised, at midnight on 19 April, Taylor told on her social platforms how it reflected 'events, opinions and sentiments from a fleeting and fatalistic moment in time – one that was both sensational and sorrowful in equal measure'. Just two hours later, she popped up again with a trademark Swiftian gift – the album was actually twice the size of what was anticipated. 'It's a 2am surprise,' she wrote. 'The Tortured Poets Department is a secret DOUBLE album. I'd written so much tortured poetry in the past 2 years and wanted to share it all with you, so here's the second instalment of TTPD: The Anthology. 15 extra songs. And now the story isn't mine anymore ... it's all yours.'

CHAPTER SEVEN

The impact of *Tortured Poets* was immediate and overwhelming: it became Spotify's most-streamed album in a single day on 19 April 2024, with over 300 million streams – breaking the record she herself set with *Red (Taylor's Version)* in 2021. Five days later, it was streamed for the billionth time – the first album ever to achieve such a feat. In the US, all 31 songs debuted on the *Billboard* Hot 100, occupying the top 14 places concurrently for the first time in history. It also sold 2.6 million copies in a week, with Taylor writing on Instagram: 'My mind is blown. I'm completely floored by the love you've shown this album. 2.6 million ARE YOU ACTUALLY SERIOUS?? Thank you for listening, streaming and welcoming Tortured Poets into your life. Feeling completely overwhelmed.' In securing her 14th US No. 1, Taylor also tied with rapper Jay-Z as solo act with the most chart-topping albums ever. In the UK, it was the fastest-selling album by any artist in seven years and by a non-British artist in 18 years, and it saw her equal Madonna with 12 No. 1 records. Five Grammy nominations followed, although unusually, she was not among the winners at the 2025 ceremony. The Taylor faithful were left shaking their heads, but as *Elle* remarked, 'In a year that felt culturally bookmarked by Swift's proliferation, the move was largely considered to be the Record Academy's way of simply allowing other stars' work to be celebrated.'

With the album blowing most other metrics out of the water, it hardly mattered, and the apparent snub certainly did not detract from the superlatives that the majority of critics had dished out. 'Heartbreak inspires anguish, anger and a career highlight,' said the *Financial Times*. 'Wildly ambitious and gloriously chaotic', raved *Rolling Stone*. 'Audacious, transfixing', was *Variety*'s verdict. And as the *Observer* noted, there was also much to mull over when it came to the latest themes and preoccupations in Taylor's lyrics. '*The Tortured Poets Department* finds Swift back on brand in various ways: nailing love to the wall and watching the ooze trickle and dry,' it said. 'Ultimately, this may be Swift's most Swiftian album: the unhappiness profound, the details generous, the lessons absorbed.'

It was no coincidence that it was Taylor's most expletive-laden album to date, and in a collection of 31 songs, a huge number were based on break-ups and bust-ups. There were, of course, two real-life sources of misery for listeners to unpick

– Joe supposedly fuelling the more remorseful tracks and Matty igniting its angrier overtones. 'So Long, London' was one of the album's most affecting tracks, seen as a mournful account of earlier attempts to save her wilting relationship with Joe, while also bidding farewell to her treasured life in Britain. 'Heartfelt, tender and poetic, this is a real tearjerker,' *The Times* weighed up. 'So Long, London' also served as a striking companion piece to Taylor's earlier song 'London Boy', which had been a far brighter reflection of her time with Joe, and the twin tracks seemed to herald both the beginning and the end of the same love story.

Rich in bleak imagery of ghosts and graveyards, the piano-backed 'Loml' arguably provided the album's most desperate portrayal of her romance with Joe limping to the finish line. It captured the realisation that what once had seemed permanent had now drawn its final breath, and by the end of the song, the 'love of my life' acronym had instead become 'loss of my life'. It left many listeners fighting back tears, and as *Variety* pointed out, 'This ballad has one gut punch after another.' Equally drenched in regret, 'Fresh Out the Slammer' appeared to stand as a metaphor for leaving behind a long, constraining relationship, even comparing it to jail time. It saw Taylor singing about trying to cater to an ex's needs while seeking a fresh start, and seemed to tie in with her *TIME* interview in late 2023 when she alluded to essentially imprisoning herself with Joe. 'Me locking myself away in my house for a lot of years – I'll never get that time back,' she said. And though it would never have been her intent, Joe found himself, unfairly, on the receiving end of abuse from fans over it. 'I'm literally so embarrassed that we rode for and rooted for joe in the way we did when he made her feel like this in the end ... like omfg ... we all trusted you,' one vociferous Taylor supporter tweeted. 'She was locked away for so long to appease his wishes,' said another. Of course, nothing could have been further from the truth. During their years together Taylor was never busier, and in that time she released five albums and two re-recordings, embarked on a major stadium tour and even appeared in a movie – albeit the critically disastrous musical *Cats*.

Even more complex decoding skills were required when it came to 'The Smallest Man Who Ever Lived'. Some Swifties were convinced that as the album's most brutal takedown it captured a sense of betrayal and disillusionment once the dust had settled with Joe, and that she was expressing disdain over a man who had slunk away from her in the face of commitment. On the flipside, others felt that the song's scathing tone and sense of lingering humiliation pointed more conclusively to Matty. The lyrics dipped into memories of a joyful summer, which was when their fling had taken place, and it included other veiled references to reckless abandon which seemed much more aligned to him. Another reference was a mention of a Jehovah's Witness suit – a close-cut style of tailoring, similar to what Matty typically wore. Ultimately, the song seemed to reveal that Taylor felt taken advantage of, and as *Vogue* put it, 'Whoever it's about, they're sure to be losing some sleep.'

It wasn't wall-to-wall hostility when it came to Matty, however, and the song 'Down Bad' was seen as a touchstone of her intense infatuation with him. 'The metaphor in "Down Bad" is that I was comparing sort of the idea of being love bombed, where someone rocks your world and dazzles you and then just kind of abandons you,' she told iHeartRadio. Taylor also likened it to being 'abducted by aliens', adding, 'The character in the song felt like, "I've just been exposed to a whole different galaxy and universe I didn't know was possible."' Similarly, 'Guilty as Sin?' was one of Taylor's raunchier songs, exploring late-night fantasies and forbidden desire, while throwing fans a Matty-shaped morsel with its line about *The Downtown Lights*, an album by one of his favourite groups, The Blue Nile.

Back on a more negative trajectory, the song 'I Can Do It with a Broken Heart' saw Taylor singing about suffering extreme lows on the Eras tour and having to fake her way through it when feeling low. It suggested she regularly took to the stage when struggling with her mental health and feelings of rejection – possibly because her whirlwind dalliance with Matty had so quickly blown itself out. Others believed the song even sounded like something The 1975 might themselves have recorded. Of course, during the later stages of the tour, 'I Can Do It with a Broken Heart' became synonymous with the fact Taylor had found Travis. As we saw on the Wembley stage on that legendary night in June 2024, he was the reason she no longer needed to put on a brave face and force herself to smile through the pain.

An even more ferocious potshot came via the song 'My Boy Only Breaks His Favorite Toys', and though some fans felt it was directed at Joe, most were convinced it was aimed squarely at Matty. Speaking to Amazon Music in a *Tortured Poets* track-by-track commentary, Taylor provided a little more context, saying the song was about 'being somebody's favourite toy until they break you and then don't want to play with you anymore'. She added, 'A lot of us are in relationships where we are so valued by a person in the beginning, and then all of a sudden, they break us or they devalue us in their mind.' Also on the track list was 'But Daddy I Love Him', one of the album's most talked-about songs in which Taylor seemed to be responding to a wave of criticism that blew up over her and Matty. It conveyed her attraction towards him and her response to being told he was wrong for her, while vowing she'd rather burn her life down than settle for mediocrity. In that sense 'But Daddy I Love Him' wasn't just about Matty, but also about accepting her own fallibility and propensity to make bad decisions. Listeners also detected echoes of their situation in 'I Can Fix Him (No Really I Can)', which dealt with the delusions of love, before ending with the abrupt and ironic realisation that actually, she couldn't 'fix' any man at all.

It was perhaps just as well that when asked for his comments about *Tortured Poets* by the press in LA, Matty drily insisted, 'I haven't really listened to that much of it but I'm sure it's good.' Still, even he can't have escaped the album's opener and first single 'Fortnight' – a runaway success featuring Post Malone. Its potential link to Matty was a touch tenuous, telling of a pair of former lovers who had moved on but ended up becoming neighbours. As Taylor elucidated in her Amazon Music commentary, it was about 'longing, pining away, lost dreams', and a 'dramatic, artistic, tragic kind of take on love and loss'. The 'Fortnight' video, starring actor Ethan Hawke in a cameo, contained a humdinger of an Easter egg, with Taylor seen sitting at an old-fashioned typewriter. Matty himself was known to be something of an enthusiast, once telling *GQ*, 'I really like typewriters ... there's kind of an element of commitment that goes with the ceremony of it.' A 2016 profile in the *Guardian* noted an Olivetti typewriter in his East London home, and in *Tortured Poets*' synth-filled title track, another fictional typewriter – thought to have been Matty's – was left behind at her apartment. For an artist so intent on scattering sophisticated clues, Taylor's repeated use of such a timeless symbol seemed to represent the irony of an item built to last, used by someone who did not.

As well as becoming her fourth UK No. 1 and her 12th in the US, 'Fortnight' broke records as Spotify's most-streamed song in a single day ever, with 25 million people accessing the track. Amazingly, that record remained intact until October 2025, when it was smashed by none other than Taylor herself, as 'The Fate of Ophelia' whipped up 30 million streams in a day. 'Fortnight' additionally won nominations for Record of the Year, Song of the Year and Best Music Video at the 2025 Grammys, and though unsuccessful there, it fared far better at the MTV Video Music Awards in 2024, winning a nifty five trophies – making Taylor the most-awarded artist in the event's history. As well as thanking the 'ridiculously talented' Post Malone, Taylor used her Video of the Year acceptance speech to mention Travis in front of a public audience for the very first time. 'Something that I'll always remember is that when I would finish a take, and I'd say, "Cut", and we'd be done with that take, I would always just hear someone like cheering and [going], "Whoo!" from across the studio where we were shooting it,' she said. 'And that one person was my boyfriend, Travis. Everything this man touches turns to happiness and fun and magic. So I want to thank him for adding that to our shoot, because I'll always remember that.'

Following the release of *Tortured Poets*, Taylor dramatically revamped her Eras setlist to incorporate her new material. It was given a first airing as the European leg kicked off in May 2024, with Taylor jokingly telling the audience in Paris that the updated section of the show could be described as 'Female rage, the musical'. But not all the songs she showcased came from the vestiges of heartbreak, and a handful of those on the new album had been inspired by the green shoots of new love. As *Glamour* declared, 'Travis Kelce has officially entered the chat' – and fans were very much there for the reboot. One number she unveiled in the Eras shake-up was 'The Alchemy', which read like the opening act of the Taylor-and-Travis story. The lyrics overflowed with footballing metaphors, including touchdowns, trophies, winning runs and even floors slicked with celebratory beer. The title of the song played on the idea of the chemistry between them, with 'alchemy' denoting a medieval practice where base metals like lead were turned into exquisite gold. Though some critics branded the track 'cheesy' and even 'weightless', it would have taken a heart of stone not to be touched by Taylor's newfound joy and blissful sincerity. As she performed 'The Alchemy' in Paris for the second time the following evening, she even threw in a little Easter egg for a special guest. After flying 11 hours from California to be there, Travis was seen in the crowd with Gigi Hadid and

Bradley Cooper, and on introducing the track, Taylor said, 'Can you believe this is our 87th show on the Eras tour?' It was, of course, a subtle tribute to her man, the proud owner of the Chiefs' number 87 jersey, as well as the counterpart to her lifelong lucky number 13.

Another *Tortured Poets* track that celebrated all things Travis was the irresistible 'So High School', which pulsed with teenage dizziness, with Taylor imagining herself aged 16 again. Much was made of the song's positioning in the extended 'Anthology' section of the album, as it came right after the track 'How Did It End?', which was broadly taken as a final postmortem on her relationship with either Joe or Matty – or both. As its total opposite, 'So High School' was her most exuberant offering in years, and *Vogue* called it an 'all-American, feel-good love song', noting that it was reminiscent of her 'young and in love *Fearless* era'. The lyrics included a nod to the game 'Kiss, Marry, Kill', which Travis was asked to play when interviewed on a TV station called AfterBuzz back in 2016. As if foreshadowing the future, he was asked to 'choose' between Taylor, Katy Perry and Ariana Grande, to which he responded, 'That's messed up; I don't want to kill any of them.' However, when pressed further, he ultimately bumped off Ariana, kissed Taylor and married Katy. The song's teasing reference to marriage became even more meaningful in 2025, when 'So High School' soundtracked the couple's social media engagement announcement. Meanwhile, when it was performed live during the Eras shows, the choreography mimicked Travis's comical trademark touchdown dances, as well as 'swag surfing', a celebratory move where sports fans sway from side to side in the stands.

Travis later called 'So High School' his third-favourite Taylor track of all time, saying it 'has sentimental meaning, I guess'. But on a more profound level, it gave some insight on their dynamic as a couple. The song compared her appreciation of works by the likes of Aristotle to Travis's athletic prowess, playing cheekily on the perception of them being total opposites. While she was the cerebral songwriter with a haul of literary references at her fingertips, he was the charismatic sportsman with an intricate understanding of precision, grit and teamwork. For his part, Travis seemed to delight in the difference between them, often joking about his girlfriend's expansive vocabulary. 'She's so hot when she says big words,' he said as Taylor used terms like 'esoteric' and 'effervescence' during their *New Heights* double act. But there was no trace of insecurity or envy, just pure admiration – and for a woman who spent years walking on eggshells around her exes, such affirmation was nothing short of revelatory. 'I've never been a man of words,' Travis told the *Wall Street Journal*. 'Being around her, seeing how smart Taylor is, has been f***ing mind-blowing. I'm learning every day.'

It was hard not to be endeared by Travis's self-deprecating manner, which seemed far removed from the manufactured polish that usually comes with celebrity. Chatting on *New Heights* with his brother in June 2024, he revealed he'd only recently discovered the title of the classic children's story was *Alice in Wonderland*, and not 'Alison Wonderland'. A bemused Jason told him, 'We've watched the movie. You know her name's not Alison,' to which Travis replied, 'Not one time did I catch that, dude.' His easy affability wasn't lost on the media. As the *Guardian* observed, 'Built like Oak Furnitureland's XXL wardrobe aisle, seemingly light on ego despite excelling at whatever a "tight end" does in American football, and touchingly delighted when Swift uses polysyllabic words, Kelce seems comfortable in his own skin in a way that's very winning.'

The juxtaposition between Taylor and Travis was fascinating on many levels, with his openness and dad-joke charm serving as a refreshing foil to her habit of overanalysing and dwelling on the past. Travis was a reminder that not everything needs to be scrutinised, and his breezy nature clearly had a levelling influence. When a series of his old tweets resurfaced, it was pointed out that at the same time Taylor was writing the snow-dusted lyrics to 'All Too Well' in 2011, Travis was firing off a misspelled tweet about feeding squirrels. 'I just gave a squirle a peice of bread and it straight smashed all of it!!!!' he wrote at the time. 'I had no idea they ate bread like that!! Haha #crazy.' But his uncomplicated energy was precisely what made him a compelling choice for Taylor, and their obvious compatibility showed how two people on contrasting frequencies could meet in total harmony. 'There's something charming about Travis Kelce's enthusiasm for everything from napping to high-fives,' argued *Grazia*. 'He's sincere, without taking himself too seriously.' Echoing other media, the magazine decreed that Travis had even joined 'an esteemed lineage of celebrity himbos', about which he told *GQ* in August 2025, 'I find it funny.' He said, 'I joke about it. It is what it is. I'm just out here living life.'

Despite the playful 'himbo' label assigned to him, Travis was anything but superficial. He was raised with a strong sense of loyalty and held the values of family and marriage above all else, despite his parents, Ed and Donna, divorcing in 2008 after 25 years together. 'The handful of my friends whose parents are still together and still thriving – those are situations I would love to have,' he stressed in his *GQ* interview. 'Why not try and do it to last forever?' There's no doubt that Donna encouraged both her sons to be courteous and kind men, and she told *Us Weekly* in 2024, 'I just wanted to make sure that they treated everyone the same ... I don't care if they're the individuals who are cleaning the toilets or they're the CEO of organisations. It's basically, treat everybody with respect, like you would want to be treated.'

Those qualities have regularly come to the fore in Travis's and Jason's podcast, and though *USA Today* called the brothers 'hulking and hairy' and the 'manliest men you can find', it also described them as an 'antidote to toxic masculinity'. Summing up their positive influence on a whole generation of young men in an August 2025 editorial, it continued, 'When they show their emotions, it gives permission for other men to do the same. When they're supportive of the women in their lives, it tells boys and young men that demeaning women isn't cool. When they model deep, lasting friendships with other men, it offers an example to men searching for connection. The world has enough men who are jerks, and we're all paying the price for it. Jason and Travis Kelce are a reminder it doesn't have to be that way.'

While Taylor's dating history had been front-page news for years, there was curiosity over Travis's romantic life, too. Before meeting Taylor, his search for a girlfriend played out to millions on TV when he fronted a reality show called *Catching Kelce*. In the 2016 series on E!, 50 women from every state in America competed for his affection, and he eventually 'chose' Maya Benberry from Kentucky. Throughout the series, Maya called Travis her 'perfect guy', and at one stage he seemed pretty keen, too. 'Even though my mind's telling me one thing, I got to go with my heart,' he said, as he picked her. They dated for a month before going their separate ways, but Travis soon voiced his regret over taking part. 'The worst thing I ever did was the dating show,' he said on the *Bussin' with the Boys* podcast in 2023. 'It didn't set me up for anything. I didn't realise what reality TV really was.' He also stressed he had only taken the gig because of needing the money, admitting in a surprisingly candid interview that he burned through cash too quickly at the start of his career. 'I was so bad financially my first couple of years,' he said on *The Pivot* podcast. 'I was having so much fun buying whatever the hell I wanted to, going wherever the hell I wanted to, I wasn't financially looking at this as I need to have money down the line. So I heard about this situation where I could make six figures in two weeks and I was like, "Ah, and 50 ladies," I'm like, "This is actually starting to sound a little better."' But he added, 'I know that I'm not going back into reality TV.'

Single once more after *Catching Kelce*, Travis got together with sports journalist and influencer Kayla Nicole in 2017, after following her on Instagram. 'I was just stalking her and then finally on New Year's, she gave in,' he told E! 'And, you know, New Year new me. She just shot her shot, jumped in my DMs, and the rest is history.' Though they were on and off for several years, they eventually broke up in 2022, and Travis was later linked to *Access Hollywood* presenter Zuri Hall – though that was never confirmed. Then, shortly before meeting Taylor, he told brother, Jason, and his wife, Kylie, on *New Heights* that he was planning to get 'back on Tinder'. Referring to his profile shot on the dating app, he asked Kylie, 'Ky, you think I should go 'stache or no 'stache?' She replied, 'This is going to sound a little harsh, but I think you should do the moustache because if they swipe right at your worst, then they'll love you at your best.' Travis laughed and quipped back, 'That doesn't even hurt my feelings, that's just smart.'

Although he knew what it was like to have a famous girl-friend, once he was on Taylor's arm it was a whole new ball game. 'I've never dated anyone with that kind of aura about them,' he told the *Wall Street Journal*. 'The scrutiny she gets, how much she has a magnifying glass on her, every single day, paparazzi outside her house, outside every restaurant she goes to, after every flight she gets off, and she's just living, enjoying life.'

Adjusting to his surreal new existence, Travis decided in October 2023 to snap up a gated mansion outside Kansas City that would offer greater seclusion than his existing home. Costing around $6 million, the house in Leawood occupied a prime spot in over three acres at the end of a quiet cul-de-sac, and had six bedrooms, a six-car garage, wine cellar, outdoor kitchen, plus a tennis court, mini-golf course and pool with a waterfall. Many months later, its lush gardens, winding paths and Insta-friendly white gazebo would provide the dream backdrop for an unforgettable proposal.

Being with Taylor was transformative on every level, and by the time Travis had settled into his new abode he was a household name to millions – many of whom had never even watched a game of football. On one occasion when a video of the Chiefs players exchanging friendship bracelets was shared on the team's official TikTok account, a viewer posted underneath, 'Can't wait to watch you guys kill it tomorrow, go Chiefs!!! (Been a fan since Sunday.)' Another commented, 'If you would have told me a month ago I would be watching football TikToks, I wouldn't believe it.' NFL bosses were no doubt rubbing their hands together in glee, and as well as a 400 per cent jump in sales of Travis's number-87 jersey, ticket platform StubHub logged a threefold increase in searches for Chiefs games. On a personal level, Travis saw his own social media following explode, with more than a million new Instagram followers in the weeks after Taylor first turned out to watch him play. Google searches for his name hit an all-time high, and the *New Heights* podcast saw a 50 per cent audience spike to make it the sixth-most popular in the whole of America. An additional 350,000 subscribers also flocked to the brothers' YouTube channel.

For all the frenzy surrounding their relationship, Travis's rise through the celebrity ranks wasn't entirely accidental. Long before his beloved 'Tay' entered the frame, his team had been laying the groundwork to take his profile to the next level. As the *New York Times* reported, his managers – brothers André and Aaron Eanes – had wanted to make Travis 'as famous as The Rock', setting him up as a crossover figure who could bridge sport and entertainment. They curated a team that included a creative strategist, community outreach coordinator, an LA-based publicist, personal chef and trainer, with André explaining, 'We positioned Travis to be world famous. We didn't know how it would happen, or when it would happen, or what would help push that further along. But it's always been the thought in the back of our minds.' However, the masterplan very definitely did not include capturing Taylor's heart – which, as Travis has always maintained, was an entirely natural occurrence. 'It happened very organically, even though from a media standpoint, it was being tracked,' he insisted in *GQ*.

One of the Eanes brothers' biggest breakthroughs was getting Travis a coveted hosting slot on *Saturday Night Live* in March 2023. It took place less than a month after his epic Super Bowl victory with the Chiefs and saw him delivering the show's esteemed opening speech. 'I was nervous about doing a monologue,' he said, as the cameras rolled. 'But then I remembered I'm actually pretty good with words. Like during games, I do these super-eloquent pump-up speeches for my teammates.' The sketch then cut to VT footage of him 'motivating' his teammates in classic Kelce style, striding among them bellowing nothing but 'More, more, more, more, more!'

In another standout moment, he looked directly at his parents and brother in the audience, saying, 'Jason and I have actually been playing football together since we were little kids, and he was always better than me at everything. In high school, he was an honours student and I got kicked off the team because I failed French ... and English, too.' Showing impressive comic timing, he followed up with a laugh-out-loud zinger: 'Then when we were in college, I actually got kicked off the team because I tested positive for marijuana. So it just goes to show you if you smoke weed and you're bad at school, you can win the Super Bowl twice.'

As the show progressed, Travis launched into a succession of skits that showed his willingness to poke fun at himself. In 'American Girl Café', he played a man awkwardly dining with children's dolls, and in a parody called 'Straight Male Friend', he took on the role of a meathead gamer offering a 'low-effort, low-stakes relationship that requires no emotional commitment'. Then, in 'Too Hot to Handle', he lampooned reality dating shows, casting a sly dig at his *Catching Kelce* days. Though it was clearly a daunting gig and he later confessed to struggling with the autocue, the reviews were highly enthusiastic, with the *Guardian* saying it established him as 'a good comic actor not only by athlete standards, but a good comic performer outright'. It added, 'He needs to become an *SNL* staple. Dude deserves to take another victory lap.'

Six months later, Travis was invited back on to *SNL* – and this time he was not alone, with Taylor also appearing in a surprise cameo slot. They had only just made their romance official, and during the October 2023 episode, Taylor introduced a performance by rapper Ice Spice, who worked with her on a remix of 'Karma' earlier that year. Travis cropped up separately, playing a pitch-side reporter in a sketch that parodied the NFL's obsession with Taylor. 'Listen, sorry, Swifties. This is a show about football. It's a sport. Ask your dad,' joked comedian Mikey Day in his role as a spoof pundit. As the gags about the hot new couple flew, another comic, James Austin Johnson, brazenly piped up, 'Hey, I'm just glad it's not Matty Healy.' He then told his co-stars, 'You're treating it like it's Joe all over again.' Taylor's and Travis's involvement in the show was especially newsworthy because neither had been billed in the run-up to transmission, and the production team only found out minutes before the live recording began. Despite it being a brief stint for them both, it demonstrated not only how comfortable Travis had become in the entertainment sector, but also how unafraid Taylor was to appear with him in such a public arena. Even at this early stage, it was a major departure from the caution and restraint seen so often in her previous relationships, when secrecy and invisibility were her guiding principles.

After the *SNL* taping, the couple were snapped holding hands en route to an afterparty at New York's glamorous Catch Steak eatery, where *Page Six* claimed they were 'kissing throughout the night', staying until after 4am. TikTok clips of Travis gallantly shepherding Taylor through a wall of waiting photographers earlier in the evening caused a tizzy among fans, with one posting online, 'I'm SO happy! She got herself a real man!' and another saying, 'Good job, Mama Kelce'. As innocuous video footage of the pair went viral – not for the first time – some claimed Travis shoved her security guard to one side amid his act of chivalry. Even Jason Kelce ribbed him about it on *New Heights* afterwards. 'Did you get any push-back from the actual security guards about pushing them out of the way?' he asked his brother. 'If I would have pushed him ... he probably would have turned around and tased me,' Travis joked, while stressing that it was important for him to shield Taylor when they went out. 'I feel like whenever I'm on a date, I'm always having a sense of like, "I'm a man in this situation". I'm protective,' he said. 'You always gotta have that feeling or that self-awareness.'

It wouldn't have been an overreaction to fear for her safety on that or any other night, since Taylor's unprecedented level of fame has always carried heightened risk. Over the years, she has had to endure multiple stalker threats and intrusions, with total strangers breaking into her homes or turning up uninvited. As a result, she travels with extensive security, and still rarely makes any unplanned public appearances. On a quirkier note, it was reported that when she was first dating Travis, she was wheeled in and out of a luxury suite at Arrowhead Stadium in a giant popcorn cart, with supporters in the vicinity calling out, 'That's her! She's in there!' Before another game, she was said to have hidden inside a recycling bin which was then wheeled into the stadium. Speaking on Radio 2 to promote her later album *The Life of a Showgirl*, Taylor joked that she would have made a good spy. 'Just put me in a garbage can and roll me,' she said. 'I don't care, honestly no ... I can fit in like a purse.' Known for some ingenious stealth moves when trying to get from A to B, one of the wackiest rumours originated in 2017, when fans became convinced Taylor was regularly transported to and from her New York apartment in oversized luggage. The bizarre theory gained traction when former One Direction singer Zayn Malik told *Vogue* in a 2018 interview that Taylor 'was travelling around in a suitcase'. The pair had duetted on the song 'I Don't Wanna Live Forever' from the *Fifty Shades Darker* movie, so Zayn was surely well placed to have inside knowledge of such things.

Anonymity effectively went out the window as Taylor and Travis grew more serious, and every sighting was a cultural flashpoint that generated acres of news coverage. Yet with

Taylor becoming a steady presence at Chiefs games through the 2023–4 NFL season, a small but vocal faction of sports fans were increasingly hostile, seeing her as a needless distraction. Hellbent on the idea that love and football could not coexist, if the team lost, they would suggest she had thrown Travis off his game. The numbers told a different story, though, and Travis's performances often improved when she attended. 'Who doesn't play better when they want to impress their girl-friend?' his teammate Justin Reid said on the sports show *Up & Adams*. 'Taylor, come to all the games. Taylor, keep coming.' It was an issue later brought to light in another *Tortured Poets* song, 'The Albatross', assumed to be about Travis. The song explored Taylor's reputation as a negative force in the life of any man she held dear; the fabled albatross around their neck – or according to the *Britannica Dictionary* definition, 'A continuing problem that makes it difficult or impossible to do or achieve something.' Travis was characteristically unruffled by the accusations she was a hindrance to his performance, telling reporters at a Chiefs press conference in January 2024, 'As long as we're happy, we can't listen to anything that's outside noise. That's all that matters.'

Away from the earnest sports chat and hand-wringing over her presence at games, Taylor's game-day outfits provided a regular shot of light relief. Every time a new set of photos landed, fashion writers microscopically examined every last detail, as if she was stepping on to a couture catwalk, not watching 22 strapping men get sweaty on a field. In the beginning, she would cheer Travis on in relaxed Chiefs merch, opting for varsity jackets, vintage sweatshirts, T-shirts and snuggly beanies. But as the weeks passed by, her style evolved from straight-up fangirl into a more designer-centric aesthetic. 'Tay's always gonna be dressed head to toe looking the flyest,' Travis observed loyally. As well as Versace tailoring and miniskirts and shorts by the likes of Balenciaga and Louis Vuitton, there were corset tops by Mugler and Vivienne Westwood, thigh-high boots by Zanotti and Stuart Weitzman, plus Dior and Chanel bags. Usually, her outfits would contain a splash of red to show allegiance to the Chiefs. Her signature bright scarlet lips coordinated immaculately, too, although few realised her preferred shade was once a bit of a no-no: make-up guru Gucci Westman, who came up with the bold look for her, had to work hard to convince both Taylor and her mum, Andrea, to run with it. 'I really wanted to do a red lip on her because I hadn't seen her in a red lip before,' she recalled on the TV show *Today with Jenna & Friends* in April 2024. 'And her mom, if I'm allowed to say this, was like: "Well, Taylor doesn't wear red." And I was like, "Oh please, can I try?"' They agreed to try it for a cover shoot for *Allure* magazine in 2009, and Taylor has been a sworn convert to the vibrant colour ever since.

'I never really get too far from red lipstick, do I?' she once said in *People*. 'I guess I just think my face looks worse without it.'

As the weeks rolled on, Taylor's matchday accessories and jewellery were on point, too, and a diamond 'TNT' bracelet gifted to her by Travis took pride of place on her wrist. As revealed by Wove Made, the Pennsylvania-based jeweller behind the design, Travis made contact in December 2023 and thoughtfully asked them to create an upscale take on a friendship bracelet. The result was a 14k-yellow-gold band adorned with custom beads and encrusted with pavé diamonds – including on the TNT lettering as its centrepiece. The company completed the bracelet in just three days, and CEO Simon Kendle later told *People*, 'Since this was for him, we were all hands on deck.' The full force of the 'Swift Effect' came into play a few weeks later when she was first snapped wearing the $6,300 bracelet, with Wove Made experiencing a 5,000 per cent increase in site traffic, a doubling of social media followers and a sales increase of over 2,000 per cent. Soon afterwards, Travis got back in touch and asked for a matching bracelet for himself.

Of all the times Taylor rocked up as Travis's biggest cheerleader, none was more pressing than 11 February 2024, when the Super Bowl rolled into Las Vegas. Only days earlier, Taylor had banked her two Grammys for *Midnights*, and now the weight of expectation was a baton passed on to Travis, whose

Chiefs' side were to face the San Francisco 49ers. 'You can't put any more pressure than I put on myself,' he said at a media event ahead of the clash. 'I told her I'll have to hold up my end of the bargain and come home with some hardware, too.' He also told how he was enjoying seeing Taylor's fans embrace the game. 'It's been fun to kind of gather the Swifties into Chiefs Kingdom and open them up to the football world and the sports world. It's been cool to just experience all that.'

As Super Bowl Sunday dawned, a crowd of 65,000 was expected to fill the Allegiant Stadium in Vegas, but for Taylor, just getting there was a feat of endurance. The evening before, she was performing an Eras show in Tokyo, a small detail that was of grave concern to fans who feared she wouldn't make it back to the US in time for Travis's big moment. Even the Japanese Embassy was alarmed by the challenge, releasing a slightly clunky, pun-laden statement about the logistics involved: 'The Embassy of Japan in the United States is aware of recent media reports concerning the steps Taylor Swift will need to take to travel from Tokyo after her concert on February 10th to Las Vegas in time to watch the Kansas City Chiefs play in Super Bowl LVIII,' it said. 'Despite the 12-hour flight and 17-hour time difference, the Embassy can confidently *Speak Now* to say that if she departs Tokyo in the evening after her concert, she should comfortably arrive in Las Vegas before the Super Bowl begins.' The tongue-in-cheek message continued, 'We know that many people in Japan are excited to experience Taylor Swift's Eras Tour, so we wanted to confirm that anyone concerned can be *Fearless* in knowing that this talented performer can wow Japanese audiences and still make it to Las Vegas to support the Chiefs when they take the field for the Super Bowl wearing *Red*.'

As predicted, when Taylor came off stage, she dashed straight to a private jet waiting at Tokyo's Haneda Airport. After flying through the night, she landed in LA late in the afternoon, and next morning hopped on another plane to Vegas, making it to her VIP box well before kick-off. Naturally, she was dressed for the part, wearing a sleek black top under a Chiefs bomber jacket and rhinestone-studded jeans, along with a $3,000 custom diamond-and-yellow-gold '87' pendant necklace by Stephanie Gottlieb. Soaking up the electric atmosphere, she was pictured with a heavy-duty contingent of her Chiefs crew, including rapper Ice Spice, Blake Lively, Lana Del Rey and one of her oldest friends, stylist Ashley Avignone. Representing the Kelce clan were his parents, Ed and Donna, plus Jason and Kylie, who, a die-hard Philadelphia Eagles fan, graciously abstained from donning any Chiefs gear. Taylor's parents, Scott and Andrea, were there, too, alongside her brother, Austin, and his girlfriend, Sydney Ness. And as Travis pointed out beforehand, the tickets had cost him a small fortune. Asked by Jason on *New Heights* what he was doing in preparation for the game, he said, 'I'm not really doing much different other than just counting how much money I'm spending on this damn Super Bowl for family and friends to come.' Contrary to popular belief, even athletes playing in the game don't automatically receive complimentary passes for their guests, and according to reports, luxury suites for the Super Bowl can cost as much as $1.8 million for 20 spots, with *DAZN* suggesting that the princely sum incudes a full-service bar, private lounge, kitchenette and all-you-can-eat goodies such as wagyu beef hotdogs, BBQ burritos and exotic-sounding carne asada fries.

With nerves jangling in what turned out to be a topsy-turvy match, Taylor was seen on the jumbotron screen downing a drink before slamming her plastic cup down, prompting mass cheers around the stadium. The NFL social media account even shared a clip of the moment, simply captioned, 'Icon'. She was also clocked biting her white painted nails, and when a last-gasp effort by the Chiefs levelled the game at 19–19 and sent it into overtime, the tension was unbearable. The 49ers edged back in front, but after Travis's best pal, Patrick Mahomes, played a touchdown pass to Mecole Hardman, the Chiefs narrowly scooped the win 25–22. It made them the first team to win back-to-back Super Bowls since the New England Patriots in 2003 and 2004. Taylor's jubilant reaction was truly one for the history books.

As cheers and screams broke out in the VIP suite, she leaped up and down with Blake Lively before racing down to the field, arm in arm with Donna Kelce. Through the swirling confetti, Taylor dashed straight into Travis's arms. 'Come here, girl,' he was heard saying as the TV cameras panned in on them hugging and kissing. 'Thank you for coming. Thank you for making it halfway across the world,' he continued. 'You're the best baby. The absolute best.' Overcome with elation, Taylor replied, 'I've never been so proud in my life. I can't believe you. How did you do that?' She also called it 'the craziest thing I've ever seen', while Travis very reasonably asked her, 'How do you not have jet lag right now?'

After leading a rendition of Queen's 'We Are the Champions' in the team's locker room, Travis took a breath to tell *ESPN* about the groundbreaking result. 'Even at this point in my career, winning makes you feel like a little kid all over again,' he said. 'This game is so beautiful when you're doing things the right way. You put in the grind, you put in the hard work, you reap those rewards. It's just a beautiful, beautiful atmosphere and I couldn't be more proud of the guys.' Asked by the reporter how he planned to celebrate, he grinned and said, 'It's going to be an absolute blast. I'm going to party my tail off.'

And that's exactly what he did, heading to Sin City's famed Strip for a raucous night with Taylor and their crew.

At Zouk nightclub, he joined The Chainsmokers on the decks and sang Taylor's track 'You Belong With Me', pointing back and forth at her. Later on, the action shifted to XS nightclub at Wynn Las Vegas, where they rocked up with Patrick Mahomes and his wife, Brittany, around 2am. Taylor and Travis kissed and cuddled as they danced to a remix of her hit 'Love Story', mouthing the lyrics about being the prince and princess. Travis was also snapped enjoying Ace of Spades champagne straight from its flashy gold bottle, and they tucked into a special delivery of chicken and chips before the party finally ended soon after 5am. During the evening, Taylor shared a TikTok of her parents, Andrea and Scott, sipping drinks in a booth, captioning it, 'It's a friends and family party they said. Bring your parents they said.' She added to her millions of followers, 'Accidentally going clubbing with your parents is something everyone should try at least once in their life.'

As the win sunk in, celebs rushed to congratulate Travis on his success, and one message in particular from former presidential candidate Hillary Clinton stood out. In her tweet, she wrote, 'Congratulations to Taylor's boyfriend – and the entire Kansas City Chiefs community.' It played on a popular joke which had seen Travis frequently referred to by fans as 'Taylor's boyfriend', flipping the old stereotype on its head and showing that women do not always have to be defined by men in relationships. Tennis champion Serena Williams used her opening monologue at the 2024 Excellence in Sports Performance Yearly awards to make the same point: 'Congratulations to the Kansas City Chiefs,' she said. 'This year, Patrick Mahomes and Taylor Swift's boyfriend won a Super Bowl.'

While many saw the good-natured humour in such takes, others bristled, and it added fuel to a ridiculous conspiracy theory which claimed the Chiefs' play-off success was all part of a covert operation using Taylor's huge influence over young voters to help re-elect Joe Biden in that November's presidential election. Neither Taylor nor Travis ever commented, and NFL commissioner Roger Goodell slammed the claims. 'The idea that this is within a script, this is pre-planned, is just nonsense,' he said. 'It's frankly not even worth talking about.' The largely right-wing theory was, of course, baseless, but the fact the allegations were repeated across talk shows and social media underscored how politicised Taylor's fame had become. What's more, a poll conducted by New Jersey's Monmouth University found that nearly one in five Americans believed such claims to be true. What began as a simple and harmless love story between a pop star and a footballer had, in some ways, morphed into a symbol of the divisive culture war running through the very heart of the US.

Unfortunately for Taylor, criticism and backlash had trailed her ever since she abandoned her long-held neutrality and made her first foray into politics in October 2018.

Taking to Instagram as she endorsed the Democrats in the US midterms, she said, 'In the past I've been reluctant to publicly voice my political opinions, but due to several events in my life and in the world in the past two years, I feel very differently about that.' Saying she could not support Tennessee Republican Senate candidate Marsha Blackburn – who had been endorsed by President Donald Trump – she wrote: 'I cannot vote for someone who will not be willing to fight for dignity for ALL Americans, no matter their skin colour, gender or who they love.' The post accrued 360,000 Instagram likes within an hour, and her plea for fans to register to vote consequently led to a surge of 160,000 new registrations in two days according to Vote.org. But when President Trump was asked about her comments the following day, he told reporters, 'Let's say that I like Taylor's music about 25 per cent less now, okay?' Having once called her 'fantastic' and 'terrific', that marked a hefty gear change for him. But as the *Washington Post* put it, her actions 'fell like a hammer across the Trump-worshipping subforums of the far-right internet, where people had convinced themselves ... that the world-famous pop star was a secret MAGA fan'. Taylor's decision to speak out was an agonising one, which was later brought to life in her Netflix documentary *Miss Americana*. In one scene, she argued with her dad, Scott, over voicing her opinion. 'I need to be on the right side of history,' she told him. 'Dad, I need you to forgive me for doing it, because I'm doing it.' She even released a song, 'Only the Young', to promote the 2020 documentary, which was seen as a protest song with its references to Trump, tragic school shootings and a call to fight the system. 'Only the Young' was later used in a campaign ad by Joe Biden and Kamala Harris, with Taylor taking to social media to endorse the pair in the 2020 election. Less successfully, she lent VP Kamala her support again ahead of the 2024 election, saying on Instagram that September, 'I believe we can accomplish so much more in this country if we are led by calm and not chaos.' This time, her post led to a 500 per cent increase in voter registration, as well as mobilisation through dedicated groups like 'Swifties for Kamala'. In a comic twist, Taylor famously signed off her social post, 'Childless Cat Lady', mocking an earlier comment made by Trump's running mate JD Vance when he described Democrats as 'a bunch of childless cat ladies who are miserable at their own lives'. Fittingly, Taylor even posed with her cat Benjamin Button in the accompanying photo, and the term 'childless cat lady' went on to top Yale University's list of 2024's most notable quotes.

Though less outspoken politically, it has often become apparent that Travis shares Taylor's values and views on the world. He has openly supported social-justice initiatives within the NFL and advocated for unity and equality.

He also publicly endorsed vaccination campaigns during the pandemic, starring in a Pfizer commercial encouraging Americans to get their shots. In 2017, he took the knee during the American National Anthem, offering solidarity to other teammates who were opposing racial injustice and police brutality. Then, when US conservatives mounted a boycott against Bud Light after it ran an ad featuring a transgender social media influencer in 2023, Travis went on to star in a commercial for the beer. His stance was anathema to certain prominent media personalities, but it pinpointed one of the reasons Taylor was so drawn to him. 'The tight end the right turned against: why Travis Kelce is the man for Taylor Swift' ran a headline in the *Guardian*. As its commentary stressed, his political beliefs struck a mighty chord with her: 'They are more progressive than those held by nearly every other prominent white American professional athlete – and therefore line up comfortably with those of the singer and most of the so-called Swifties who support her.'

For all their chemistry and mutual sense of fun, it was clear that Taylor and Travis were bound by something deeper; an instinct to stand up for what mattered, even as the bluster around them often grew deafening.

CHAPTER EIGHT

During their first year together, much of the media emphasis was on Taylor's steadfast support for Travis during months of intense NFL games. But he was just as devoted, and literally crossed continents to watch her hold court in multiple Eras tour shows. Amid a congested roster of matches and training sessions, he managed to get to several of her biggest international dates, including a show in Argentina in November 2023 – the first on the tour to take place outside North America. During the concert at River Plate Stadium in Buenos Aires, fans spotted him in a VIP tent alongside Taylor's dad, Scott, who filmed him joining in with thunderous chants of 'Olé, olé, olé'. Travis was also seen dancing and singing along to tracks like 'Blank Space' and 'Karma', and when Taylor changed a lyric in the latter to include a reference to the Chiefs, the crowd duly erupted. Later, leaked video footage showed the sweet moment when Taylor ran off stage after her final bow and jumped into Travis's arms for a kiss – leading one fan to write on X, 'This is the best thing I've ever seen in my life!' Another said, 'Will be forever known as the "Kiss heard round the world!"'

Buoyed by his Super Bowl glory in February 2024, Travis flew over 8,000 miles to Australia to be reunited with Taylor. At Sydney's Accor Stadium, he exchanged friendship bracelets and posed for selfies with fans, and when she ended the first night's show by greeting him with a kiss, social media took off again. During their time in the city, the pair petted kangaroos at Sydney Zoo, and reportedly enjoyed a stay at the $25,000-per-night presidential villa at the Crown Hotel. Split over two levels, the 800-square-metre residence comes with views over Sydney Harbour, a terrace with an infinity pool, plus a kitchen and dining area for ten, a bar, small gym, media room and even butler's quarters. Sadly for Travis, he could only stay a couple of days before duty called him back to the Chiefs. The following month, he and Taylor had another Eras rendezvous in Singapore, where they were snapped exploring the city's Gardens by the Bay, wandering hand in hand among the illuminated trees. 'I'm a big plant guy,' Travis said in his winningly goofy way on *New Heights* afterwards. 'Loved seeing f***ing enormous trees. It was cool as f***; they had the world's biggest waterfall in a greenhouse, too. It was awesome, man.'

The passion shown by Travis whenever he turned up on the Eras trail was infectious and, as he told *GQ*, he was proud to step into a 'fanboy' role. 'I get to be the plus one,' he said. 'I get to go and be that fan. Because I am a fan.' And showing how it was a feeling that ran on both sides, he added, 'It's so cool that I get to experience her being that plus one for me on the football field ... I feel that same enjoyment every time she comes to my shows.' Reflecting on the effort he witnessed Taylor putting into each concert, Travis called her work ethic 'pretty remarkable', and said the operation behind her was 'an absolute machine'. He stressed he could 'take a lot of notes' from her performances and that they were 'arguably more exhausting than how much I put in on a Sunday, and she's doing it three, four, five days in a row'.

But, as was often the case, the loyalty Travis showed Taylor was not popular with everyone. Some commentators felt he was not in tip-top shape for the Chiefs at the start of the 2024 season, and that the frequent travel to Eras shows had detracted from his training. Travis contested such claims months later during an appearance on *The Stephen A. Smith Show*, saying, 'You have to be true to yourself. You've got to be able to reflect and look at yourself and see, "Why are they saying these things?" I was still playing at a high level knowing all that. We were winning football games, which is all I ever care about.' He also pointed out that in the end, what mattered most was being there for Taylor, because it allowed her to thrive. 'That's the beauty of being in a very strong relationship,' he insisted. 'You get that support to be able to come in and focus on your craft, focus on being the best version of you. You know, that's why I wanted to be at the concerts supporting her and being there for her and making sure she feels comfortable and supported in everything she's doing in life.'

After the Asia leg of Eras wrapped in March 2024 and Taylor geared up for the release of *The Tortured Poets Department*, she and Travis were the star attraction at America's Coachella festival. While in the Californian desert, they were spotted dancing – and smooching – through sets by Ice Spice and Bleachers, fronted by Taylor's co-writer Jack Antonoff. Explaining why they chose to immerse themselves in the crowd rather than watch the acts from side of stage, Travis said on his podcast, 'I like to see it from the fans' perspective ... It's more of an experience if you're in the pit and the madness with all the fans.'

During a two-month tour gap for an exhausted Taylor, she and Travis also escaped to Harbour Island, a tropical paradise in the Bahamas. According to reports, they stayed at the ultra-swanky Rosalita House – a six-bedroom beachfront villa with $15,000 nightly rates and a dedicated team of staff, including a private chef and housekeeper. Savouring a rare break from the spotlight, they spent sun-drenched days strolling along sandy beaches and splashing in the crystal waters, and they also took a 32-foot power boat out for a spin. But when photos surfaced of Taylor wearing a glam yellow bikini and Travis in blue swim shorts, the tabloid press homed in on his so-called 'dad bod'. Jason Kelce wasted no time in teasing his brother about the pictures on *New Heights* on his return, but he laughed it off, reminding him it was the offseason. 'It's March!' he said. 'I got a couple weeks to get back into the routine.'

In any case, the jokes didn't last long, because as he set his sights on the start of the following football season, Travis overhauled his diet and fitness regime and soon dropped several pounds in weight. His leaner, sharper look was certainly noticeable when he joined Taylor in all his finery during her long-awaited Eras stint at Wembley Stadium in June 2024. The London run of shows had begun with a brush with royalty, as the Prince of Wales attended the first night in the capital with his two older children, Prince George and Princess Charlotte. William was celebrating his 42nd birthday, and though Princess Kate was unable to attend due to her ongoing cancer treatment, TikTok footage of him dancing his heart out to 'Shake It Off' became an instant hit and generated over 19 million views. 'OK slay Prince William,' remarked one appreciative fan, while another comment said, 'Nice moves your highness'. Kensington Palace later shared an Instagram snap of Taylor posing backstage with William, George and Charlotte along with the caption, 'Thank you Taylor Swift for a great evening!' which set a new bar for the street cred of the monarchy. Even more buzzworthy was a photo Taylor posted of herself with the royal trio, which included a beaming Travis in the frame, too. Surprisingly, it was the first time she had ever shared a picture of him on her main Instagram grid. The post garnered over 10 million likes, and fans were thrilled at the development. 'Hard launching your boyfriend on Instagram with the British royal family is INSANE,' wrote one. Taylor's caption – 'Happy Bday M8! London shows are off to a splendid start' – also caused widespread merriment thanks to her uber-casual address to the future British king.

For that opening night, Travis watched the show in a VIP tent with a host of famous faces, including Cara Delevingne, Jonathan Van Ness and Salma Hayek, while also accompanied by his former Chiefs buddy Ross Travis, plus Jason and Kylie, who were seen handing out friendship bracelets to fans. For night two at Wembley, the celebrity guest list was even beefier and could almost have been mistaken for a lavish Hollywood awards show. Jostling for space alongside the likes of Tom Cruise, Ashton Kutcher and Mila Kunis were Liam Hemsworth and Greta Gerwig, and Phoebe Waller-Bridge and pal Andrew Scott were seen rocking out to 'Shake It Off'. Actor Hugh Grant was also there with his wife and daughter, and after the gig he offered his gratitude on social media, letting slip he had enjoyed an impromptu drinking session with Travis. 'Dear Taylor, you have an incredible show, an amazing and v hospitable team and excellent if gigantic boyfriend (#tequilashots),' he wrote on X. 'Thanks so much from one ageing London boy, wife and thrilled 8-year-old.' An evidently chuffed Taylor replied, 'As a long time Hugh Grant stan this tweet is very important to my culture.' Some weeks later, Hugh revealed more about his evening boozing with Travis at the gig. 'We were doing tequila shots. We got absolutely smashed,' he told *NME*. 'I thoroughly enjoyed it.'

But night three at Wembley was the real headline grabber – and not just because the legendary Sir Paul McCartney was clocked in the audience dancing to 'But Daddy I Love Him' and swapping friendship bracelets with fans. Even that was eclipsed by the jaw-dropping moment a tuxedoed Travis stepped into the Wembley mayhem and caused tens of thousands of spectators to collectively lose their minds. His surprise appearance during 'I Can Do It with a Broken Heart', carrying Taylor in his arms and fanning her dramatically back to life, remains one of the tour's most unforgettable moments. In the days after his cameo, Travis spoke to various media and news outlets about the experience. 'I've been on a few stages in my life, [but] that one was definitely the most shocking,' he told radio network Westwood One Sports. 'The stadium, the lights, the crowd and how they went insane. The whole time I'm thinking, "Oh, snap, I have a job to do. I gotta lock in and I gotta make this fun."' Elaborating further on *New Heights*, he told Jason, 'It was an absolute blast. It was such a fun, playful part of the show and it was like … the perfect time for me to go up there, just be a ham and have some fun.' When Jason asked how it compared to playing football at Arrowhead Stadium, he explained, 'It's nothing like this. I felt like an ant. I felt like the smallest piece of life ever … I'll never forget being on a stage in front of what felt like a million people.' Though he lapped up the reaction he received from the 90,000 fans, his main motivation was not to let the side down. 'I didn't disappoint Taylor, so that's all that really matters,' he concluded. For Taylor, who revealed in her Instagram post afterwards how it left her 'cracking up' and 'swooning', the moment highlighted one of the qualities she valued so much in Travis; his love of rooting for her at every opportunity. Like she had said in her 'Person of the Year' interview with *TIME*, 'We're showing up for each other, other people are there, and we don't care … We're just proud of each other.'

Taylor's Wembley Stadium residency was notable for another major reason, too, as she shattered a record set by Michael Jackson back in 1988 of performing seven concerts there in one tour. 'You just made me the first solo artist to ever play Wembley eight times in a single tour,' she told the crowd during her final performance on UK soil on 20 August. 'We will never, ever be able to thank you enough for it.' On that final Wembley night, she kept a few surprises up her sleeve, bringing out Ed Sheeran and Florence Welch as special guests. She also played 'So Long, London' from *The Tortured Poets Department* for the very first time on the road. 'I've never played this on the Eras tour before,' she said, before launching into what was the most apposite farewell to the city she still cherished.

That same month, Taylor and Travis found themselves battling rumours that their relationship was about to become a whole lot more serious. In an apparent showbiz exclusive, *Page Six* stated that Travis was preparing to propose, and that he had already asked Taylor's dad for permission to pop the question. 'The engagement is happening soon,' it quoted an insider as saying. 'Scott has been asked for his blessing and has wholeheartedly given it, and Travis has been talking to friends about a ring.' However, a representative for Travis was quick to shut down the claims, saying there were not 'any official engagement plans in place'. Of all the questionable stories that trailed them, none was more spurious than a fake document leaked on to social media in September 2024, which claimed to be a 'break-up contract' advising a full media strategy. Alarmingly, it had been created with the letterhead for Travis's PR agency Full Scope, and it stated that his split from Taylor would be officially announced on 28 September, and that it should be framed as a 'mutual' decision. To the relief of Swifties, Full Scope condemned the document as 'entirely false and fabricated', and speedily launched legal action to identify its source. On social media, fans suggested it could have been an AI-generated hoax, noting its amateur style and misuse of industry jargon. Though absurd, the episode reinforced the persistent scepticism around Taylor and Travis, and even a year into their relationship they had not quite been able to see off all the 'showmance' whispers. To some, their romance was too all-American and sports-movie-like to be genuine, and they could not believe that someone like Taylor – the force behind such thoughtful works as *folklore* and *evermore* – would have chosen such a partner.

Still, the week following the leak, Taylor and Travis attended the final of the US Open in New York, where footage of them looking loved up as they sang and danced to The Darkness's 'I Believe in a Thing Called Love' went some way to showing doubters how happy they were. And if further proof of their commitment were needed, that came in spades in December 2024, when Travis threw a huge party to celebrate the end of Taylor's Eras tour and mark her 35th birthday at the same time. Pulling out all the stops, he assembled a wide circle of close friends and family at the Kansas City bash, including his teammate Patrick Mahomes and his wife, Brittany. Also present were Taylor's bestie, Ashley Avignone, who revealed the unexpected nature of the event on Instagram. 'When she thought she was going to a small, quiet dinner but it was actually a giant surprise party with her friends and family,' she wrote. For obvious reasons, Taylor hadn't got the memo about the Eras-themed fancy dress, but she still wowed in a $4,300 black mini-dress by Balmain, paired with DeBeers diamond earrings, while Travis wore a smart tux and top hat to replicate his scene-stealing Wembley garb. Other guests rocked feather boas and colourful clothing to match Taylor's various career eras, and there were friendship bracelets scattered across the tables. Travis helped oversee a range of kooky props, too, including a replica cleaning cart stacked with mops and brooms, like one Taylor often hopped on to speed around the Eras set. She and her guests also took to the dancefloor wearing hooded green capes resembling the one she wore when performing 'willow' on stage. In another thoughtful gesture, Travis presented Taylor with the black fedora she wore for each performance of her song '22' on the tour. It was always one of the most treasured rituals from the show, with Taylor donning the hat as she shimmied down the runway before kneeling down to place it on the head of a chosen fan. Famous recipients had included Selena Gomez's younger sister, Gracie, and Bianka Bryant, the daughter of Kobe and Vanessa Bryant. By returning the '22' hat to its rightful owner, Travis turned the Eras tradition on its head, poignantly honouring Taylor for having brought so much joy to others.

Despite entering the 2025 Grammy Awards with five nominations for *The Tortured Poets Department* and one for the song 'Us', a duet with Gracie Abrams, Taylor left the LA event without a single trophy. Yet the night didn't feel like a loss. Dressed in a glittery red Vivienne Westwood minidress and an eye-catching Lorraine Schwartz thigh chain with a tiny 'T' dangling from it, she certainly did not spend the evening sulking. She swayed along to a medley performance by her tour buddy Sabrina Carpenter, then screamed with genuine joy as her friend picked up the Grammy for Best Pop Vocal Album. As Billie Eilish performed her hit 'Birds of a Feather', Taylor held hands and danced with pal Margaret Qualley, and she was also seen clinking champagne glasses with several big hitters from the music world, including rapper Jay-Z.

One of the biggest moments of the night came when Taylor presented the Best Country Album Grammy to Beyoncé for *Cowboy Carter*. Recalling her own win for the same award back in 2010 for *Fearless*, she said, 'They say you never forget where you came from, and I will never forget standing here right on this spot almost exactly 15 years ago accepting the Grammy Award for Best Country Album.' The moment felt like a passing of the torch from one icon to another, and the mutual respect between the two was clear to see as they embraced on stage.

At the afterparty later, a backstage clip of Taylor individually tipping four event workers with cash went viral. 'Thank you so much for your hard work,' she told them, as one employee replied, 'We appreciate you so much.' Once again, it showed Taylor's quiet but instinctive belief in trying to make others feel seen and valued, and also her recognition of the small armies involved in keeping her professional world turning.

Though many were disappointed by the distinct absence of Travis on Grammys' night, he was somewhat preoccupied, with the 2025 Super Bowl taking place just a few days later. The Chiefs had booked their place in the world's biggest sporting contest for the third successive year after a crunch championship victory against the Buffalo Bills at the end of January. Wrapped in a Louis Vuitton hoodie and beanie on that bitterly cold winter's day, teary-eyed Taylor was seen hugging Donna Kelce before running down to the pitch and congratulating Travis. 'I love you so much,' she was heard telling him on camera. 'I'm so proud of you, I can't stand it. Look what you did!' With confetti raining down on them as they hugged, Travis replied, 'New Orleans, Louisiana, baby!' referring to the destination of the upcoming Super Bowl.

In a rematch of the 2023 spectacle, the Chiefs had to face the Philadelphia Eagles once again – and the head-to-head caused some consternation within the Kelce contingent as

Jason had spent his entire career with the rival side, only retiring the year before. Amid frenzied speculation over which team he would root for, he finally put sports fans out of their misery, telling Travis on *New Heights*, 'Obviously, you're my brother. I always root for my brother. That's the reality of it. Even though I'm decked out in Eagles gear, I'm always going to root for Travis.' But he added, 'No matter what on game day, I'm going to be happy for one of those sides.'

As expected, Taylor's presence at Caesars Superdome dominated much of the coverage on 9 February. When she took her place in a VIP suite with Ice Spice, Ashley Avignone and the Haim sisters, fans spotted she had recycled the ruby T chain from the Grammys, this time wearing it around her neck instead of her leg. Very much owning stadium chic, she wore a white Alaïa bodysuit with embellished denim shorts, an oversized Saint Laurent blazer and knee-high boots.

On the pitch, the game did not offer quite the same edge-of-seat drama as 2023's 'Kelce Bowl', and in the end, the Chiefs were soundly beaten 40–22 by the Eagles. As a gutted Travis admitted to reporters afterwards, his team simply 'couldn't find that spark'. He added, 'We haven't played that bad all year.' The night was also marred by the unpleasant reaction Taylor received from some Eagles fans, who noisily booed her when she appeared on the jumbotron. Looking bemused by the hostile reception, she gave Ice Spice a flash of side-eye and, according to a lip-reader, said, 'What's going on?' Though it was laughed off, the incident provoked some serious debate afterwards, with many unsettled by what seemed like an unprovoked act of misogyny. Even fellow attendee President Trump – who conversely attracted cheers when he appeared on the big screen – muscled in, falsely claiming on his social platform after the game that 'She got BOOED out of the Stadium', and that 'MAGA is very unforgiving!' Many rightly dismissed his inflammatory words, but as *Glamour* pointed out, 'It's still worth calling out how gross – and frankly ridiculous – this sort of conduct is. And when the Twitter rant becomes real life, in the form of a stadium full of thousands and thousands of people, it's chilling.'

One notable absence from the Super Bowl was Blake Lively, who had been such a prominent figure at the previous year's event. As one of Taylor's closest confidantes, their friendship stretched back to 2015 when they met in Australia, just as Taylor was finishing her 1989 world tour. The following summer, Blake was a guest at her Fourth of July party in Rhode Island, along with husband Ryan Reynolds, where they messed about in the sea and on water slides. Then in 2017, it emerged that the child's voice heard on Taylor's track 'Gorgeous' belonged to Blake and Ryan's eldest daughter, James. She and her two little sisters, Inez and Betty, also featured in the lyrics for Taylor's *folklore* song 'betty', and it later transpired that she was godmother to all three girls. When *folklore* won the Album of the Year Grammy in 2021 Taylor gave the family a shout-out in her acceptance speech. 'I want to thank James, Inez and Betty and their parents, who are the second and third people that I play every new song that I write,' she said. The same year, when Taylor performed her haunting ten-minute version of 'All Too Well' on *Saturday Night Live*, Blake and Ryan were both in the audience to cheer her on. Straight afterwards, Taylor unveiled her new video for 'I Bet You Think About Me', which Blake had directed for her. 'I finally got to work with the brilliant, brave, & wickedly funny @blakelively on her directorial debut,' she posted on Instagram. 'Join us as we raise a toast, and a little hell.' In the video, which Taylor's brother, Austin, produced, she played a woman attempting to sabotage an ex's nuptials, and she and Blake crammed it with Easter eggs – including the long-lost red scarf, and the number 13 iced on a wedding cake, which she proceeded to destroy.

As the friendship bloomed, Ryan chatted about Taylor's 2022 album, *Midnights*, on *Entertainment Tonight*, saying, 'She's a genius', and that the entire family was 'obsessed' with it. 'All of us, whole house, I'm not kidding. I love it so much,' he said. 'I do, Blake does, my daughters. We love it.' When Taylor split from Joe Alwyn in early 2023, Blake was on speed dial to help her through it, and like many of the

Swift squad wanting to show their solidarity, she and Ryan both unfollowed Joe on social media. Once Taylor's Eras tour was under way, Blake proved the ultimate Swiftie, attending shows in Philadelphia, Detroit and New Orleans, as well as two separate concerts in Madrid – one with her daughters and then a different night with Ryan. After the New Orleans show, Ryan could not hold back his admiration, and he wrote on Instagram, 'When I'm 95 yrs old and my wife and kids wheel me outside and into the sun so I can drink a sandwich, I'll still be talking about seeing this show in New Orleans.' Adding that Taylor's show felt like the Super Bowl or Mardi Gras 'had a baby with music', he said, 'The only bummer is she can't be in the audience to experience what everyone else sees and feels.' With Blake and Ryan regularly attending Chiefs matches, too, and stepping out for double dates with Taylor and Travis in New York, it seemed like the foursome were solid as a rock. So when reports a year later suggested that Taylor and Blake were no longer speaking, the revelation struck like a thunderclap.

Tensions between the two women had arisen as a result of Blake's protracted legal battle over her film *It Ends with Us*. She had accused its director and her co-star Justin Baldoni of on-set sexual harassment and claimed he then orchestrated a retaliatory smear campaign to damage her reputation. He denied the allegations, calling them 'false, outrageous and intentionally salacious with an intent to publicly hurt'. In court documents, Blake cited a number of A-list stars as potential trial witnesses, including Taylor, who was said to have felt uncomfortable over the situation, with a source telling *People* she 'wanted no part in the drama'. The two were then said to have had no contact for many months, and a bond that was once seen as a rare example of genuine Hollywood sisterhood seemed to be broken. However, hinting at a possible thawing, Blake 'liked' one of Taylor's Instagram posts around the launch of *The Life of a Showgirl* in early October 2025. It was then thought that the song 'Cancelled!' from the album may have been intended as an olive branch from Taylor. Seen as a kickback against cancel culture, the lyrics were widely interpreted as a show of support for friends who had been hit by public backlash, and fans hoped it might lead to eventual reconciliation and a resumption of the friendship.

At the end of the 2025 NFL season, Taylor and Travis took some time out, heading on a snowy getaway to Montana. While in the mountains, they hung out with pals, including sports presenters Erin Andrews and Charissa Thompson – who had played a hand in first getting them together via their podcast appeal. Speaking after the trip, Charissa told listeners, 'They are so happy and adorable and all things, so when the opportunity came about for all of us to spend time together and go on vacation, we were elated to just have time with them and in general see what she was all about ... She's a dream and I adore her.' During Travis's offseason the couple also made what was their first ever official red-carpet appearance together at a footballing summer camp in Nashville. The event, called Tight End University, was co-founded by Travis in 2021 and takes place annually at Vanderbilt University as a training and networking hub. Walking hand in hand on arrival, the VIP pair smiled for the cameras and later in the evening, guests were taken aback when Taylor took to the stage to perform an acoustic version of 'Shake It Off'. DJ Mike Fresh, who was compering, wrote on Instagram, 'There are Monday fun days, and then there are Monday fun days when Taylor Swift is in the building partying to your set.'

The early part of summer 2025 was spent in Florida, where Travis rented a $20 million mansion in Boca Raton for a combination of relaxation and high-intensity training. And in July, he used the downtime to finally 'hard launch' their relationship on Instagram, posting a series of 13 belated photos of them together – including the Montana trip and lazy days in Florida. He captioned the shots, 'Had some adventures this offseason'. The post attracted over a million likes in an hour, and drew comments like, 'Swifties' heads and hearts exploding right now!' and 'Travis broke the internet'. That was tasty enough, but for fans and the wider world, an even more exciting development was just around the corner.

On 12 August 2025, the *New Heights* Instagram account dropped a teaser clip which showed Taylor on the podcast's set, complimenting Travis on his blue hoodie. 'Such a nice colour on you,' she told him. 'Yes, I know. It's the colour of your eyes, sweetie,' he replied. 'It's why we match so well.' The video then cut to Taylor saying, 'We're about to do a f***ing podcast!' The Swiftiesphere barely had time to draw breath before the episode landed the following day – and it delivered in unimaginable ways. Whereas so many celebrity podcasts sometimes drown under the weight of PR fluff or right-on worthiness, this one felt like a genuine glimpse behind the velvet ropes. It was candid, intimate and supercharged with the chemistry they had become so revered for. As the pair chatted naturally and without barriers to Jason for more than two hours, the golden nuggets just kept on coming. On a personal level, they revisited the beginnings of their romance, replaying Travis's pursuit of her in vivid, technicolour detail and speaking about each other's magnetism with unprecedented candour. 'I'm the luckiest guy in the world,' he said, kissing her hand. Speaking of the day they met with disarming tenderness, he said, 'I had never experienced something so mesmerising on stage and then so real and so beautiful in person.' Jason broke the spell, joking, 'Should I leave?' to which Taylor replied, 'At this point,

I think everyone should leave.' But she was equally effusive, saying, 'I love this new world that Travis has shown me. It's so fun. It's so exciting. You manifested it. You summoned me – here I am.' Comparing the demands of their careers, they found a few unexpected likenesses. 'Our job is to entertain people for three-plus hours in football stadiums,' said Taylor. She noted some debilitating physical parallels, too. 'I'm not getting hit by huge 300-pounders, but the heels ...' she grimaced. 'When I saw the recovery station in the hotel room, with the toe-spacers ... I'm telling you, dude, the similarities were crazy,' agreed Travis. 'I was like, "Oh my gosh. She does more than I do."'

Painting a picture of the domestic harmony they had created together, Taylor admitted an obsession with baking sourdough, saying she was 'thinking about bread about 60 per cent of the time'. She told how she had been baking rainbow bread for Jason's four daughters, too, saying, 'Because they love sprinkles, you know we put sprinkles in everything when we hang out.' Spilling the beans on other interests outside music, she admitted to 'hobbies you could have had in the 1700s', adding somewhat surprisingly, 'I like to sew – I specialise in children's purses and baby blankets. I love to paint. I love to cook.' For Swifties and neutral observers alike, these soundbites were riveting, showing how the world's greatest show-woman was equally content to potter at home with a paintbrush and knitting needles, or to tend to a dish bubbling away on the stove. There were some important family updates, too, and Taylor revealed that her mum, Andrea, was recovering from a recent knee replacement, while more concerningly, her dad, Scott, had undergone invasive quintuple bypass surgery following the discovery of five blockages in his heart. 'This was the summer of my parental upgrades,' she said. 'Making sure that they live to be at least 186 years old.' Although Andrea and Scott are no longer thought to be together, they appear to remain extremely civil as co-parents, and Taylor told how much she valued the time with them both. 'They're two of my best friends and I just adore them,' she said. 'It was actually one of the most special things that's ever happened to me, spending all that time with them this summer.'

One of the most emotional parts of the podcast came when Taylor revisited the upheaval of finally buying back the master recordings of her first six albums. She had first announced it happened at the end of May 2025, when a deal was struck with Shamrock Capital who had purchased her works from Big Machine Records five years earlier. In a letter to fans, she spoke of her overwhelming relief. 'I almost stopped thinking it could ever happen, after 20 years of having the carrot dangled and then yanked away,' she wrote. 'But that's all in the past now. All of the music I've ever made ... now belongs

... to me.' The conclusion of years of wrangling meant she had ownership of not only her first six albums, but also her videos, concert films, album artwork and photography. 'I can't thank you enough for helping to reunite me with this art that I have dedicated my life to, but have never owned until now,' her letter continued. In her *New Heights* heart-to-heart with Travis, she explained how the settlement had come to pass, saying that after her Eras tour she'd tasked Andrea and brother Austin with negotiating with Shamrock. 'Rather than send lawyers or management in a big crew, I sent my mom and my brother,' she said. 'They told them what this meant for me, they told them the whole story of all the times we've tried to buy it, all the times it's fallen through.' Taylor then tearfully recounted the longed-for moment when Andrea rang to let her know the sale had been agreed: 'I just, like, very dramatically hit the floor,' she said. 'I started bawling my eyes out.' She remembered dashing to share the news with Travis, who was playing video games in another room. 'He thought something was wrong; I started absolutely heaving,' she said. 'I had no power in my legs to support myself.' Travis chimed in at that point, saying she had been a 'dead weight' in his arms, and that he felt just as overwhelmed. 'I started crying, too,' he confessed.

Aside from all the intimate stories and snapshots of life chez Swift–Kelce, there was, of course, another purpose to their debut on-air appearance as a couple. Partway into the episode, Taylor took a breath and announced, 'So, I wanted to show you something.' She reached for a mint-green brief-case inscribed with the initials T.S. and, after unlocking it, pulled out a record that she proudly held up to the camera. 'This is my brand-new album, *The Life of a Showgirl*,' she said, prompting Travis and Jason to roar their approval.

Though a fairly monumental reveal, it wasn't a total surprise to Swifties. Over the preceding days, Taylor had already sent the internet into overdrive with a series of cryptic online countdowns, all leading to 12:12am on 12 August when her 12th album was first announced. The teasers featured a glittering orange backdrop on her website and a familiar image of the door she'd walked through on the final night of her Eras tour. Fans had also been speculating for weeks about an imminent release using the codename 'TS12', and with suspicions that her orange-hued phase would be focused on Travis, her decision to formally confirm the news on his podcast, on the 13th of the month, felt beautifully apt. Travis himself had dropped a few clues, and even back in January 2025, during an appearance on *The Pat McAfee Show*, he'd let slip he'd heard some new songs by Taylor. 'There might be a few,' he said. 'I don't know. There might be a few.'

Despite being so embedded in her Eras tour, Taylor revealed she wrote and recorded the album during fleeting breaks in her schedule. 'I would be playing three shows in a row and have three days off,' she said. In those gaps, she would fly to Sweden to work with producers Max Martin and Shellback. 'I was basically exhausted at this point in the tour, but I was so mentally stimulated and so excited to be creating.' As Travis suggested, she was 'literally living the life of a showgirl', to which she replied, 'I was! Which is why I called it that.' But even Travis seemed to be in some disbelief about her work rate, saying, 'How on earth did she do this on the tour is still blowing my mind.'

Describing the album as 'a complete 180' from *Tortured Poets*, Travis said it was filled with '12 bangers', and it was 'a lot more upbeat.' Taylor concurred, adding with a smile, 'Life is more upbeat.' She told how the theme of *The Life of a Showgirl* captured 'everything that was going on behind the curtain', but while it was unlike anything she had made before, she insisted there would be no extra songs or extended-album versions. 'There aren't other ones coming,' she clarified. This time, there would be 12 songs 'and that's it'. The album's artwork depicted Taylor in a jewelled dress, lying in water, representing her precious alone time after coming off stage. 'My show days are the same every single day; I just have a different city,' she said. 'And my day ends with me in a bathtub – not usually in a bedazzled dress.' In tandem with the podcast announcement, she showcased the album cover art on her Instagram page, along with the caption, 'And, baby, that's show business for you. New album *The Life of a Showgirl*. Out October 3.' The album was simultaneously made available for pre-order on Taylor's website, which immediately started crashing. In the end, she broke her own record with 5 million pre-saves on Spotify. Such was the hype that Google wriggled in on the action, with searches for her name bringing an explosion of orange confetti. An emoji of a heart in flames then rose from the bottom of the screen along with her own words, 'And, baby, that's show business for you'.

Following the announcement of the album, the Empire State Building in New York was even doused in an ethereal orange glow, with its official X account saying, 'See you next era'. Keen to jump on the trend, too, various brands posted orange memes on their social media, and Pinterest reported an 8,000 per cent surge in searches for 'bold orange glitter'.

When Jason pressed Taylor for more intel on the album's orange theme, she said, 'I just always liked it.' But linking the shade to the newfound energy she had been relishing, she added, 'This album is about what was going on behind the scenes in my inner life during this tour, which was so exuberant and electric and vibrant.' She also referred back to leaving her final Eras show through an orange door, and the unfailing alertness of the Swifties. 'That actually was an Easter egg,' she said. 'I was happy that they noticed that.

I trained them well.' And speaking of the grander meaning behind the colourful exit, she stressed it was 'a subliminal hint to the fans that I may be leaving the Eras tour era, but I was also entering a new era'. All the way through the conversation, she made it clear how much the release meant to her. 'I care about this record more than I can even overstate,' she said. 'This is the record I've been wanting to make for a very long time.' And with her passion for her latest recording so palpable, she said, 'I just love it. I love it a lot.' For Taylor, this wasn't just another album, it was a unique undertaking that she had managed to create while in perpetual motion, turning every stolen hour into a new tale.

With such transfixing content, the astonishing stats resulting from *New Heights* that day were only to be expected. Shattering a Guinness World Record as 1.3 million viewers concurrently watched it live, the episode amassed more than 10 million views in its first 24 hours and became the most-seen podcast stream in history. But it was groundbreaking for more than just the numbers; the fact Taylor and Travis chose to present themselves so openly – and in an environment they owned – lent the broadcast a rare authenticity. 'I think [people] tuned in because Taylor gave the world two hours that she's never given them before,' Travis later said. Calling it 'a masterclass in marketing in the digital age', business title *Forbes* summed up its unique impact: 'In an era where media, sports, and politics compete for attention, Taylor Swift has shown us just how cultural influence is evolving. For two hours, Swifties and sports fans shared a moment that made her more than a performer: she became a connector, wielding a form of soft power rarely seen so visibly from women.'

By speaking on her own terms, Taylor had rewritten the rulebook once again. Yet even as the *New Heights* delirium began to recede, the next page in her story had already been mapped out, and it was just waiting to be turned.

CHAPTER NINE

After packing away their *New Heights* headphones and mics, Taylor was looking forward to a planned night out with Travis: dinner in the city, a few glasses of wine, maybe a Netflix movie afterwards. But he had a very different idea, and it was one that would once again stop the world in its tracks. Unbeknown to Taylor, he had been working on a plan to propose to her for a while, and he chose to put it into action that very evening, knowing she'd already be camera-ready from the podcast.

Thanks to an A-grade effort by his personal team, the garden of his Leawood mansion was transformed into a romantic haven when they were recording inside the house. Florists had to work quickly to arrange thousands of flowers, positioned around a 20ft floral arch centrepiece and planted in stone urns. Experts suggested that at least 1,200 pink and white roses were brought in for the occasion, along with willow, delphiniums, ivy, vines, hydrangea, lilies and peonies. The other-worldly result clearly amazed and delighted Taylor.

'He really crushed it when it came to surprising me,' she told TV host Graham Norton, appearing on his BBC chat show in October 2025. 'There was a wall of hedges in the garden that weren't there before and inside the hedges was my tour photographer hiding. Travis went all out.'

Though she had always been good at keeping her own secrets, she apparently had not suspected Travis was hiding such a big one, and he managed to keep it below radar by ensuring the curtains in every window of the house were firmly closed. Despite thinking it was odd, Taylor assumed the windows were blacked out so as not to interfere with the recording. Speaking on *The Tonight Show Starring Jimmy Fallon* a few weeks later, she said, 'I think for Travis, the podcast was just sort of a distraction, sort of a ruse, to keep me not looking out the windows of the house.' But she admitted she should have twigged because he began pacing around the house. 'He's walking around sort of nervous about the podcast,' she said. 'He's like, "My heart is racing … I know how much this means to you. I really want this to be what you hoped it would be."' But as she pointed out, 'I'd never seen this dude nervous,' she said. 'He's professionally not a nervous person.' She also recalled what happened after the recording ended. 'He was like, "Do you want to go and just walk around the backyard and have a glass of wine?" I'm like, "I'm always gonna want to do that."' Once outside, it wasn't long until the penny dropped.

'They were going to go out to dinner and she was ready to go,' Travis's dad, Ed Kelce, later told reporters. 'They went out there and I think she knew something was up because as they approached, as they walked out there, she could see suddenly there's a lot more flowers.' But the organisers only just managed to finish their handiwork in time. 'They actually saw them coming,' Ed added. 'They hid in the bushes so they weren't part of it.'

The moment Travis got down on bended knee and asked Taylor to marry him was captured in an intimate photo that barely needed any explanation: the look between them said it all. She cradled his head in her hands, and everything about it looked like the kind of fairytale moment she had so often conjured up in her music. We will probably never know the exact words Travis used to propose, but we do know Taylor was over the moon at the prospect of becoming his wife. On announcing their joyful news on Instagram, she picked the now immortal ten words – 'Your English teacher and your gym teacher are getting married' – playfully alluding to her penchant for storytelling and his athletic genius. She signed off with a dynamite emoji, which referred to their famed 'TNT' initials.

The post contained five pictures in all, including one of the smiling couple locked in an embrace, their foreheads gently touching. Another shot saw them sitting beneath a flower-strewn chandelier, with Taylor's legs draped over Travis's lap. There was also a close-up of her vintage-inspired engagement ring, which he had designed personally with one of her favourite jewellers, Kindred Lubeck of Artifex Fine Jewelry. Set in yellow gold with filigree detail work on the side, the centre stone was an elongated, cushion-shaped old-mine hand-cut diamond. Unlike more modern machine-cut diamonds, this variety tends to give off a softer glow. The ring was valued by some experts at around \$550,000, but others thought \$1 million was a more realistic price tag. During a subsequent interview on *Heart Breakfast*, Taylor told DJs Emma Bunton and Jamie Theakston she had given Travis a not-so-subtle hint about Kindred Lubeck months earlier. 'I had shown him a video – I just thought her stuff was so cool,' she said. 'He was just paying attention to every-thing, it turns out, because when I saw the ring, I was like, "I know who made this, I know who made this," and also, "You listen to me!"' She added, 'He did amazing. It was like, "You really know me." I didn't know what I would want, but he did somehow, and that's kind of a flex.' Showing off the ring to Jimmy Fallon, Taylor admitted she could barely take her eyes off it. 'I look at it constantly,' she said. 'It doesn't feel in any way normal for me. I'm just sort of like, "Oh, man! Whoa!"' She also said of her new fiancé, 'He's just my favou-rite person I have ever met – no offence to everyone else. The fact that this is the person that I get to hang out with every-day forever, that's the whole thing of it.'

Looking radiant in the engagement photos, Taylor was wearing a black-and-white striped silk-blend sundress by Ralph Lauren, which predictably sold out 20 minutes after the news became public. As *Glamour* suggested, it had the effect of 'immediately moving the American designer to the top of the list for who could potentially make her wedding gown'. Within two days of the photos dropping, the global buzz about Ralph Lauren – which included online articles, social posts, TV mentions, reposts and tagged images – was claimed by marketing buffs to have had a total advertising value of some $6.8 million. Boosting the stats further, Travis was also clad in a Ralph Lauren navy polo shirt and khaki shorts, although he looked far more relaxed than he was probably feeling on the inside. Taylor paired her dress with tan-coloured Louis Vuitton heeled sandals and a diamond-encrusted Cartier watch, and her lips were painted a dusky pink coral. It was noted that Taylor's nude nails were an ideal match for the garden aesthetic, prompting some half-baked online theories that she knew about the proposal in advance, and even that she had helped mastermind the whole thing. That seemed extremely unlikely, but it was a reminder of the way in which even the most life-affirming gestures can still be prey to cynicism and conspiracy in the feisty social media age.

The Instagram reveal, which was not published until 26 August, inevitably sent shockwaves around the world, racking up more than 18 million likes in four hours and soon passing the 37 million mark. Meta also confirmed it had surpassed 1 million reposts – more than any other post on the platform ever. On her Stories, Taylor soundtracked the news to 'So High School' – the song suddenly seeming all the more relevant with its reference to marriage and all-consuming infatuation.

As the hunt for Easter eggs pepped up, much was made of the date of the announcement. Not only did Taylor post the news at exactly 1pm – the 13th hour of the day – but the proposal had taken place 13 days earlier on 13 August, with the reveal date of the 26th equating to 13 + 13. 'I love numerology, I love math stuff, I love dates, that stuff I just find really fun,' she had said on *New Heights*. Some fans also noted that as well as resembling a photoshoot for Taylor's 2019 album *Lover*, the engagement setting looked like a scene from her 'Bejeweled' music video. In the 2022 promo, Jack Antonoff pretended to propose to her, kneeling in front of an arch lined with flowers.

As more details began to surface, it became clear that Travis had stuck to the tradition of asking Taylor's dad, Scott, for permission to propose, as he wanted to make the occasion more meaningful. Speaking on *The Jimmy & Nath Show with Emma* a few days after the story broke, Ed Kelce let slip,

Chapter Nine

'It's kinda funny, I was talking to Scott Swift and Travis went to ask him for permission. And this was probably a month ago. Scott said, "Oh come on, when are you gonna get this done?"... But, you know, [he] wanted to make it special.' Ed then revealed that he and Scott both gave Travis similar advice. 'I told [him] the same thing Scott told him, "Asking her is what's going to make it special. Not where you do it, you know?" You can do it on the side of the road ... And Scott adds on, "Just get it done. Don't worry about any special date. Just, you're ready. You got the ring. Go do it."' In a separate interview with Cleveland's News 5 station, Ed also suggested that Travis had abandoned plans for a larger, more 'grand' proposal because Taylor was feeling impatient. 'I think she was getting maybe a little antsy,' he said. Asked by reporters where he was when he found out, Ed recalled, 'They started FaceTiming me and their mother and her folks to make sure everybody knew. As soon as I saw the FaceTime, I saw it was Travis, and then I saw Taylor there with him. I knew what they were going to say.' Although Travis's mum, Donna, did not speak publicly about the engagement, she changed her Facebook background to a picture of Travis and Taylor as children, along with the words, 'THEY ARE GETTING MARRIED'.

Shortly afterwards, Travis thanked fans for the outpouring of good wishes, saying on *New Heights*, 'It's been really fun telling everybody who I'm going to be spending the rest

249

of my life with.' And in a Chiefs pre-match interview a few weeks later, he told just how nerve-shredding the proposal had been. 'The palms were definitely sweating,' he said. 'I'm an emotional guy so there were a few tears here and there.' The day after the engagement share, Jason Kelce called it a 'gigantic piece of new news' on the podcast, and in his brother's absence he added, 'We felt it necessary here as a team on *New Heights* to get together and send Travis and Taylor a giant congratulations.' There were also warm wishes from the Kansas City Chiefs, with a message on X saying, 'Today is a fairytale. Congrats to Travis and Taylor – we're excited to have you as a permanent member of the Chiefs Kingdom family!'

The wider reaction to their betrothal was, in some cases, wonderfully creative. In Kansas, a cornfield was carved into a maze depicting the couple embracing and two intertwined rings with their lucky numbers 87 and 13. An accompanying message in the corn read 'Kansas City is Enchanted' – echoing Taylor's 2010 hit. Elsewhere, social media teams for big brands had a field day, firing off an artillery of so-called 'trendjacking' memes. Krispy Kreme was bang on the pulse, wittily posting on X 'FREE doughnuts for the class', and Hershey's announced wedding-ready bulk bags of its chocolate Kisses. Lego created tiny Taylor and Travis figurines complete with microphone and football helmet, calling their relationship the 'greatest love story ever built'. Urban Outfitters hastily compiled English teacher and gym teacher 'starter packs', featuring a selection of natty fashion items and accessories, and language app Duolingo posted a message saying, 'But when will it be your Spanish teacher's turn?' along with a weepy-eyed emoji. US takeout service DoorDash also cleverly offered a 13 per cent discount on all food orders – 'since her love finally delivered'. Highlighting the importance of seizing the momentum for any brand, the company's head of social told NPR, 'These days, to know your audience is to know pop culture. If you want your audience to love you, you have to understand what they love – and a good majority of them probably love Taylor Swift.'

The impact of the engagement brought a resurgence of the Swift Effect, too, through a sharp spike in retail trade. Within hours of Taylor's post, jewellers reported an astonishing surge in interest, with searches for engagement rings – particularly vintage and yellow-gold designs like Taylor's – soaring worldwide. Shares in Ralph Lauren jumped, and wedding-planning consultations took off in the days that followed, with couples spurred into action by Travis's sumptuous proposal. Lifestyle guru Martha Stewart, who had promptly offered her wedding services to Taylor and Travis, reported an uptick in 'styled proposals', with hikes in bookings for professional photographers and floral installations. Quick off the mark, apparel retailer American Eagle then announced a limited-edition collaboration with Travis's own sportswear and lifestyle brand, Tru Kolors. On the day of the launch, American Eagle's shares rose by around 8 per cent. Meanwhile, sales of his number-87 Chiefs jersey shot up by 200 per cent post engagement, and digital sales of Taylor's entirely unrelated song 'Dress' surged by 8,000 per cent, with listeners wondering if it held hidden wedding clues. Betting markets also lit up, and large wagers were placed on the timing of their nuptials, as well as more flighty predictions, such as the likelihood of them announcing a pregnancy in 2026 and, ridiculously, the chances of them breaking up before even tying the knot.

With the engagement dictating conversations across every corner of the planet, celebrities who rushed to congratulate the pair included Julia Roberts, Kate Hudson, Avril Lavigne, Cara Delevingne, Demi Lovato and Gracie Abrams. And the Prince and Princess of Wales broke ranks by liking the engagement post, too. One of the most vocal reactions came from actress Reese Witherspoon, who said in a social media video, 'Guys, we're trying to concentrate and do work here and Taylor Swift got engaged and it's very exciting!' Footage showed her jaw fall open on seeing photos of the ring, while she dramatically mouthed, 'Oh my God!' Sabrina Carpenter took to Instagram Stories to reshare Taylor's post with several white heart emojis, and fellow footballing WAG Brittany Mahomes wrote,

'Two of the most genuine people meet & fall in love. Just so happy for these two.' Even President Trump wished them 'a lot of luck', saying of Travis, 'I think he's a great player. A great guy. And I think she's a terrific person.' That was quite some U-turn from the man who only a couple of weeks earlier had attacked Taylor – yet again – for being 'woke' on Truth Social, sniping, 'I can't stand her (HATE!). She was booed out of the Super Bowl and became, NO LONGER HOT.'

It goes without saying how much the engagement meant to diehard Swifties, and one fan wrote on X, 'Big day for girls who believe in love'. Another said, 'I am more excited for Taylor than I was for my own engagement, lol'. The TikTok brigade were equally jubilant: 'It gives us all hope that we will someday get there,' said one user. 'The girl who wrote all the songs we cry over boys to finally has her happily ever after and so will we,' commented another. Those fans who felt maternally connected to Taylor were even more profoundly moved. 'MOTHER IS GETTING MARRIED,' was a much-shared reaction, accompanied by emojis of crying, brides and champagne bottles. The euphoric response also saw her husband-to-be anointed with the nickname 'Travis Swift', signalling mass approval and the fact he had not only won Taylor's heart, but his place at the core of the fandom. As the *Guardian* suggested, 'It's a bit of a retro move, a throwback to the super-couple era of the 90s and early aughts, when celebrity matches had their own portmanteaus (Bennifer, Brangelina, Posh and Becks). Now, it comes with a pop feminist spin: they are known online as Travis Swift, with him taking her last name.'

While a shorthand for gender equality, 'Travis Swift' was confirmation that 'Mother' had at last found someone worthy of becoming her mate for life. It was unusual for a celebrity engagement to be so deeply felt, but it seemed to touch the hearts of all those who had ridden the ups and downs of Taylor's rollercoaster romances over the years. 'It feels personal,' said a commentary in *Vogue*. 'First love, unrequited love, on-and-off-then-on-again love. Love that is cruel, manipulative, hopeful, comfortable, addictive, frustrating, depressing and a giant red flag. The Swiftie internet is one giant parasocial relationship at present.'

In the days and weeks that followed, the frenzy changed course, shifting from initial celebration and delight into a global guessing game about when, where and how it would all unfold. Most seemed to agree that it would be the celebrity wedding of the decade, likely to even eclipse the extravagant Venetian nuptials of Jeff Bezos and Lauren Sánchez in June 2025. *People* magazine billed it as 'America's royal wedding', although speaking on *The Late Show with Stephen Colbert*, comedian John Oliver asserted, 'This is better.'

As the couple entered what fans denoted Taylor's 'bridal era', she and Travis made their first public appearance as future Mr and Mrs at a college football game between the Cincinnati Bearcats and Nebraska Cornhuskers at the end of August. In a possible nod to her newly engaged status, Taylor wore white, teaming a Ralph Lauren sweater with a denim miniskirt and knee-high boots by Louis Vuitton. Speaking about it on *New Heights* afterwards, Travis told Jason, 'It was my first time introducing Taylor as my fiancée to a few of my teammates. So yeah, it was pretty cool. I still get giddy, exciting times.' Jason later asked his brother what they might have in store for the wedding, saying, 'I cannot wait to hear more ... Travis, you're about to embark on the wedding planning phase of a relationship.' Under no illusion about what lay ahead, he replied, 'Oh, it's gonna go crazy. That is the next step, yeah, I've heard about that.'

As that craziness took hold, every possible detail became a point of fascination, beginning with theories around a likely date. Swifties pinpointed Saturday, 13 June 2026 as an obvious contender, not only because of the lucky-13 connection, but also because it would be the only Saturday in the whole year to fall on the 13th. Traditionally, couples prefer weekend weddings as they are more convenient for guests and generally allow for a more relaxed vibe. The year '26 also carried extra Easter-egg value, both as the sum of 13 + 13, and its link back to the couple announcing their engagement on 26 August. Although the mooted June date would only allow for around eight months of planning, it correlated with reports that Taylor and Travis were keen to move on apace – especially with mounting rumours over their hopes of becoming parents before too long. 'They don't want a long engagement,' an insider was quoted in *Us Weekly*. '[They] very much want to start a family in the next year or so. Family means everything to them.'

On the small matter of potential venues for their big day, Taylor's Rhode Island mansion at Watch Hill was initially the frontrunner – not least because it has its own private beachfront with sublime views over the Atlantic Ocean and Little Narragansett Bay. Taylor reportedly paid $17 million for the colonial-style property in 2013, with its eight bedrooms, large pool and more than 5 acres of grounds. Already known for hosting her famous Fourth of July parties – dubbed 'Taymerica' – the pad was reportedly undergoing renovations to the tune of $1.7 million throughout 2025, with a new bedroom suite, extra bathrooms and a modified kitchen all part of the upgrade. However, it was then suggested that Taylor and Travis were eyeing up an alternative venue nearby. The Breakers in Newport, also in Rhode Island, is one of the region's most spectacular estates, and once served as the summer home for the American socialite Cornelius Vanderbilt II. Completed in 1895, the 70-room property has soaring 50-foot ceilings, Italian-inspired gardens and crystal chandeliers so heavy they had to be hung from reinforced steel beams. Valued at some $400 million, the mansion is a National Historic Landmark and is today owned and operated by the Preservation Society of Newport County. It was alleged that another bride and groom who had booked the estate for a wedding on the same date were offered compensation to change their plans, but the society denied all such rumours. 'Taylor Swift is not getting married at the Breakers, or any other property the society runs,' it said in a statement.

Another historic property thought to be in the frame was Ocean House – a Victorian-style beach resort located virtually next door to Taylor's Watch Hill home. Boasting multiple lawns and ocean-front backdrops available for ceremonies, its wedding packages include optional extras like private yacht cruises, champagne towers, firework displays and, appealingly for any sunny afternoon spent toasting newlyweds, a Whispering Angel rosé cart.

With a seaside wedding seeming eminently possible, interiors and décor experts began forecasting a 'romantic coastal' theme, suggesting elements like driftwood, seashells, sea glass and linen fabrics to match Rhode Island's serene maritime setting. However, with the location far from confirmed, a destination further afield was also in contention, and Italy's Lake Como was mentioned by several media pundits. Taylor and Travis took a brief holiday there in May 2024 in between Eras shows, and they were believed to have fallen in love with the peaceful setting. Staying in a suite at the ultra-private, $20,000-per-night Villa Sola Cabiati, they enjoyed candlelit dinners on the terrace and took time to explore the pretty, arabesque gardens. And despite some unseasonal spring weather, they headed out for a rain-soaked boat ride across the lake, sipping champagne as they huddled together on board. They were so taken with their visit that it was reported they were considering snapping up a property on the shores of Como, where George and Amal Clooney have a lakeside home.

When actor George appeared as a special guest on the *New Heights* podcast in December 2025, he quizzed Travis about his and Taylor's trip there. 'Me and Tay danced around Lake Como for a little while. I loved it out there,' Travis said. Revealing that they enjoyed 'the best pasta you can imagine,' he also told how he refused to let his fitness regime slip during their short stay. 'Every morning, I was throwing my shoes on, running up and down the water,' he said. With the location clearly leaving a big impression on Travis, he added, 'We had gloomy days, we had beautiful days. Every single day was a new epic realisation of what's really around the world. I have never imagined that place in my dreams.'

During the same interview, Travis drilled down on claims that *Out of Sight* star George had not had an argument with human rights activist Amal in over a decade. 'Are you lying?' Travis joked. Amusingly, George responded, 'No, I'm not lying!' before turning the tables back on Travis. 'Should we ask *you* the same question?' he said brazenly. With barely a flicker of hesitation, Travis insisted he and Taylor had never had a tiff in their entire time together. 'Well it's only been two and a half years and you're right, I haven't gotten in an argument. Never once,' he said. When Jason Kelce chipped in, asking George what his secret to a tension-free marriage was, he replied, 'Dude, I'm 64 years old, what am I going to argue about at this point?'

The guest list has been another red-hot topic, with plenty of shoe-ins for an invite, including Gigi Hadid, Cara Delevingne, Florence Welch, Sabrina Carpenter, Zoë Kravitz, Gracie Abrams and Ice Spice. Other key members of Taylor's inner circle, such as Lana Del Rey, Emma Stone, Sophie Turner and the Haim sisters have also been widely tipped for a coveted spot, as well as the likes of Max Martin and Shellback, her long-serving publicist, Tree Paine, and actor Hugh Jackman. She once called the *Wolverine* star one of her 'best friends on the planet' after they met when she auditioned for the 2012 film *Les Misérables*. One couple who can clear their diary for the event are Jack Antonoff and wife, Margaret Qualley, whose New Jersey wedding Taylor attended back in 2023. Jack may, in fact, be hellbent on revenge after she teased him mercilessly in a 15-minute speech that *Page Six* dubbed a 'roast'. With a social circle spanning the entire entertainment industry, Taylor joked to chat-show host Graham Norton that she planned to invite 'anyone I've ever spoken to'. Insisting she wanted to avoid the stress of a small wedding where people end up being excluded, she said, 'You have to evaluate or assess your relationship with them to see if they should be there. I'm not going do that.'

That could be good news for Prince William and Princess Kate, also singled out as probable guests. As well as hobnobbing backstage at her London Eras show, William and Taylor memorably had an impromptu singsong together at a charity gala at Kensington Palace in 2013. During the event for the Centrepoint homeless organisation, she was sitting next to William when she persuaded him to join her and Jon Bon Jovi on stage for a surprise rendition of 'Livin' on a Prayer'. Though it may have seemed like a meticulously planned photo-opp, royal aides claimed it was entirely spontaneous, and William later recalled the evening with some degree of horror on the Apple Fitness+ series *Time to Walk*. 'To this day, I still do not know what came over me,' he said in the 2021 episode. 'Honestly, even now, I'm cringing at what happened next, and I don't understand why I gave in. But, frankly, if Taylor Swift looks you in the eye, touches your arm, and says, "Come with me ..." I got up like a puppy and went, "Yeah, okay, that seems like a great idea. I'll follow you."'

One person who was knocked for six after receiving an in-person invite from Taylor live on air was Radio 1 DJ Greg James. Though he'd known her for many years, he was yet to meet Travis – a fact they were discussing on his breakfast show. 'He's a really easy-going guy. You will absolutely love him when you meet him,' said Taylor. 'He's a real vibes guy.' Greg said he'd love to 'play catch' with Travis or have him 'do a wrestling move' on him, to which Taylor casually responded, 'He's going to do that as soon as he sees you at our wedding. That's gonna happen.' As her comment sank in, Greg threw his hands in the air and said, 'Woah, am I coming?' to which Taylor replied, 'Obviously.'

Much debate also ensued over bridesmaid and flower-girl candidates. Jason and Kylie Kelce's daughters, Wyatt, Elliotte, Bennett and Finnley, were thought to be leading the pack, and Taylor's closest friend from high-school days, Abigail Anderson, was said to be in the frame, too. It would be a fair swap, since Taylor was bridesmaid at her Martha's Vineyard wedding in September 2017. Her stylist pal, Ashley Avignone, was also suggested for a major supporting role, partly because the two have been inseparable for years. On Taylor's 30th birthday in 2019, Ashley wrote on Instagram, '30 years of life for you, 11 years of friendship for us. Thanks for being the bestest friend, listener, dance party-starter, story teller, haircut enthusiast, with the biggest, warmest, and most generous heart.' Back in 2021, Taylor was a brides-maid for Lena Dunham at her London wedding, so there were reports she might ask the *Girls* actress to return the favour. There were dozens of rumours around Selena Gomez being in the mix, too. Taylor attended the *Only Murders in the Building* star's wedding to music producer Benny Blanco in September 2025, and delivered a heartfelt speech at the Santa Barbara bash. Afterwards she said, 'Not just the most beautiful bride, just like the most beautiful thing I've ever seen. I'm just so happy, and she deserves it so much.' Selena then posted photos of her and Taylor from her happy day, writing, 'Blessed to have you by my side almost 20 years later gator! I love you.'

On the groom's side, Travis's teammate Patrick Mahomes, his wife, Brittany, and other Chiefs stars, like Chris Jones, Mecole Hardman and coach Andy Reid, were said to be dead certs for the wedding. Also destined for an invite were his personal chef, Kumar Ferguson, and childhood best pal, Aric Jones, plus ex-Chiefs player Ross Travis. Naturally, Jason Kelce was instantly touted as best man; speaking on the *Bussin' with the Boys* podcast he admitted he was more than keen for the job. 'Hopefully, I'm the best man. We'll see,' he said. 'Trav has a lot of friends, I'm just hoping to get the opportunity.'

Travis himself showed he was unfazed about the wedding planning, telling TV host Jimmy Fallon it was 'gonna be easy', and that he just had to 'figure out winning football games first'. Appearing on *New Heights*, Jimmy asked if he and Taylor would prefer a DJ or a band to get guests up on their feet. 'I think we're live-music kind of people, you know?' Travis said.' Of course, one of the musicians linked with filling that brief was Taylor's old friend Ed Sheeran. When she was chatting on Hits Radio to promote the release of *The Life of a Showgirl*, she told host Fleur East, 'He's like, "I'm always being asked to sing at weddings," and you're like, "Ed, if there's a stage, you know that you'll be on it!"'

When it came to Taylor's all-important dress, style insiders had much to say about which designer would be assigned the once-in-a-lifetime responsibility. Ralph Lauren seemed to be in pole position, but some suggested Taylor would opt for a gown by Elie Saab, one of her go-to outfitters. That would certainly make sense, since the Lebanese designer provided two bridal-inspired gowns for her Eras tour – including one with white florals and a sequinned bodice. Others felt a more likely choice was the late British great Vivienne Westwood, whose creations also featured in the Eras shows. Taylor has often worn her vintage couture for awards shows and red-carpet events, and trend-setting Charli xcx, Demi Lovato and Miley Cyrus all wore Westwood gowns at their weddings. Oscar de la Renta was floated as a strong possibility, too, and as the *Standard* said of the

American designer, 'Lace overlays, floral appliqué, perhaps even a nod to the woodland fantasy of *evermore*. It is bridal-wear at its most romantic, and it would not feel out of place for a woman who has spent much of her career reimagining the concept of the modern princess.' Taking a bolder view, iconic designer Vera Wang suggested that Taylor may opt for multiple dresses. 'I don't think there'll be just one,' she told *E! News*. 'That'd be my guess.' With no definitive answers, bridal specialists enjoyed sketching out their own visions of what Taylor could wear to walk down the aisle, with lace and corsetry featuring prominently, as well as crystals and celestial motifs to reflect her love of stories and romance.

Across platforms like Pinterest, Instagram and TikTok, a new trend was born, with Swifties creating mood boards, collages and Reels that dreamed up every conceivable wedding detail – from the dress and décor to colour palettes and floral schemes. Some of the more imaginative ideas included personalised friendship bracelets that would also direct guests to their seats, a wedding guestbook made from vinyl records, and a punchy cocktail list with drinks named after songs like 'You Need to Calm Down' and 'Look What You Made Me Do'. Other fans spent hours designing mock-ups of everything from the invites to seating plans, as well as Taylor's bridal hair and make-up, wedding favours and even hen-party accessories. Far from a simple wedding, it began to feel like a cultural spectacle that everyone could lean into and help script.

But of course, all the conjecture, hype and hearsay were jumping the gun by anyone's standards. That was made abundantly clear when Graham Norton asked Taylor, as she sat on his esteemed red sofa, if she had begun making any plans at all. 'No, I just am doing the album thing now, which is a big thing,' she replied honestly. 'And then I think the wedding is what happens after that in the scheme of the planning, but I'm so excited about it.' She gave the same impression on Scott Mills's Radio 2 breakfast show when he asked if she would be hiring a wedding planner. 'I'm doing one thing at a time,' she told him. 'Right now, I'm just stoked about the idea that I get to marry this person. So I'm going to think about that, and then I'm going to put out this album, and then I'm going to think about other things after that.' In interviews, she seemed keen to point out that she had not, as some might have assumed, been planning her wedding since she was five years old. 'You'd think I'd be the type of person who would have obsessed over the idea of a wedding my whole life,' she said on *Heart Breakfast*. 'But I actually never thought about what I would do, what I would want, until I met the person.' While that person was undoubtedly Travis, she was at pains to show there was no need to rush full steam ahead with anything. Before any of that, her music would do the talking – and, it turns out, it had plenty to get off its chest.

CHAPTER TEN

Some 51 days after it was first announced, *The Life of a Showgirl* finally crash-landed on 3 October 2025, instantly bathing social feeds in an orange-and-turquoise glow. In the US, where the release was timed for midnight eastern time, fans congregated in bars and clubs for listening parties and vinyl unboxings, many dressed in fringed flapper dresses and feathers, to match the album's cabaret aesthetic. Newly crafted friendship bracelets were exchanged in their thousands, and themed cocktails with names like 'Ophelia's Juice' and 'Showgirl Slushy' fuelled the dancing long into the night. In the UK, fans set their alarms for 5am to wake up to the release, and similar patterns were seen across international time zones. In Australia, lunchtime gatherings brought menu choices like 'Eggs (Taylor's Version)', and in Asia, *Showgirl*-based afternoon teas were quite the thing. Ensuring all Swifties could feel part of the action, mass global online listening parties were also organised by Taylor's official social team, Taylor Nation. There was even a big-screen launch event, with *The Official Release Party of a Showgirl* film premiering at more than 8,000 cinemas globally on release day. The 89-minute film, which had a limited three-day run, featured lyric videos, behind-the-scenes footage and personal song commentary from Taylor, as well as the video premiere for lead single, 'The Fate of Ophelia'. 'I hereby invite you to a dazzling soirée,' she said by way of introduction, and many fans – having already learned all the words – sang along ecstatically to every frame.

Marking a sharp gear change, *The Life of a Showgirl* veered away from the confession and introspection of *Tortured Poets*, swapping heartbreak for pure, unadulterated pop. Standing as the very epitome of her self-christened 'Glitter Gel Pen' genre, it was as buoyant as she had ever sounded. Taylor told how Eras was the driving force behind the album's carefree spirit, saying in the accompanying film, 'The way that that tour felt, the way it lit up my whole life, was such a through line for making this music. So thank you for being that unknowing inspiration. Behind the scenes, I was internalising all that love and putting it into that record.' Working with Swedish producers Max Martin and Shellback for the entirety of the album and recording with them during tour gaps, she said their reunion 'felt like catching lightning in a bottle'. It had been several years since they last collaborated, and she said, 'By the time we came back together, I feel like we had so much more dexterity to what we do. This was the time where it felt like all three of us in the room were carrying the same weight as creators and it was really special.' At just 41 minutes in length, *The Life of a Showgirl* was her shortest album since her 2006 debut, and having decided she wanted a different sound, it was her first record in over a decade not to feature production by Jack Antonoff. Incredibly, though, she kept the whole thing secret from Republic Records until it was completed. 'The label didn't know at all until the record was done, and we had made, and we'd shot all of the art, we'd done everything,' she told Scott Mills on Radio 2. 'I think it's fun to surprise them, honestly, it's really fun.'

Stylistically, she wanted the album to align with the characteristics of a showgirl, which she described as 'mischievous, fun, scandalous, sexy, fun, flirty, hilarious'. During an intense run of promo activity that began the day the album launched, she reiterated to Apple Music's Zane Lowe that this was a record she had long dreamed of making. 'I have always wanted to have fun in this type of way,' she said. 'To exhibit mischief and be flirty, and fun, and make jokes, and get to have that side of my personality. That's a huge part of my personality.' The shift in tone was clearly inspired by her happiness with Travis, and his larger-than-life energy directly influenced the exuberance of the album's 12 songs. He even had an indirect role in shaping *Showgirl*'s development, with

Taylor revealing she played him clips whenever she returned from recording sessions in Sweden. 'As soon as I got back, I would play it. I knew that this was the kind of album that he was going to love the most,' she told Greg James on Radio 1. Speaking to *Heart Breakfast* presenters Emma Bunton and Jamie Theakston, she admitted just how much Travis had infiltrated the songs. 'This person came into my life, and everybody's like, "Yeah, you've never been so you,"' she said. 'I think that comes through in music. People who fuel you, they fuel every part of you, and they make you walk taller, and they make you present in a more vibrant way and so hopefully that bleeds into the music, too.'

From the outset, fans and critics alike pored over the lyrics, keen to prise out every possible Kelce-shaped allusion. Few can have been disappointed on that front, and album opener 'The Fate of Ophelia' kicked straight off with a portrayal of Travis as the man who saved Taylor from the tragic end that befell Shakespeare's heroine in *Hamlet*. Just as she did with her Romeo-and-Juliet-inflected song 'Love Story' some 17 years earlier, Taylor rewrote the tale so that it ended well for Ophelia, and not in a catastrophic drowning. 'I fall in love with those characters so much that it hurts me that they die,' she said in her making-of film. 'I'm just kind of putting this romantic spin on the fact that Ophelia was driven mad; they drove her mad – but not me.' *The Life of a Showgirl*'s cover art made subtle reference to Ophelia, too, with Taylor partially submerged in water. In the song's video, she also re-enacted the classic 1850s' painting by artist John Everett Millais of Ophelia, lying in a pool of water in a long white dress. Written and directed by Taylor herself, the opulent video saw her playing showgirls from different eras and, as some of her most impressive choreography to date, it spawned a whole new TikTok craze. Even Travis was seen doing the video's dance as he scored his 100th career touchdown against the Washington Commanders.

Taylor also revealed there were a whopping 100 Easter eggs in the four-minute clip, including a shot of her catching a football in honour of Travis. It was a move that was evidently most *un*-Taylor-like, and when the production crew asked whether she preferred to catch the ball on her right or left, she humorously replied, 'I don't know, I've never caught a ball!' Another sequence took place in hotel room 87, again invoking his Chiefs identity. Their combined number of 100 was namechecked, too, and the lyrics described him using a megaphone to broadcast his public declaration about wanting to meet her. Observant viewers additionally spotted a small black-and-white photo of Travis pinned to a dressing-room mirror in one scene. Another Easter egg conjured up Taylor's real-life sourdough passion via a loaf of bread on a pedestal, while on a more poetic note, an orange bird was seen perched on her hand before flying away. It was thought to hark back to Taylor's 'Look What You Made Me Do' video, when she swung inside a gilded birdcage, wearing an orange outfit. Fast forward eight years and the bird had at last been freed. One of the most puzzling motifs were two green emergency exit signs which top and tailed the video. Despite inducing minor fears in some fans that it could signify a dramatic goodbye, the wider assumption was that the signs symbolised her exit from the old part of her life and her entry into a bright, new phase. Her marriage era, no less. 'She has exited from the game; she has found her match,' said one fan on a Facebook thread. Another Easter egg in the video's final scene took the form of an opal stone, which neatly cross-referenced the album's third song – 'Opalite'. The track was an equally Travis-centric slice of pure pop, viewed through a spectrum of healing and growth. 'Travis loves it,' Taylor told Jordan North on his *Capital Breakfast* show. 'I think that's his favourite.' Explaining how she had 'always fixated' on opals, she added, 'I've always loved that stone and I thought it was a kinda cool metaphor that like, it's a manmade opal. And happiness can also be manmade.' Travis confirmed his liking of the song on *New Heights*, telling his brother, Jason, 'I think "Opalite" might be my favourite … Every time it comes on, I always catch myself.' And of the album overall he said, 'It's just so much fun to listen to, man. I've been dancing throughout the house.'

Other songs with an overt Kelce connection included 'Wi$h Li$t', in which Taylor vowed that a life centred around marriage and kids would be far more valuable to her than any material riches. 'When I met Travis, I started to feel a little bit like I could be the person who could have romantic whims and have these dreams,' she told Zane Lowe on Apple Music. 'The song "Wi$h Li$t" is me just describing what my happy place is.' She elaborated further on *Heart Breakfast*, saying, 'There's a line in a song that says, you just wanted a best friend who you think is hot – and that's kind of it.' When Taylor was asked by NBC to name her favourite track on the record, she replied, 'I think it might be "Wi$h Li$t." It was actually the last song that we made for the album, and it was the song where, after we finished it, I was like, "Oh, we're done. We're good."'

The track 'Wood' caused mild hysteria among Swifties who quickly realised it was Taylor's most sexually explicit song ever. The cheeky lyrics saw her reflect on being unlucky in love until she discovered Travis – and more pertinently, his manhood. The meaning was barely concealed under lyrical references to redwood trees and knocking on wood, but Taylor attempted to play it down in her *Official Release Party of a Showgirl* film. She insisted the track was 'about superstitions ... black cats, stepping on cracks, things like that', but after a momentary pause, she gave a coy smile to camera which had cinemagoers giggling into their popcorn. A little less saucy but packed with meaning, the track 'Elizabeth Taylor' explored the pressures of fame and scrutiny, and Taylor's overriding hope that she and Travis could withstand them. It also drew parallels between her life and that of the late Hollywood starlet and, as she said on *The Tonight Show Starring Jimmy Fallon*, 'I just wanted to make a song that felt as luxurious and glamorous as she was.' Then there was the song 'Honey', which highlighted the different ways in which language can be used. 'Words that have been meant to hurt you in the past can be repurposed by someone who loves you in a way that feels totally different,' she said in an album run-through with Amazon Music. As she pointed out, when Travis calls her 'Honey', it is never in a 'passive-aggressive, evil, critical way', but instead 'feels great'.

Not every song was about Travis, though, and 'Actually Romantic' was seen as the album's core diss track. Taylor called it 'a love letter to someone who hates you', and the internet and everyone on it decided it had to be about the singer Charli xcx. The pair had supposedly been estranged for years after Charli said in a 2019 interview that opening for Taylor on her Reputation stadium tour felt like 'getting up on stage and waving to five-year-olds'. She later apologised, but things escalated in 2024 with Charli's song 'Sympathy Is a Knife', which listeners believed was dismissive of Taylor's relationship with Matty Healy – a bandmate of Charli's now-husband, George Daniel. Charli denied it, saying the song was about 'my feelings and my anxiety', but when 'Actually Romantic' landed, it was framed as a countermove by Taylor. In a step that seemed to be very much turning the tables, it saw her singing about someone who appeared resentful, but still kept talking and thinking about her. There was no confirmation of who the track really was about, but Taylor said cryptically, 'In this industry, attention is affection and you've given me a lot of it so ... mwah.'

'Actually Romantic' skewered professional rivalry, but the song 'Cancelled!' offered an acerbic take on reclaiming social outrage. Partly thought to have been prompted by Taylor's falling out with Blake Lively, it was a defiant anthem that showed how conflict can be transformed into control. 'I wanted to write a song about how you can become wiser for it and you can become sharper, and I definitely judge people a lot less now that I've been kind of under the microscope for so long,' she said in her album release film. Elsewhere on the album, the George-Michael-inspired 'Father Figure' was thought to be a take on Taylor's difficult relationship with former label boss Scott Borchetta, while the poignant 'Ruin the Friendship' was believed to be a tribute to her late school friend Jeff Lang, who passed away in 2010. It saw her wishing she had risked the friendship for a chance of a relationship, rather than experiencing regret that would last forever. 'It was exploring that idea of like, was it so consequential?' she said. 'Would it have been so crazy if you were younger and you just took some chances that you didn't take?'

Falling right at the end of the album, rousing title track, 'The Life of a Showgirl' with Sabrina Carpenter, served as the ideal curtain call. Taylor had known there was only one person she wanted to duet with, and when she asked her to do it, Sabrina's reaction was, 'Are you kidding? I'm dead. Yes, of course.' In a sign of her commitment, she spent her well-earned days off from touring in the studio. 'And that is a showgirl for you,' said Taylor in the making-of film. Their duet told the story of a fictional showgirl called Kitty who found herself paying the price of a life on stage, and Taylor explained that it was a metaphor for the music industry and a 'manifesto of how I've had to operate'. Speaking to Jimmy Fallon, she revealed exactly why she wanted to partner with Sabrina. 'She's such a funny person, she's tough in the right ways, and soft and vulnerable in the right ways.' She felt Sabrina knew how to deal with the 'absolute mayhem' that artists are subjected to, and added, 'I kind of wrote it for her.' Having long been nicknamed 'Taybrina' by the fandom due to their ever-strengthening bond, the coming together of the two friends conveyed a genuine sense of solidarity, as well as hope for the future. Just as the *Independent* stated, the grand finale served to unite them 'in shimmering harmony as Swift symbolically takes a bow and hands the spotlight to the next generation'.

On an artistic level, *The Life of a Showgirl* was a veritable tour de force, with the artwork, marketing and visuals fully leaning into the outrageous glitz and glamour of the genre. The flamboyant styling was brought to life by fashion photographers Mert and Marcus, who were also behind the imagery for Taylor's *reputation* album. Following an 'extraordinary' photoshoot, which saw her wearing designer headdresses, bedazzled bras, sparkly bodices and even a dress made of chainmail, she decided to max out what they released. 'I just wanted the fans to have as many images from this sort of world, this album era, as possible,' she said. 'We chose this really high-gloss finish which I've never done before, and I think it looks so cool. We wanted this album to feel really luxurious and kind of as a nod to the luxury that a showgirl puts on when she's on stage.' The album rollout was even more dynamic, with a bewildering array of 27 physical formats – including multiple vinyl colourways, collectible CDs and limited-edition cassettes – some with extras like posters, jewellery and photo cards. Though the choice was unprecedented, not everyone embraced the strategy and Taylor faced accusations of commercial excess and even of exploitative behaviour. Yet others felt the variations were a key part of the album's immersive and theatrical experience, and as with her previous releases, she was praised for helping generate record-breaking physical sales and revitalising parts of the music industry that had been decimated by digital streaming.

Wherever you were in the world, there was no escaping the album's deployment, and after 2023's *Barbie* pink craze and the lurid green Brat summer of 2024, autumn 2025 belonged resolutely to *Showgirl* orange. Brands of every kind scrambled to ride the trend, with Dunkin' Donuts trading its classic logo for a sparkly orange version, its caption crowing, 'We've always been in our orange era'. Official partner, Spotify, led a three-day pop-up at High Line Nine in New York, where fans entered through a giant orange door to explore theatrical sets, Easter-egg installations and flower-filled bathtubs reminiscent of 'The Fate of Ophelia'. The campaign also saw lyrics projected on to billboards in New York, LA, London, São Paulo and Las Vegas. Keeping the orange theme ablaze, KitchenAid released a limited-edition 'Tangerine Twinkle' mixer, with only 12 made, to tie in with it being Taylor's 12th album. Krispy Kreme also saw commemorative boxes of a dozen orange-glazed doughnuts fly off the shelves, at $12 a pop.

Another album partner was TikTok, and the platform hosted a month-long series of events and missions. These included a pop-up at LA's Westfield Century City mall, where fans could step into Taylor's cinematic world, courtesy of dressing-room sets and a theatre backdrop. In Nashville,

Starbucks created a temporary 'Showgirl Starbies' branch, complete with a record shop, friendship-bracelet station and glitter-sprinkled coffee. One of the quirkiest activations came from Uber Eats, which launched a 'Showcats' initiative to reflect Taylor's feline passion and famed 'childless cat lady' persona. The adoption event helped rehome 28 cats and attracted more than 1,000 visitors, who were invited to make their own jewelled cat collars and, of course, snap cute selfies with the kitties. Collectively, these collaborations once again blurred the line between marketing and fandom, transforming *Showgirl*'s launch into an all-out cultural carnival and sacred communal experience.

The hype was off the scale, but whether *The Life of a Showgirl* truly lived up to it remains one of the most debated questions of Taylor's career. Though many lauded the record as her boldest reinvention yet, others dismissed it as all spectacle and no substance. Some critics felt its Travis-tinged sentiment was a hollow diversion, but on the flipside, it was argued that Taylor had never sounded lighter, freer or more genuinely joyful. The reviews varied wildly as a consequence, with *Rolling Stone* seeming most enamoured of all, devoting its first ever 'homepage takeover' entirely to the album. It also issued a five-star rating that said Taylor had 'reached a whole new artistic and personal peak'. *Variety* was similarly effusive, saying it was 'contagiously joyful' and that 'nobody does it better, now or at any recent time, when it comes to delivering world-dominating pop'. *Billboard* hailed its 'wall-to-wall bangers', and despite calling the album 'one of her most uneven', the *Independent* still found Taylor 'as compelling as she's ever been'. The *New York Times* described it as a 'catchy and substantive but unflashy album', while *Pitchfork* was a little underwhelmed, saying, '*Showgirl* sounds like much of the pop music you have heard over the past 10 years and throughout your lifetime.' Worse came from the *Guardian,* which branded *Showgirl* 'dull razzle-dazzle from a star who seems frazzled'. In particular, the Travis-imbued song 'Wood' was lambasted for its steamy undertones, with the review stating that it amounted to 'weak writing from someone who made her name, at least in part, by being a sharper, wittier, more incisive lyricist than her peers'.

In a similar vein, a minority wondered if Taylor's provocative showgirl costumes were a departure too far from her more modest image of old – which she had always seemed proud to uphold. In 2015 she told the *Washington Post,* 'It's fine, I've accepted it. I'm a lot of things, overtly sexy is not one of them.' But even sympathetic critics – particularly females who were wary of policing another woman's choices – suggested that the raunchiness of *Showgirl* felt slightly at odds with Taylor's long-cultivated girl-next-door persona. A writer in *The Times* wrestled with just such tension, saying, 'While I'm all for women celebrating their sexuality, particularly if they've been relentlessly slut-shamed for most of their adult and teenage lives, I can't help but feel that this sultry new era is out of sync with everything Swift has told us about who she is: the one we can relate to rather than look up to, the goofy best friend rather than the unapproachable hot girl, the one in the bleachers rather than the cheer captain.'

The Swifties' reaction to *Showgirl* was unusually polarising, too. On social media, many were absolutely convinced it was among her best work ever. 'One of Taylor's most self-aware and emotionally layered projects,' claimed a rapt listener. 'Christmas morning vibes,' another said. 'Her happiness shines through so beautifully on this album,' enthused one fan. But the glowing praise could not temper the disappointment expressed by others – or the grief over what some saw as a decline in the quality of Taylor's songwriting. 'There's no way the woman who wrote *folklore* wrote these lyrics,' said a TikTok user. Equally disheartened, one fan lamented a 'distinct lack of yearning on this record', and another said, 'Not bad, not great, just ... serviceable'. The term 'rare misstep' was shared on several forums, and 'boring and basic' was one especially harsh verdict.

Such discussions could have raged for an eternity – and are probably still smouldering in the far reaches of the Swiftiverse today. But whatever anyone thought of *The Life of a Showgirl*, musically or otherwise, Taylor was willing to hear it. 'I welcome the chaos,' she told Zane Lowe on Apple Music. 'The rule of show business is if it's the first week of my album release, and you are saying either my name or my album title, you're helping.' She also welcomed the wider debate around music and performance more generally. 'I have a lot of respect for people's subjective opinions on art – I'm not the art police. Everybody is allowed to feel exactly how they want and what our goal is as entertainers is to be a mirror.' It was clear in that moment that Taylor's skin had become thicker than it once was – no doubt through necessity; but the less-than-universal adulation for *Showgirl* certainly did not put her off. 'I'm playing for keeps,' she added. 'I have such an eye on legacy when I'm making my music – I know what I made, I know I adore it.'

At any rate, the commercial impact of *The Life of a Showgirl* served as the ultimate 'up yours' to her detractors. The album didn't just sell by the bucketload and dominate charts across the world, but in Taylor's unrivalled way, it steamrolled its way into the annals of history. As well as being the fastest-selling album in America ever, it set new single-day streaming records across Spotify, Apple Music and Amazon Music, and it was 2025's bestselling album on iTunes. Securing Taylor her 15th No. 1 album on the *Billboard* 200 – the most for any solo artist – the album tracks also occupied the top 12 spots of the *Billboard* Hot 100, led by 'The Fate of Ophelia'. In the UK, the album logged the biggest open-ing week of Taylor's career, and as well as becoming her 14th No. 1, it was the fastest-selling UK vinyl debut since modern records began in the 1990s. 'What an incredible week for Taylor Swift,' said the Official Charts' chief executive, Martin Talbot, in a statement. 'Taylor is bigger than she has ever been in the UK – and shows absolutely no sign of letting up.' The figures were all the more impressive with album sales in perpetual decline, providing the strongest possible vindi-cation for her decision to release so many different variants of the record. Still, even she seemed surprised at *Showgirl's* impact, and writing on Instagram after a colossal 4 million copies were either bought or streamed in the US, she said, 'I have 4 million thank yous I want to send to the fans, and 4 million reasons to feel even more proud of this album than I already was. Thank you for going out to celebrate this project in the movie theatres, investing in vinyl, streaming, watching the video, buying CDs, reading the poems I wrote inside the packaging, and immersing yourselves in The Life of a Showgirl. I'll cherish this feeling forever. Just wow.'

On 12 December, the day before her 36th birthday, Taylor's next venture was poised to deliver an early burst of festive sparkle, with two new Eras-related projects set to roll out on Disney+. In addition to a six-episode, behind-the-scenes docu-series, *The End of an Era*, a full-length concert film called *The*

Final Show was to bring the last night of the tour in Vancouver – AKA 'Swiftcouver' – to the small screen. Announcing the double whammy on Instagram, she told fans, 'It was the End of an Era and we knew it. We wanted to remember every moment leading up to the culmination of the most important and intense chapter of our lives, so we allowed filmmakers to capture this tour and all the stories woven throughout it as it wound down. And to film the final show in its entirety.' Within the first hour, her post gathered 1.5 million likes, and in a tantalising trailer for the docuseries, she and Travis were seen kissing backstage and practising the eye-opening moment he carried her across the Wembley stage. The teaser clip also included childhood footage of Taylor and guest cameos from the likes of Ed Sheeran, Sabrina Carpenter and Florence Welch, while it was also revealed that the *Tortured Poets* section of the show would feature for the first time. As Taylor said in the trailer, 'We broke every single record you can break with this tour. The only thing left is to close the book.' The announcement on her Taylor Nation Instagram account prompted a heady blend of excitement and nostalgia, though some clearly had mixed feelings about the finality of it all. 'So this is where the exit signs have been leading us,' posted one follower. 'Taylor talking about closing this book makes me very emotional,' said another. 'I knew this day would come, but it's still bittersweet.' Still, as one final flourish, it seemed like the most fitting legacy for the Eras age – a welcome gift and a tender goodbye rolled into one.

Following Taylor's conquering every chart, stadium and record imaginable, there has been great intrigue over her plans for 2026 and beyond. As it stands, she appears to have ruled out any large-scale tours for the foreseeable, telling Radio 1's Greg James, 'I'm gonna be really honest with you. I am so tired, when I think about doing it again. I would want to do it really well again, you know?' She stressed that since she was last on the road, she has come to rediscover old parts of herself. 'My joints are good. I bake, I have hobbies again,' she said, before referring to Eras as 'two years of just having no other hobbies'. But that's not to say she has any intention of easing off from writing or recording songs, and suggestions that married life with Travis might affect her professional output understandably hit a raw nerve. Asked on *The Scott Mills Breakfast Show* on Radio 2 if there was any truth to fan speculation that *Showgirl* could be her final album, she was visibly horrified. 'That's a shockingly offensive thing to say,' she fumed. 'That's not why people get married – so they can quit their job.' When Scott said he thought 'the fans were just panicking', and that their concerns came from a good place, she agreed. 'They love to panic sometimes.' But she insisted there would be no slowdown in her work rate, largely because

Travis was so supportive of her career. 'I love the person I am with him because he loves what I do and he loves how much I am fulfilled by making art and making music,' she said. 'There's no point in time where he's going to be like, "I'm really upset that you're still making the music."' The fact Taylor was even having to fend off such nonsensical rumours was obviously one of the most frustrating byproducts of her engagement to Travis. As the *Guardian* so effectively put it, 'Music critics are already gloomily debating whether marriage will kill her creativity, or whether she'll be left for dust by one of the younger rivals already nipping at her heels if she does take time out from music to have the children she's always said she wanted. Poor Taylor, mummy-tracked before she's even pregnant.' It was a moment that exposed the rampant sexism at play – why should a female pop icon disappear just because she chooses to marry, when presumably, a male star would never be subject to the same kind of appraisal?

Of course, conversations around motherhood need not be reductive, and Taylor has long spoken about wanting a family one day. Since the engagement announcement, fans have wondered when they might feasibly hear the pitter-patter of little 'Tayvis' feet, and thankfully, most view the prospect of them starting a family as an organic next step, rather than an existential threat to her career. 'I want a bunch of [children] running around, minimum four,' Taylor said when she was still in her early twenties. 'The idea of pouring everything you are into another person when you become a parent has always been amazing to me.' Travis is said to be equally keen to have children, and his brother, Jason, has called him an 'outstanding uncle' to Wyatt, Elliotte, Bennett and Finnley. Speaking on *New Heights* in February 2025, Jason told how they were in 'the thick of it' in terms of parenting, and Travis joked that he was looking forward to having 'fun with those girls and handing them right back to you'. Jason replied, 'That's the benefit of the uncle, Uncle Travi ... Travis has great advice.' In video footage of Travis chatting away to his young niece Wyatt on Instagram, his natural ease and warmth were almost too much for some fans to bear. 'Ugh my ovaries,' posted one, and another said, 'Uncle Travi looks like the best funcle'. Taylor has shown an affinity with the four girls, too, and on *New Heights* she revealed how she bonded with them after introducing them to her cats. 'As soon as I got the kids around the cats, it was my goal to prove to them that they weren't poisonous,' she said. 'And there's no better way to prove that than to just hand them Benjamin, my rag-doll cat, who lets humans hold him like he's a baby.'

For now, though, any talk of parenthood remains part of the longer vision. Between their thriving careers and a slate of new projects on the horizon, Taylor and Travis already have more than enough to keep them busy. For starters,

2026 marks 20 years since the release of Taylor's self-titled debut album, which arrived in October 2006. Many believe an anniversary version could surface to mark the milestone. 'I've already re-recorded my entire debut album,' she revealed in May 2025. 'And I really love how it sounds now.' She hinted the project – along with a long-awaited re-recording of *reputation* – would have 'a moment to re-emerge when the time is right'. Though with Taylor at last having ownership of her masters such re-recordings are no longer required, the symbolic pull of going back to where it all began may prove too strong to resist. With much of *Showgirl* written in 2024, fans also suspect work on her next album – her 13th, no less – is already under way, especially as Taylor has often said she never stops composing new material. 'Writing songs is my life's work and my hobby and my never-ending thrill,' she said in a speech in Nashville in 2022.

Another creative prospect lies in a planned feature film debut for Searchlight Pictures, for which Taylor wrote the script. She is expected to direct the project, too, and this will position her not just as a performer but as a fully fledged film-maker. After its initial announcement in 2022, Searchlight presidents David Greenbaum and Matthew Greenfield said in a statement: 'Taylor is a once-in-a-generation artist and story-teller. It is a genuine joy and privilege to collaborate with her as she embarks on this exciting and new creative journey.'

Since his *Saturday Night Live* triumph in 2023, Travis has also been dipping a toe into the world of film and TV, and he made a noteworthy leap into drama, care of Ryan Murphy's Disney+ horror *Grotesquerie*. Appearing as a hospital orderly called Eddie in the 2024 series, his performance won solid reviews, but when Jason told him he had 'killed it' on *New Heights*, Travis was a little bashful. 'I can't watch it; I can't even listen to it,' he said. During filming, he had also told Jason it was a major step outside his comfort zone. 'I feel like an amateur, but I haven't gotten fired yet,' he said at the time. 'I'm just taking it scene by scene and making sure I remember my lines.' In October 2024, Travis went on to front the quiz show *Are You Smarter Than a Celebrity?* on Prime Video. 'I never in a million years thought I was ever going to be an actual host of a gameshow,' he said on the brothers' podcast. But he admitted being 'terrified' about the prospect, revealing he threw himself into doing extra prep because he was 'a terrible reader'.

With his reputation in the entertainment industry growing, Travis was brought in as executive producer of the indie film *My Dead Friend Zoe,* which premiered at the South by Southwest Festival in Austin, Texas in March 2025. The comedy drama, starring Morgan Freeman and Ed Harris, told the story of an army vet, played by Sonequa Martin-Green, dealing with PTSD after the death of a fellow soldier. It was ranked by *Variety* as one of its ten best films of the year, and *Deadline Hollywood* called it 'a powerful testament to the resilience of the human spirit'. Travis described his producing role as 'an incredible experience', and added, 'My hope is to continue working on meaningful projects like this – stories that entertain, inspire and make a real impact.' The director, Kyle Hausmann-Stokes, said Travis brought 'a tidal wave of energy' to the film, while producer Paul Scanlan was also full of praise. 'He's such a likeable guy and he's a good actor,' he told *People*. 'He's a good producer ... he made a difference to our project.'

Travis then got a chance to appear on the opposite side of the camera in *Happy Gilmore 2*, which hit Netflix in the summer of 2025. His role as a waiter in the sports comedy was written especially for him after Adam Sandler watched his show-stealing hosting gig on *Saturday Night Live* in 2023. Though the film was largely panned by critics, Travis called his film debut 'a dream come true'. Speaking on *The Pat McAfee Show*, he said, 'I thought SNL was going to be the peak of my acting and showman or entertainment career ... Working with Happy Gilmore himself, the Sandman and Happy Productions, it was off the chain.' Adam returned the compliment in an interview with *Entertainment Tonight*: 'Travis is such a gentle, nice guy, and funny as hell. He's like the guys I grew up with,' he said. 'It reminded me of my buddies in high school and just being able to laugh and say the things you want to say.' Meanwhile, director Kyle Newacheck singled out Travis's 'natural charisma', and said of his performance, 'Kelce was fantastic ... He's a hard worker, and he wanted to do right by the film.' In one surreal dream sequence that got some viewers frantically reaching for the rewind button, Travis was seen stripped to the waist as he was tied to a pole and smeared in honey by rapper Bad Bunny, who played a rival waiter. The scene was apparently appreciated by Taylor, too, who added a sneaky honey emoji to an Instagram Story saying, '*Happy Gilmore 2* had me cackling and cheering the whole movie! An absolute must watch.'

Stepping into the bright lights of Hollywood might not seem like an obvious next move for someone who has spent over a decade immersed in NFL, but it's a transition Travis appears eager to embrace. After 13 seasons with the Chiefs, talk of him retiring from football has been gathering pace, and he seems intent on proving that his charisma and discipline can translate just as well to a film set as to game day. After scoring his 100th touchdown back in October 2025, he told a TV reporter, 'I'm just the old lucky dog, still able to do this thing. I'm putting on the pads like I'm 15 years old again, I'm loving every single bit of it.' But a decade older than the average NFL player, he also admitted earlier in the year that 'football only lasts for so long'. And when asked in November 2023 if he thought about life after the game, he replied, 'More than anyone could ever imagine ... The discomfort. The pain. The lingering injuries – the ten surgeries I've had that I still feel to this day.'

Travis's confidence took a knock, too, after the bruising Super Bowl defeat to the Philadelphia Eagles in February 2025, and he admitted suffering 'wear and tear' on both body and mind. As questions around his retirement gained momentum, he told Jason on *New Heights*, 'I'm kicking every can I can down the road. I'm not making any crazy decisions.' Mid-season, Travis seemed hopeful of at least getting to one more Super Bowl. Asked by actor Keanu Reeves on *New Heights* who would win the big prize in 2026, Travis showed no trace of hesitation. 'The Kansas City Chiefs are rolling right now, big guy,' he said. 'That's all I have to say.' However, after a run of defeats in the ensuing weeks, the Chiefs were eliminated from the all-important play-offs in December. As Taylor watched on nervously from the family's private box at Arrowhead, the team narrowly lost to the Los Angeles Chargers, brutally ending the prospect of Travis earning a fourth Super Bowl win with his beloved team.

For many months, it seemed that Taylor might even play the prestigious 2026 Super Bowl halftime show, following in the footsteps of acts like Beyoncé, Lady Gaga, the late Prince and Michael Jackson. But she eventually closed the rumours down, saying she couldn't imagine performing during a stressful game that Travis could potentially be competing in. Explaining the dilemma she faced to Jimmy Fallon, she said, 'He would love for me to do it,' before adding, 'I am in love with a guy who does that sport on that actual field. The whole season, I am locked in on what that man is doing.' Bad Bunny was booked for the slot in the end, but the smart money is still on Taylor agreeing to the illustrious gig in future years. 'We would always love to have Taylor play,' NFL commissioner Roger Goodell told *Today*. 'She is a special, special talent, and obviously she would be welcome at any time.'

Few artists have the luxury of being able to call the shots and dictate their own terms in quite the same way, but as we have seen, Taylor has spent years earning it. Her imprint on modern life is such that she is no longer just a performer and songwriter, but a global force whose influence ripples through entire industries and populations. As sports-and-pop-culture website *The Ringer* observed in 2024, 'So much of the Taylor Swift phenomenon is how woven she is into the fabric of people's lives. Families with multiple generations of fans. Inside jokes that work for an audience of millions. She's a reference, she's a punchline, she's a historical text.' Even as far back as 2014, a striking *Bloomberg Businessweek* front cover summed up her reach with a clarity that still holds true 12 years later. 'Taylor Swift IS the music industry,' it declared. Such a grand statement was no gushing exaggeration, and when Taylor topped *Billboard*'s annual 'Power 100' list of the most influential music executives in 2024, she was only the second artist to do so after Beyoncé and Jay-Z. Reflecting on her own learnings within the tough profession, she told the publication, 'The biggest crossroads moments of my career came down to sticking to my instincts when my ideas were looked at with scepticism. When someone says to me, "But that has never been done successfully before," it fires me up. We have to take strategic risks every day in this industry, but every once in a while, you have to really trust your gut and take a flying leap.'

That sense of conviction has made her not only a creative visionary, but a proven changemaker of our times. As the *Wall Street Journal* noted in 2023, she has 'outmanoeuvred music executives vying to control her song rights, sparred with tech giants and sold record numbers of albums'. What's more, according to music trade magazine *Pollstar*, if Taylor was a country, she would rank as the 199th largest economy on earth, comparable to a small Caribbean nation. Market research company QuestionPro also valued the worth of her Eras tour as being bigger than the GDP of 50 nations. But her dominance is as much cultural as financial, and she has managed to become the most streamed artist of all time, while singlehandedly driving the vinyl renaissance for a generation that consumes everything digitally. At the same time, she has used her platform to champion and nurture other musicians – Sabrina Carpenter and Gracie Abrams among them – proving she's as comfortable being the mentor as she is the megastar. Meanwhile, her ability to maintain a fandom that bridges nationalities, genders and age groups remains unsurpassed, with Swiftmania described as the 21st-century equivalent of Beatlemania.

Given her position, it's no surprise that universities around the world now offer courses on Taylor's work and influence, examining her through lenses of celebrity and internet culture, feminism and capitalism, as well as Americanism and post-postmodernism. And yet, even at this pinnacle of her career, Taylor continues to evolve – and with Travis by her side, that evolution is heading for a new stratosphere. Together, they represent a rare fusion of star power, where they are not only mutually supportive and mutually ambitious, but mutually bankable. Thanks to sponsorship offers, TV and film opportunities and the staggering cross-pollination of their respective fanbases, we're no longer dealing solely with the Swift Effect, but the 'Swift–Kelce Effect', too. As Nicole Tidei, vice president of communications firm Pinkston stressed, 'Swift and Kelce are no longer just individual powerhouses building influence in separate lanes. They're a merged brand ecosystem with unparalleled reach.' The full scope of their commercial potential is still to be discovered, but what makes them so compelling beyond that is the authenticity and realness underpinning it all.

Speaking at a pre-Super Bowl press conference in 2024, Travis was asked why he thought people were so fascinated by them as a couple. 'I think the values that we stand for and just, you know, who we are as people,' he said. 'We love to shine light on others, shine light around the people that help and support us. And on top of that, I feel like we both have just a love for life.' That sentiment encapsulates exactly why they resonate: Travis's affable, big-hearted presence has helped humanise Taylor in the eyes of many who once viewed her as untouchable, and their shared sense of kindness and humility has made them eminently relatable to the masses.

Taylor's story has always been one of reinvention. Each of her former selves – the fearless, the heartbroken, the defiant, the dreamer – has helped her become the woman she is today. And now with Travis, there is ease where there was once effort, and assurance where there was once uncertainty. The teenager who ached to be chosen has found someone who chooses her, every single day. All her years of songwriting and soul-searching have led her not to a fantasy ending spun from her school notebooks, but a grown-up partnership grounded in light, laughter and respect. More than anything, Travis has become the co-architect of Taylor's freedom. He doesn't overshadow her story; he steadies it. And wherever their next era takes them, we're left with an overriding sense that it will be impossible to ignore.

ACKNOWLEDGEMENTS

Thank you to all the Swifties, whose endless curiosity and devotion made telling this story such a joy.

My gratitude also goes to the team at Ebury – in particular, Charlotte Hardman and Michelle Warner – for this opportunity, and for guiding the project home with such enthusiasm and trust.

All materials and sources consulted are credited within the pages of the book.

IMAGE CREDITS